The
Marvellous
Century

The Marvellous Century

Archaic Man and
the Awakening of Reason

George Woodcock

Fitzhenry & Whiteside

A Godwit Paperback

Dedication
To Tony Phillips in friendship
and in appreciation of his continuing
interest in the subject and the book

The Marvellous Century
© George Woodcock 1989

Fitzhenry & Whiteside
195 Allstate Parkway
Markham, Ontario L3R 4T8

Editors: Theresa Griffin
         Frank English
Maps: McCalla Design Associates
Cover art: 1972.22 Black figure krater,
           6th Century B.C. Greek pottery
           Courtesy of Dallas Museum of Art, Gift
           of the Jonsson Foundation of Mr. and
           Mrs. Frederick M. Mayer
Cover design: Ian Gillen

Canadian Cataloguing in Publication Data
Woodcock, George, 1912-
The marvellous century
(Godwit paperback)
Bibliography: p. 245
Includes index.
ISBN 0-88902-739-0.
1. Civilization, Ancient. 2. Reason.
3. Thought and thinking. I. Title.
CB311.W66 1988   930   C88-095035-8

Printed and bound in Canada

Table of Contents

Greece and the immediately surrounding area in the 6th century B.C.

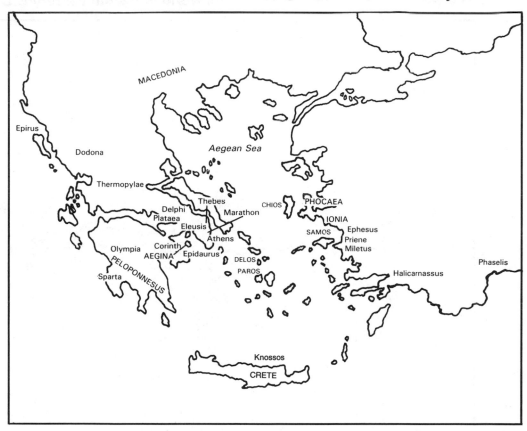

The western half of the known literate world in the 6th century B.C.

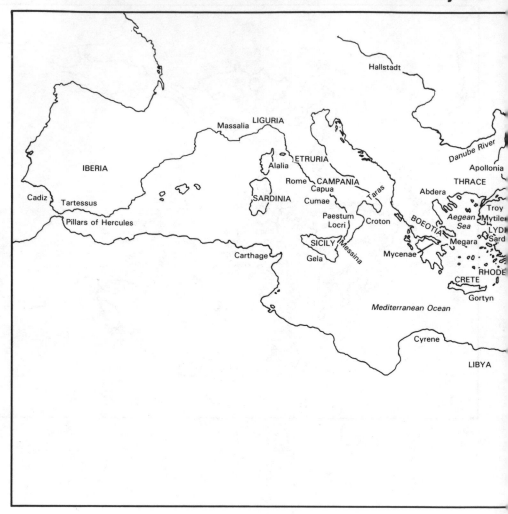

The Times Concise Atlas of World History (Fitzhenry & Whiteside) and Michael Chelik's *Ancient History* (Barnes & Noble) are excellent aids in finding the many places noted in the text.

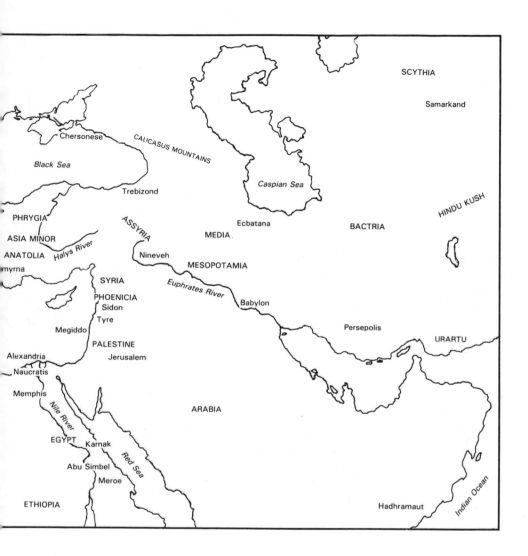

SCYTHIA

Samarkand

Chersonese

CAUCASUS MOUNTAINS

Black Sea

Trebizond

Caspian Sea

HINDU KUSH

PHRYGIA

ASIA MINOR

ANATOLIA

Halys River

ASSYRIA

Ecbatana

MEDIA

BACTRIA

Nineveh

myrna

MESOPOTAMIA

SYRIA

Euphrates River

PHOENICIA

Sidon

Babylon

Persepolis

URARTU

Tyre

Megiddo

PALESTINE

Alexandria

Jerusalem

Naucratis

Memphis

ARABIA

Nile River

EGYPT

Karnak

Red Sea

Abu Simbel

Meroe

ETHIOPIA

Hadhramaut

Indian Ocean

PART I

INTRODUCTION

Chapter 1

The Marvellous Century: A World Awakening

> Thus should we talk around the fire in winter, with a strange guest among us, all bellies satisfied, sweet wine beside us, and filbert nuts to chew. Then we can ask: "Pray tell us, sir, your name. What was your home? How old are you? How old were you the year the Persians came?"
>
> *Xenophanes*

I

Xenophanes is as good a man as one could pick to speak the opening words in a book about the extraordinary period in which he lived out his long and eloquent life. Xenophanes was an Ionian Greek, a poet and philosopher deeply affected by the political events of his time and deeply involved in the intellectual movements that made the sixth century BC a time of awakening in the whole world of ancient civilization from China westward to the Pillars of Hercules. He came from the little city of Colophon a few miles inland from the Aegean coast of what is now Turkey, and lived out the latter half of his life a wanderer in the Greek cities that had been established in southern Italy. He was one of many men in many places who during his lifetime challenged the old mythological concepts of the nature and process of the universe. He was

1

one of the first to recognize the relativity of religions, and, himself a deeply religious man, he sought to found both his faith and his knowledge of the world on reason rather than fable and on fact rather than dream.

For Xenophanes, and for all the other Greeks who inhabited the Hellenic cities of Asia Minor, the year the Persians came was 546 BC. It was a date that deeply affected their personal lives, sending many of them, like Xenophanes and Anacreon the poet, into exile; it was also a notable date in the history of the whole western civilized world. For then Cyrus, the Great King of Kings, founder of the Achaemenid dynasty, defeated Croesus, the ruler of Lydia, who until then had been the over-lord of the Greeks who built their highly civilized cities in Asia Minor.

Cyrus established the largest empire the world had yet known. He described himself as "lord of all men from the sunrise to the sunset." Like most royal titles, it was an exaggeration, yet the Persians, starting out from the little kingdom of Anshan not far from present-day Shiraz, absorbed all the great empires that had preceded them — Assyria and Babylon, Egypt and Media, Lydia and Urartu. They spilled over the Hindu Kush into northeastern India, beyond it into Turkestan, and over the Bosporus into Thrace, which was the beginning of Europe; thence they chased the elusive Scythians over the boundless steppes of the Ukraine until their advance lost its impetus in the scorched earth of the citiless spaces. Even if their vast realm did not stretch from sunrise to sunset, it did extend from the Punjab in India westward to Libya, and from the shores of the Black Sea and the Caspian south to the Indian Ocean. To all this vast area they brought a new concept of government that replaced the sacred kingships of the past with a secular rule based on the realities of power, and a dynamic monotheism in which religion became a matter of positive action rather than passive resignation.

Yet the Persians never conquered the whole civilized world; other powers and cultures shared with them the sixth century's astonishing vitality and the developments that then changed the ancient world. They did not penetrate the Ganges valley or southern India. They did not conquer the tribes of Arabia, though as independent rulers the Bedouin chiefs assisted Cyrus' son Cambyses in conquering Egypt. They may not even have known of the Chinese or the Chinese of them, though rumours of these two great peoples could have reached each other through the Scythians of the Siberian Altai, who remained in contact with the Scythians of Crimea, or by the ancient routes along which even in prehistoric times the trade in lapis lazuli was conducted. And it was only an edge of the rapidly spreading Hellenic world that the Persian Empire, even at its greatest, overlapped.

If the Persians were the great imperialists of the archaic world, the Greeks were its great colonizers. Crowded by rocky hinterlands into small cities that loom large in the glow of history, they experienced a perpetual need for trade, for living room. From the early eighth century they hived off like bees, rowing their long vessels like the legendary Argonauts in search of places where they could establish trading posts or colonies on lands more ample than the meagre toeholds their mainland of Hellas offered. Hundreds of Greek colonies appeared around the Black Sea and the Mediterranean, and almost every one of them was a true *polis*, a city state independent of the community whence its people originally set out.

The contrast between empire and independent *polis* sharply differentiated the Persians from the Greeks of this period. It produced a division of outlook and a tension of wills which explain much that happened during this vital and turbulent era.

The Persians created an empire in which many races and cultures could live together, practising their own customs, worshipping their own gods and even to an extent sustaining their own laws. These disparate peoples were united under the aegis of a single monarch whose rule, in comparison with the rule of the earlier Assyrians and Babylonians, was relatively benign and reasonably just.

The Greeks shared a single culture yet were never united. They developed their civilization in the tense ambience of small communities, often no more than a few thousand people, who were often at war, city against city and Greek against Greek, and who sometimes treated each other with a cruelty that might go as far as massacre and often involved enslavement. Yet when they talked of Hellas, they thought of a community, a common range of myths and traditions and social assumptions, which they celebrated when they came together on all-Greek occasions like the games at Olympia and Delphi and Nemea.

The people, ideas and events I shall be discussing are linked mainly with the literate civilizations I have mentioned — those of the countries verging on the Mediterranean, of the Middle East between the Persian Gulf and Libya, of India and China — but at least in passing I shall refer to contemporary developments in hinterlands like Scythia and Central Europe, and even in remoter regions like Siberia and Central and South America, where new civilizations were at this time stirring awake.

There are similar flexibilities in the time scale I follow. History never arranges itself in neat capsules of a hundred years each, and what I am writing about when I name the sixth century is a period of between 120 and 130 years, characterized by a cluster of events that changed irrevocably the way men looked upon the universe and even upon themselves.

The period effectively begins in 612, when the Medes and the Babylonians destroyed Nineveh, and the Assyrian Empire, the last of the totalitarian realms of the archaic world, came to an end. The fall of Assyria opened the way for the rise a few years later of the Achaemenid dynasty in Persia. As for my terminal date, I had first thought of making it 490, the year of Marathon. But the Persian threat to the Greek mainland and hence to Europe was not averted until the sea battle of Salamis in 480 and the land battle of Plataea in 479; these victories, even more than Marathon, made the differences between Persia and Hellas irreconcilable, for all the Hellenes, not the Athenians alone, had by now become involved. From these years dates the historic opposition between Europe and Asia which casts its shadow over the world to this day. This was also the time, as tradition tells us, of the departure from life of the Buddha and Confucius and Xenophanes, the last of the great seminal thinkers of the archaic age.

II

The Buddha, Confucius and Xenophanes had been the survivors of an amazing group of original minds that appeared in the sixth century, scattered over the world like Auden's "ironic points of light." Among the Greeks, mainly in Ionia, emerged the thinkers whom Aristotle called the *physiologi* and we call the pre-Socratics. These quiet iconoclasts discarded the mythology of Homer to observe phenomena as they saw them, and to classify them rationally; they sought physical explanations of what happened in the universe rather than accepting tales of divine whims; they saw Godhead moving through phenomena rather than externally directing them. The pioneer historian and geographer Hecataeus, master of Herodotus, spoke for all of them when he declared, "The stories of the Greeks are manifold and, in my opinion, absurd," and proposed to establish his own truths.

The first natural philosophers of Miletus, Thales and Anaximander and Anaximenes, were followed by Xenophanes and Hecataeus, and, slightly later, by Heraclitus and — last of the true archaic philosophers — Parmenides. They stand at the dawn of rational philosophy, and also, as we see them trying to explain logically the motions of the stars, the reasons for eclipses, the origins of fossil fish found in the quarries of Syracuse, they represent the beginnings of scientific thought. Beside them, manifesting the spirit of the age in different ways, we see other mental giants of the time, like Solon, the poet and practical philosopher who inspired Athenian democracy, and Theodorus, the technological polymath from Samos, and the more shadowy figure of Pythagoras, who first discovered the rules of music and, through his belief that numbers were the key to open the secrets of the universe, laid the foundations for mathematics as we use it.

Farther east, in Asia, the dawn of enlightenment was also breaking. Among the dry mountains of Bactria appeared the prophet Zoroaster, who gave the Persians a religion based on the great natural powers of the universe considered as the emanations of Godhead. The great Cyrus of Persia liberated the

Jews at this time from their Babylonian captivity, and for them it was the age of men of intellectual power, like the anonymous author of the final chapters of Isaiah, and like the prophet Jeremiah, whose real virtue lay in his clear perception of the world as it was. Even the captivity had its positive side, for it provided the circumstances in which a rigorous monotheism finally became the nucleus of Judaic thought and the Old Testament as we know it emerged to form the basis of all the three great religions of the Book, Judaism, Christianity and Islam.

Over the mountains in India, a ferment of philosophic speculation had already been stimulated by the treatises known as the Upanishads, with their efforts to determine the relation between the individual being and the All. In the sixth century widespread heresies emerged against the dominant Brahmin orthodoxy. They found expression not only in the rational teachings of the Buddha and Mahavira, out of whose doctrines emerged the world religions of Buddhism and Jainism, but also in lesser-known ascetic philosophers whose determinist teachings gave rise to the earliest atomic theories. In China also this was a time when great teachers emerged whose influence survives even today in the attitudes of their countrymen, despite the structural changes that Communism has brought to Chinese society: Confucius, who sought the harmony good government could provide, and the more shadowy Lao-tzu, the Taoist sage who taught the other harmony, between man and nature, which he called *tao*, the Way.

Everywhere in the sixth century the old polytheistic and anthropomorphic attitudes were thus being criticized by thinkers who looked at their world directly, seeing it in terms of concrete phenomena and subjecting those phenomena to critical logic. In the fragments that survive from the works of Xenophanes, who mocked the Homeric concept of the gods as magnified and amoral human beings, such criticisms of ancient beliefs acquire a special potency, since this poet-philosopher not only showed how men's religious beliefs are relative to their circumstances, but also made one of the earliest deist arguments for the idea of God as no more and no less than the universal, unifying intelligence:

The Ethiop thinks his gods are black;
the Thracian sees them blue-eyed and red-haired.
If cows and horses had hands as we do,
and could draw and carve images,
they would make gods like cows and horses.
But God is unlike beasts or men.
He is one, undifferentiated, undivided,
sees all, hears all, and without labour
sets all things in vibration
with a thought.

Xenophanes put his philosophy into verse, as Solon put his politics, and indeed this was one of the great periods of Greek poetry. In lyric verse the voices of great singers, chanting their poems to lyres they often designed, were heard throughout the Greek world: Alcaeus and Theognis, Sappho and Anacreon, Pindar and Simonides, performing at popular festivals and in the courts of tyrants. In Athens rhapsodes working under the protection of the tyrant Peisistratus prepared the written versions of the *Iliad* and the *Odyssey* that we know today. In Athens also the festival of the Great Dionysia developed, and there the Greek drama was initiated by the great early tragedians whose names are known to us but whose works are lost.

But the sixth century, with its need for exact expression of observations and of rational thought, was also the beginning of the age of prose. The grand vaguenesses of Hesiod's stories of the gods could be effectively rendered in the verse of his *Theogony*, but when the pioneer physical scientists and geographers began to set down their perceptions, and the earliest historians began to record facts rather than dynastic legends, they found they needed a new form in which rational speech could be made literate, in the same way as oral poetry had been made literate a century or so before.

Pherecydes of Syros, the philosopher who taught Pythagoras, and Anaximander of Miletus, the early scientist who flourished in the mid-sixth century, were the pioneers in prose, for Thales, the first of the pre-Socratic philosophers, left nothing in writing. Of their successor Hecataeus we have only tantalizingly brief fragments. He was a notable pioneer map-maker as well as a geographical writer whom his contemporaries described as a "much-travelled man," and also a historian whom later scholars described as "the only authoritative predecessor" of Herodotus. The sophisticated prose and the developed historical sense Herodotus showed in the fifth century when he narrated the conflicts between the Hellenes and the Persians must have been derived from a line of talented predecessors, and so, by a kind of inverse reflection, Hecataeus and the other early historians whose works are lost shine through the achievements of their successors, first Herodotus and then Thucydides. History as we know it — an account of the past as near to objective as possible — emerged from the prose narratives of the sixth century which, whatever their subject, were generally classified under the title of *historia*.

For the Greeks the sixth century was a great artistic as well as a great literary age, the time of the haunting archaic sculptures whose evident derivation from Egyptian models so eloquently hints at the rich oriental-occidental connections of the period. It was an era of great architectural advances, when both the Doric and the Ionic styles were developed and temples were built, like the Artemesium at Ephesus and the Heraeum on Samos, that became the wonders of the ancient world. At the same time newly developed scientific and mathematical notions were being applied in areas like engineering, metallurgy and shipbuilding by such widely dispersed peoples as the Greeks, the Etruscans and the Phoenicians.

Elsewhere, except among the Persians and the Babylonians, the monumental architectural developments of the Hellenic world were not rivalled, and archaeology presents the record of life in such countries usually on a more modest and intimate scale. Nor, except among the Jews and the past-oriented Babylonians, was the literary record as developed as among the Greeks. The Persians wrote in stone the deeds of kings, but how those deeds affected the lives of ordinary men we learn from Hellenic historians. What we know of such great Asian sages as the Buddha, Mahavira and Confucius, who never wrote down their teachings, was recorded generations after their deaths.

Yet their names, their teachings, and some sense of their personalities survive. They were historic figures as no men before them had been. We are aware of the sixth century as a period teeming with enterprising and originative men and women; they exist for us as recognizable figures like the people of our own times, and not as semi-mythical figures like Agamemnon the king and Odysseus the voyager, on whose authenticity and identity we can only speculate. In the sixth century Cyrus the king and Scylax the voyager, who first explored the Indus, were real men, and so was Solon, the poet-politician of Athens, who celebrated in his verse the restless spirit of the times that seemed to fill men with superabundant energy as they moved in so many different directions:

Everywhere you meet them, men in a hurry.
One man wanders over the fish-filled seas,
Beaten by fearful winds, careless of life,
All in the hope of bringing back a profit.
Another ploughs his lands, year after year,
Curving his share between the laden trees.
Others have learnt their skills from artisan gods
And live by deftness of the eye and hand,
And some have won the Muses' gifts
And sing in verse the wisdom of the ages.

Solon himself was as much an example of archaic energy as the other men he describes in his poem. Early in the sixth century, called in by the Athenians to reform their economic system, he gave them a group of laws that not only laid the foundations of democracy in Athens but also included some of the world's earliest social legislation. But when he had framed the new system, he immediately left the city and travelled for ten years. He said he wanted to see the world, and see it he certainly did, visiting the Greek cities in Italy and Sicily, and the rich kingdom of Lydia, and Egypt, whose decaying civilization — artificially frozen in a semblance of its glorious antiquity by the Saite kings, the last native dynasty — fascinated the archaic Greeks and deeply influenced both their architecture and their sculpture.

Solon embodied one of the great contradictions in the thought of his age: he acted as if the will were free, according to the strong current of individualism flowing in his time, yet he held to the older belief that men's lives are governed by destiny.

In their actions and in their philosophy and art the Greeks at this time showed unprecedented qualities of independence, the signs of a dawning age when men would be recognizable individuals and not particles in a tribal personality or a hieratic order. Yet at the same time they still felt man alone did not have the power to shape his world or even completely control his own life. In different ways the contradiction appeared among the oriental sages, the contradiction between belief in an ineluctable karma and the teaching of individual release epitomized in the Buddha's deathbed remark to his disciple Ananda, "You are your own light, your own refuge."

Fate, for the Greeks, always lay in wait for man, and for statesmen like Solon it could assume the form of great political events that unpredictably changed the lives of men and of whole societies. That is why the year the Persians came assumed such a special importance in the minds of Greeks. The Persians seemed to come from nowhere, and when they struck they seemed to carry the power of an irreversible destiny. That the Greeks did in the end check that fateful tide is a sign of how strongly by the end of the sixth century men had come to resist the idea of a world ruled wholly by necessity.

Everywhere, indeed, the century was marked by the conflict of wills and forces. Everywhere it was a time of change and apparent chaos, and perhaps, as happened in other such germinal periods, like the Renaissance, the instability of the era was somehow connected with its fever of achievement. The Greeks warred, city against city. In the China of Confucius the ancient kingdom of Chou had disintegrated into a pattern of warring principalities. The India of the Buddha and Mahavira was in political as well as intellectual flux as large new kingdoms like Magadha and Kosala began to take shape in the Ganges valley, gradually swallowing the small principalities and republics of the Vedic era, while the warriors of the Kshatriya caste resisted the growing power of the Brahmin priests. In the Middle East the upheaval was the greatest of all, for one after another the traditional powers, Assyria and Lydia, Babylon and Egypt, were swept into history by the incursion of the Iranian mountain tribesmen who created first the kingdom of Media and then the Persian Empire and eventually overshadowed the whole world known to the Greeks even where they did not rule it.

III

Of the character and consequences of the Persian Empire, and the way it set Greek and Asian traditions in opposition, I shall have much to say. Yet when we consider from a distance the sixth century and the modern world's debts to it, it seems as impossible to separate Greeks and Persians as it is to consider in isolation the Jewish prophets or the Indian heretical philosophers or the Chinese sages of the same period, or even the small group of angry men who chased out an alien king and founded a republic in the obscure Italian city of Rome.

Together they created the moulds in which the world's great civilizations have taken shape. Whether our political ideas are autocratic or democratic or even anarchist, they find their ancestral types in Greece and China; in the contrasts between Athens and Sparta; in the disagreement between the ordered world dreamed of by Confucius and the free life according to the rhythms of nature preached by the Taoists.

The great religions that still dominate the world also have their roots in that age when men broke away from tribal myths and sought a broader concept of the ordering of the universe as well as a more universal morality. Christianity and Islam, as well as modern Judaism, sprang from a resurgent Hebraic monotheism that had been purged of impurities during the exile and given an eschatological purpose through the influence of Persian Zoroastrians. Zoroastrianism, now a vestigial minority religion, in fact left its mark both on all the religions of the Book and on the secular messianic creeds of the West like Marxism and anarchism: it contributed a progressive vision dominated by the idea of a final struggle between good and evil that would lead to a new paradisial order on earth, and it accompanied this vision with a stress on action as a sign of moral purposiveness, a stress that had been absent in the more ancient religions of the East.

Farther into Asia, there emerged out of the philosophic insurrection of the Buddha and Mahavira and the other Indian heretical teachers a movement that went far beyond the institutionalized traditions of Buddhism and Jainism. The success of this movement led the best of the Brahmins to reform their own creed and practice; their example was followed in later generations, particularly among the followers of Vishnu, who sought to purify and humanize religious institutions and moral codes, and who often repeated in different settings and different terms what the original heretical teachers had taught. Gandhi's unique fusion of politics and religion in our own century grew ultimately out of this movement.

Similarly, despite recurrent attempts in imperial as well as revolutionary China to suppress them, the doctrines of Confucius and Lao-tzu, as well as a modified Buddhism that reached the country seven or eight centuries after its founder's death, have wielded a profound and lasting influence on Chinese political structures and social mores; they have also created a special relationship with the natural world that over the centuries has encouraged a persistent moral and philosophic pragmatism among the Chinese and has also deeply affected the character of Chinese, and by derivation of Japanese, art and poetry.

In the Mediterranean world, and in somewhat different ways in India, the sixth century saw the emergence of scientific philosophy and, in a rudimentary way, of scientific practice. Mathematical and astronomical knowledge spread out from the ancient Middle East, and became empirical as well as secular because it was no longer subordinated to the religious demands of the Babylonian and Egyptian hierarchs. Geography, geology and physics all developed, and in India atomic theories emerged before they appeared in Greece. These developments were the products of minds examining the world in the light of reason rather than of myth.

In later ages, as Europe extended its political power and its cultural influence, taking over and settling the largely empty land of continents unknown to ancient Greeks or Chinese, other communities were created, in the same way as the Greek colonies had been founded in ancient times, and these infant cultures, notably in the Americas and Oceania, were in their turn shaped by the changes in human society and in human consciousness that took place in the sixth century BC. The same applied in other parts of the world, even though the lines of inheritance might be different. Whether we live in San Francisco or Gorki or Xi'an, whether we inhabit the Islamic world or the Christian, the way we live and the way we see our world has been largely shaped by the extraordinary century which forms a bridge between a past haunted by the ghosts of mythology and a present lived in the light of history.

IV

The intangible heritage of the sixth century, translated into political and social and artistic forms, is still part of our common experience; it has helped to shape our world. But tangible remains and written records are scanty, and this is the inevitable result of the century's character as a transitional period between the mythological and the historical.

When you visit the archaic lands and try to seek out the places where the men of the sixth century lived and thought and acted, you immediately become aware of this fact. The buildings which were their homes have vanished long ago, and so for the most part have the buildings connected with their public lives. In many parts of their world the custom of construction in lasting materials had not even begun. The Indians did not start carving their great sacred caves, let alone building stone temples, until at least four hundred years after the Buddha's death. The only durable buildings of the Chinese in the sixth century were tombs hidden well underground. Even among the Greeks, the stone temples which we associate especially with their classical culture were a comparative innovation. It has been established that less than forty such temples were built before 600 BC, including some very small shrines, while even in the sixth century itself, despite the erection of some of the largest Greek temples ever built, at Ephesus, Samos and Acragas in Sicily, it seems likely that no more than a hundred were built in the whole Hellenic world.

Of these, few remain. Earthquakes and other natural disasters, political storms and conflagrations, invasions and revolutions, and the quiet attrition caused by peasants taking building stones and contractors taking road metal have worn away at their fabrics, and when some great building of the period has survived in a recognizable physical shape, it is usually the result of some untypical circumstance. Along the sacred way of Paestum, the old Greek city of Poseidonia to the south of Naples which began as a colony of Sybaris, the great sixth-century Doric temples of golden stone do still stand, almost intact except for their fallen roofs. They do so not because men cared for them, but because men were forced to leave them alone. The presence of the anopheles mosquito preserved them for many centuries from the kind of people who in the Middle Ages and even later combined Christian fanaticism with an eye to personal profit as they pulled down the pagan temples and used the stones for their own purposes.

But few sixth-century centres are so well preserved as Paestum. Sybaris, its mother city, has gone without a trace. It is hard to find a single foundation on the site of Miletus that dates from the time when it held the trading hegemony of the Black Sea before being destroyed by the Persians in 494 BC. Of the temple of Artemis in Ephesus a single pillar, reconstructed out of bits by the archaeologists, stands in the middle of a murky pool which has filled the site of this building once celebrated among the seven wonders of the ancient world. One of the other wonders, Nebuchadnezzar's Hanging Gardens, constructed in Babylon also in the sixth century, has so completely vanished that historians actually debate what the phrase "hanging gardens" really described.

And even the traditions that survive are not always suffi-

cient to make up for the missing structures. The ancient Greeks
were much aware of the importance of a good name left for
posterity. The poet Pindar emphasized the feeling when he
compared Croesus, the barbarian king whom the Greeks loved,
with Phalaris, the notorious tyrant of Sicilian Acragas, who
roasted his enemies alive in a bronze bull and was himself so
cooked in the end:

When we are alive and gone away
how men speak of us is all
chroniclers and poets will have to go on.
Thus open-hearted Croesus is remembered
in all his generous grace,
but ruthless Phalaris who burnt men live
in the bronze bull of Sicily
they speak of with revulsion,
and so the poets chanting in the halls
have not a word for him;
he lives not in the dreams of boys.
Good fortune is the best of gifts;
the next is to be thought of nobly.
Good fortune and good fame
give life its perfect crown.

The importance to the Greeks — and equally to the Persians and the Chinese — of leaving a good name behind makes
it all the more ironic that we know so little in terms of human
details about so many of the men and women who lived at
this time when the foundations of the world we know were
being laid in the thoughts of men and in human institutions.

Partly this was because the written word was everywhere
young at this time, and in many places distrusted. Literacy
was not general even among the Phoenicians and the Greeks
at the beginning of the sixth century. Most of the great men-
tors of the age were oral teachers; the Buddha and Mahavira
in India, Confucius in China, Zoroaster in Iran, even Thales
and Pythagoras among the Greeks taught in spoken homilies
and never wrote their doctrines down; perhaps that is why
modern paper-oriented scholars sometimes wonder whether
such a palpably real figure as Zoroaster ever existed.

Yet hundreds of books were written in the sixth century,

in verse and, by mid-century, in the new medium of prose. Copies of many of them were among the half-million manuscripts which Ptolemy Philadelphus gathered into the great library he built three centuries later in Alexandria; they are often mentioned by Hellenistic and even Roman writers. But most were burnt by the Romans during one of their civil wars in the third century AD, and those that survived were destroyed by the Christians in 391. In this way almost the entire record of scholarship, speculation and poetic creation during the early centuries of Greek literate culture was wiped out.

Some of the books of the archaic Greeks survived only in fragments, and sometimes in such a ghostly way that the names of writers and the titles of their books may be known, but nothing of their contents. We know that Anaximander and Hecataeus, Xenophanes and Heraclitus all wrote elaborate treatises setting out their visions of the nature of the physical universe, but we know of their teachings only through short passages that survived on scraps of papyrus inscribed after their time and preserved in the dry desert climate of the Nile valley or that were kept alive in quotations by later authors. Among the poets Theognis, whose works survive in some quantity, was an exception. We piece together the poems of Sappho and Anacrèon and their rivals from single poems and scraps of poems, often only a few lines in length. Some sixth-century poets, like the Tanagran lyricist Corinna, are represented only by one or two lines and some wisps of anecdote.

Even those who practised the public art of the drama, which developed so vigorously in the later sixth century, usually left little that has survived. In the early days, when tragedy was emerging from the ceremonies in honour of Dionysus, there were many playwrights — Thespis and Phrynichus are only the best known — whose names have lived because they were admired by the Athenians and won prizes in the festivals. But except for a few lines here and there and a few reminiscences passed on to scholars writing three or four centuries later, their works have vanished. This has left us with perplexing questions. Was it merely chance that preserved the later works of Aeschylus, who seems to have learnt a great deal from

Phrynichus, and that made us think of him as the greatest
Athenian playwright of that early period? Is Aeschylus perhaps
merely the survivor, unchallenged because the works of his
rivals were lost?

We shall probably never have the answers to such questions.
But the fact that we ask them is a tribute to the greatness of
the age. For if, when so much has vanished, it still projects
such a sense of expansive life and achievement through what
remains, may not the time itself have been even more creative, even more important in its contributions to human
development, than we now know?

As it is, we must often proceed obliquely, through indirect
as much as through direct witness. We know more about the
Persian Empire from information accumulated by the Greek
Herodotus than we do from the Achaemenian records. Much
that we know about the early Buddhists comes from the traditions of their contemporary rivals, the early Jains, and vice
versa. And often, combining the anecdotes written by Hellenistic *littérateurs* with the one or two or three hundred lines that
may remain of a poet's verse, we can create what are probably
authentic images of the great Greek lyricists, not only as lyricists, but even as personalities. Sappho lives in the mind with
her tortured amorous intensity, as does Alcaeus with his
ancient Tory bitterness, and sweet-voiced Anacreon with his
own version of *carpe diem*. But when we try to seize the shape
of the age as a whole, it is by intuition as much as by information that we grasp it, and conjecture becomes as important as established fact. This has been the experience of all
historians of the archaic world, whether or not they have
chosen to admit it.

V

In most of this book I shall be discussing *how* so much that
was vital to our civilization came into being during the sixth
century. But the description of *how* always merges into the
question of *why*. History is the record of causes as well as
of consequences.

And speculation about causes brings us inevitably back to

the old controversy between the diffusionists, who saw all civilization moving out from one originative centre, and their rivals, who maintained that old civilizations which were geographically far removed from each other must have evolved independently.

For a long time the diffusionists seemed to be having it their own way. Stylistic similarities between cultures seemed to out-weigh the material problems of how contacts could have taken place. More precise dating methods helped to change the situation. It was shown, for example, that Stonehenge had actually predated the Pyramids, and so the diffusionist argument that the megalithic cultures of northern Europe were degenerate derivations from ancient Egypt was made untenable. In the same way, recent archaeological discoveries relating to early periods have reinforced the arguments of Chinese historians that their civilization developed over a period of continuous growth extending so far into the past that there was no possibility of the culture of the Yangtse and the Yellow River valleys having been derived from the ancient cultures of the Euphrates and the Nile.

We are talking now about the remote origins of civilizations. But long before the sixth century the situation may well have changed to the extent that communications between independently developing civilizations had been established. Once men passed out of the unitary hunting and gathering economy of palaeolithic times, there emerged a different, pluralistic culture, which gave rise to a kind of primitive Adam Smithian economy, with division of labour relating to locally available raw materials or precious commodities, and with a pattern of exchange and trade routes. The trade in useful and decorative materials like tin and silver, amber and lapis lazuli and salt began in neolithic times and extended over Europe and far into western Asia. Even before the sixth century this primitive commerce had been expanded into a trade in manufactured articles, including pottery from Corinth and bronzeware from Tuscany and textiles from Miletus, that extended from Cadiz in the west to the Altai Mountains in the east, where a carpet of Achaemenian design was found preserved in a frozen tomb, and from Britain in the north to Ethiopia in the south. Though the Chinese records have nothing to say of this, it may have extended even farther, for a piece of Chinese silk was found in a late seventh-century tomb of the Hallstadt culture near Stuttgart.

But it was the cultural exports of the sixth century, like the alphabet from Phoenicia and coined money from Lydia, both transmitted to the Greeks, that most deeply affected the later history of the civilized world. Linked to them were changing political patterns, which moved over the known world in the wake of the collapse of the ancient civilizations of the Euphrates and the Nile. The Achaemenian Empire became the model not only for Alexander's Hellenistic successors and the Roman emperors who imitated them, but also for the empire of the Mauryas in India, which in its turn was the predecessor of the Moghul realm and eventually of the British Raj.

Stylistic as well as political influences flowed through the ancient world, carried on the currents of trade. The trading post of Naucratis was established on the Nile as a co-operative venture of Greek commercial cities, and the Greeks began to build massive stone temples like the Egyptians and to carve the beautiful standing statues of the archaic period — the *kouroi* and the *korai* — that so subtly echo the statuary of Memphis and Thebes. And from Ionia the same architectural-sculptural line passed in the hands of Ionian craftsmen to Persia, where it flourished in the great halls of Persepolis and found its final expression in the sculptures of Ashoka's Buddhist India.

These influences, imported and exported, changed the way cultures would operate. Money would take the place of barter; words would be written and hence recorded as well as spoken; fluid speech would become frozen statement. But the essential nature of each culture, which separated it from the rest, would not be changed. The Greeks might borrow an alphabet from the Phoenicians, and the Etruscans in turn borrow it from the Greeks, but there was never any assimilation of Greek with Phoenician life, even in Sicily where they lived beside each other for centuries; and however much the Etruscans might owe to the Greeks, when political showdowns came it was with the Carthaginians that they entered into alliance against the Hellenes. Similar examples abound. The sixth century may have brought about the fruitful interaction of cultures, but they remained distinct cultures, developing their own traditions with a modicum of help from outside.

This makes all the more surprising the simultaneity with which, in all these distinct cultures, there appeared currents of thought that challenged the inherited assumptions of a myth-dominated past and led men to look at themselves, their world and their universe with clear and critical eyes.

I cannot claim that I shall give any definitive explanation why this synchronization of thought took place. Perhaps at this stage it is more important to establish the questions that have to be asked, and that I propose to do.

PART II

THE ARCHAIC GREEKS

Chapter 2

Hellas: The Unity of Diversity

I

When we look back on fifth-century classical Greece, the
Greece personified for us in the achievements of men like Pericles and Phidias and Socrates, we think of its centres as the
powerful cities of Athens and Sparta, which in the end virtually destroyed Greek democracy as a result of their rivalries
and internecine wars. But in the sixth century no city had yet
attained the political ascendancy claimed by these two great
rivals, and if the Greek world had real centres they were to
be found in the spiritual enclaves of Olympia and Delphi; the
sacred stone of Delphi, the omphalos, was in fact held to be
the centre of the world. At festival times the roads to these
centres were protected by ancient taboos, and men travelled
along them not only from the cities of the Greek mainland
and the Aegean, but also from the outlying colonies of Italy
and Africa, of Crimea and the delta of the Rhône. There they
competed in the great Olympic and Pythian games, sacred to
Zeus and Apollo respectively, and one of the signs of being
a true Greek was to be accepted as a competitor.

Of the two Olympia's fame has perhaps been the more
enduring, owing to the revival after many centuries of the
Olympic games. But at the time Delphi was possibly the more
important because its great temple of Apollo was the home
of the most famous oracle of antiquity whose word was sought

by barbarians as well as by Greeks. Apollo was the most ambivalent of all the Olympian gods, and in many ways he projected the mental duality of men in that period of transition. He was the patron of law, of intellectual activity, and hence of the use of reason in the conduct of human affairs. But at the same time he was closely linked with the powerful sources of the unconscious, and by right of conquest he had taken over the powers of the chthonian deities, the underground gods with their power over the elemental forces; it was this aspect of Apollo that was manifested in the oracle.

The priests of Delphi had many stories about their ancient shrines that show how by the sixth century mythology and fancy were gradually merging into history and stone-solid fact. The first small shrine at Delphi is said to have been made of feathers and beeswax. Its successor was made out of fern-stalks bound into bundles, and a third shrine was built, according to the legend, of laurel stems; in fact, like most ancient Greek shrines, they were probably all rather primitively built of wood. The artificer god Hephaestus agreed to oblige Apollo by constructing a temple of bronze decorated by golden singing birds like those Yeats dreamed of in Byzantium, but the seeming permanence of this structure was brought to an end when Poseidon, jealous of Apollo, set the earth quaking, and the bronze temple sank into a great fissure, with its birds still singing, like the passengers of the Titanic.

It was now, they said, that the first stone temple was built, and this was the temple with which Delphi entered into history and importance, a Doric structure which seems to have been built about the end of the seventh century. Its priestess was the pythoness, named after the great serpent Python whose powers Apollo assumed when he slew him; Apollo's victory can be regarded as a symbolic stage in the progression from the myth-shrouded irrationality personified in Python and the other earth deities to rational consciousness. In very early days the pythoness sat over a cleft in the rock and spoke when she was bemused by the sulphurous vapours that rose up. Later the priests placed her in a closed room and brought her into a trance by burning barley corns, hemp and laurel over a lamp.

They listened to her incoherent words and interpreted them in equivocal verses out of which the recipient was left to make the best sense he could.

That first temple burnt down in 548 BC, and its replacement took the oracular mysteries into the heart of Greek political struggles. It was built by an aristocratic Athenian clan, the Alcmaeonids, who had been sent into exile by the tyrant Peisistratus. Constructed between 513 and 505 BC, the new temple earned Cleisthenes, the head of the clan, the allegiance of the powerful Delphic priests and, indirectly, that of Sparta, whose military power was called upon in the expulsion of Peisistratus' son Hippias from Athens in 510, while the new temple was being built. An equivocal relationship had been established between oracular prophecy and practical politics that would have lasting consequences.

Delphi was only the first among the great oracular temples. The Ionians had their own temple of Apollo at Didyma near Miletus, where one can still gaze into the deep well in whose water the priestess saw visions as she dizzily chewed laurel leaves and made her enigmatic pronouncements. Far-off Cumae in southern Italy had her oracle, who became famous in Roman history as the Cumaean Sibyl. There were even more ancient and primitive oracles, like that of Zeus in the lonely sanctuary of Dodona on the borders of modern Albania, whose priests slept on the ground, never washed their feet, and gave their oracles as interpretations of the sounds of the wind in an enormous ancient oak.

The contradictions involved in the survival of such cults were exemplified in the fact that the Greeks of the period built very rationally planned temples, marvels of the technology of their times, to serve beliefs that emanated from an irrational past and that were even then being subjected to the rigours of critical analysis by the philosophers of Ionia. On the very walls of the temple of Delphi where the pythoness swooned and blabbered her garbled statements appeared the two great maxims of Hellenic rationality, "Know yourself" and "Nothing to excess." They are said to have been inscribed when the famous Seven Sages made a visit together to the shrine; one of the Seven Sages was Thales, the great sceptic credited with the foundation of scientific thought, and he is said to have composed the maxims.

Thus archaic Greek society remained largely dominated by the past of myth even when the philosophers worked within it to change the cast of human thinking. Around the temple at Delphi stood the richly carved little shrines or treasuries that were built not only by the Greek mainland cities, but also by colonies as far away as Cyrene in Libya and Massalia, which is now Marseille. The treasuries were filled with rich gifts presented by the cities either at the Pythian games held every fourth year in honour of Apollo, or on special occasions when they hoped for a favourable prophecy from the oracle. There seems to have been an underlying feeling that the oracular words not only foretold the future but also indicated how the god had been persuaded to influence it. With all the gifts it received, which often included large quantities of bullion from barbarian monarchs, Delphi eventually became very wealthy, and, like the temples of Babylon, it made usurious loans out of its vast funds, so that with the other great sanctuaries it established a financial network that resembled a modern banking system and ironically helped to change the archaic world by reinforcing the economic revolution caused by the Lydian invention of coinage in the early sixth century.

The priests of Delphi acquired a good deal of political as well as economic *savoir faire*, and they became experts in gauging the forces at work in their world. They began to shape their prophecies to favour what seemed to them the side likely to win, though they always built in enough ambiguity to allow for error. As Heraclitus ironically remarked, ''The Lord to whom the oracle at Delphi belongs neither speaks nor hides but signifies.'' At the same time they sought to encourage enquirers who were lavish with gifts, so that the winning side was not always the side that paid most generously.

The classic case of the loser whose hopes — and whose folly — were encouraged by the ambiguity of the oracle is that of Croesus. When the Persians overthrew the empire of the Medes, Croesus felt that his martial alliance with the king of

Media, as well as his own fear of a Persian attack, obliged
him to attack. But since it was obviously a perilous undertak-
ing, he sent his envoys to Delphi. He paid for a vast holocaust
of sacrificial animals, and offered thousands of pounds of the
gold washed from the River Pactolus, made up into images
and ingots and ceremonial bowls and weapons. His message
ran:

> Croesus, the king of Lydia and lord of many other
> nations, believes the oracles of the Lord Apollo are the
> truest in the world. So he sends the gifts your powers of
> divination command, and asks if he should march against
> the Persians.

And the oracle answered:

> If you cross the River Halys and attack the Persians, a
> great empire will be destroyed.

Croesus interpreted the prophecy according to his own wishes.
He crossed the Halys to attack the Persians, and it was his
own empire that was destroyed, in 546 BC, "the year the Persians came."

But it was usually the winning side that Delphi encouraged,
and its favour often helped to assure victory by demoralizing
the opposition. Inevitably, there were accusations of corrupt-
ing the oracle, and in at least one famous instance the charge
was proved. Cleomenes, one of the two kings who shared
ceremonial power in Sparta, bribed the pythoness in 491 to
declare that his fellow king Demaratus was illegitimate and
therefore unworthy to rule. Demaratus was dismissed on the
strength of the oracular pronouncement, but later the true facts
were revealed, the priestess was stripped of her office, a priest
of Apollo was exiled, and Cleomenes fled and killed himself,
a fate attributed to the wrath of Apollo over his sacrilege.

Such scandals helped to discredit not only Delphi but other
great oracular centres, and those who practised the new art
of history became overtly or obliquely critical of them.
Herodotus would talk of oracular pronouncements with a kind
of ironic objectivity; Hecataeus was boldly sacrilegious. When
the Ionian Greeks revolted against the Persians in 499 BC,
he suggested to the delegates of the rebel cities, who were

assembled at Priene, that if they were serious about their rebellion they should impound the treasure of the Branchidae, the priestly clan that operated the oracle at Didyma, and use it to build themselves a fleet. Hecataeus clearly believed that arms were more effective than oracles.

Yet at the same time as distrust and even derision towards the oracles was spreading, the mystery religions were on the increase, notably the famous cult of Demeter at Eleusis and the more obscure Orphic cults. Both the Eleusinian mysteries and the Orphic cults were linked with the worship of Dionysus, which also led to the creation of the Athenian drama, in which the people participated publicly instead of secretly as at Eleusis. These developments, I suggest, should be seen as parallel to rather than in opposition to the secularizing tendencies of the new natural philosophers.

To begin with, they represented a break with the old Olympian deities and the customary ways of worship. Both Dionysus and Orpheus were outsider deities whose cults originated in Thrace and came to Greece late; Dionysus is not even mentioned in the *Iliad*. Demeter was an Olympian deity, but the Eleusinian mysteries emphasized her relations with the underground deity Kore and with Dionysus under the name of Iacchus, in ceremonies that were clearly linked to popular pre-Olympian fertility rites.

The very beliefs projected by the mysteries differed from the Olympian religion in important ways, particularly in their view of the nature of the soul and its adventures after death. The idea of future life, even of eternal life, appeared in them as something more real and positive than the mere survival in misery of the shades whom Odysseus called up from Hades in the *Odyssey*. The concept of sin and the need for atonement also appeared; it was associated with the idea of the suffering and death of a man-god, who in the case of Dionysus goes through a resurrection, linked with the annual reappearance of the grapes to be harvested, which became a symbol of the rebirth of the human spirit. In their own ways the mystery cults represented a re-examination of the human condition on a spiritual level that paralleled the re-examination of the world on a phenomenological level conducted by the Ionian philosophers.

In ritual, as in beliefs, the mystery cults differed from those of the Olympian deities, whom men sought to propitiate by sacrifices that implied individual deals with a god who had most of the attributes of a human absolute monarch. The mysteries — in which secret knowledge and rites were shared — were by definition fellowships in which the social distinctions of the ordinary world were dissolved, and the initiates, by their very participation in congregational ceremonies, were held to facilitate the resurrection of the god. The god was as dependent on his worshippers as they on him.

In all this there was a strain of populism, a threat to the established aristocratic and oligarchic orders, which had vested interests in the Olympian temples and the traditional oracles. It is not surprising that the cult of Dionysus and the mysteries in their various forms spread widely under the tyrants who then ruled so many Greek cities, since tyranny, like the totalitarian movements of the twentieth century, contained strong populist elements.

II

In politics, as in religion and other aspects of public life, the sixth century was a transitional time. Often it is simplistically portrayed as a time of struggle between tyranny and democracy. But it would be wrong to see it merely as a contest between past and present or even, adopting modern terms, between conservative and liberal or right and left. Both tyranny and democracy were products of the great social changes taking place in the archaic order. Writing barely two generations after the end of our era, Thucydides remarked:

The old Greeks were ruled by hereditary kings, and rights and limitations were built into the monarchy. But as the Greeks became more powerful and more and more concerned to gain money, tyrannies came into being in nearly all the cities, the revenues of the state increased, trade flourished, and shipbuilding with it.

So also did the arts and sciences. Tyrants were the employers of architects and engineers, the patrons of poets and sculptors. Athens under Peisistratus was the birthplace of drama, Samos under Polycrates was the home of the Ionian high technology of the time, and Miletus under Thrasybulus and his successors became the leading intellectual centre of the Hellenic world.

The Greek *tyrannos*, a word that seems to have been borrowed from the Lydians, did not mean what the word *tyrant* means to us today — according to the OED, a ruler who conducts himself in "an oppressive, unjust or cruel manner." For the Greeks it had an innovatory flavour in a world whose ideas of monarchy were derived from Homer, with his warrior kings like Agamemnon, who were really rather similar to North American Indian war chiefs — tribal leaders on a large scale, ruling with the consent of other warrior chiefs, like Achilles and Nestor and Odysseus, who were sovereign in their own domains. As Greece evolved from a warrior towards a mercantile society, the kings became obsolete. They survived on the edges of the Greek world in more primitive regions like Macedonia and Epirus, and in Sparta there was a curious limited monarchy consisting of two kings who shared ceremonial functions and led the army in battle like Blackfoot war chiefs.

But the real government of Sparta was in the hands of a military oligarchy, and here and there other transitional forms of government existed. In Massalia there was a mercantile oligarchy limited to 500 men which lasted into Roman times, and in Thessaly there was a landholding knightly aristocracy whose cavalry regiments were famous in ancient times.

But all these realms belonged to an economically less advanced world than the seacoast cities in which the first tyrannies appeared almost at the same time as Solon was carrying out his democratic reforms in Athens; it is significant that even in Athens this early democracy gave way to the tyranny of Peisistratus, and a lasting democratic system was not established there until late in the sixth century.

Often the circumstances that might produce a tyranny in

one city and a democracy in another were strikingly similar, arising from discontent with the privileged rule of a few power-ful families who had replaced the old kings. The typical tyrant was a popular leader who took power with the support of the disaffected lower classes and tried to hold it by furthering their interests. Most tyrants, it is true, became corrupted by the authority they wielded, but so, even in Greece, did most democratic leaders. A few tyrants, like Phalaris, became cruel despots and were responsible for the modern connotations of the word *tyranny*; on the other hand, some of the most ener-getic communities of the archaic age were ruled and spurred to activity by the tyrants who began to appear late in the seventh century.

One such community was Corinth. There Periander ruled as tyrant for forty years, from 625 to 585, and managed affairs so astutely that the Greeks afterwards talked of him as one of the Seven Sages of antiquity. In later years he seems to have become ruthless in dealing with opposition, and he always dis-trusted men of exceptional abilities who might become rivals. The tale goes that when he was new in office he sent a mes-senger to Thrasybulus, the tyrant of Miletus, asking his advice on how to rule. Thrasybulus took the messenger into a poppy field and silently gave his lesson by knocking off the heads of the tallest flowers with his stick; Periander apparently took the hint.

Whether the tale is true or was concocted later when tyrants had become unpopular, Corinth flourished in Periander's day as one of the great commercial centres of Hellas, and his peo-ple for the most part were content. Corinth built up an export trade in painted pottery that not only made the city's fortune but sparked off the great sixth-century commercial expansion of the cities of Greece and of the outlying colonies on the Mediterranean and the Black Sea. Corinthian ceramics were exported in quantity to "barbarian" countries like Etruria, whose craftsmen quickly imitated them. The modelling of clay ornaments for temples was first developed in Corinth, and the pottery industry was so well organized that when the tem-ple of Apollo at Calydon was re-roofed in the late sixth century, the tiles were brought ready-made from Corinth, each one numbered to be fitted into its place. The Corinthians also excelled in shipbuilding, which they carried on in the interests of both trade and naval power, for Periander had a large war fleet; they were the first Greeks to adopt a new invention of the Phoenicians and to build triremes, large warships propelled by triple banks of oars.

Corinth owed much of its prosperity and strategic advantages of the fact that, lying on the isthmus that unites the great pensinsula of Peloponnesus with the rest of Greece, it faced on two seas. The isthmus is narrow, but travelling by open sea from one side to the other involves a long voyage around the whole peninsula. Many centuries later the problem was solved by cutting the deep canal on which one now looks down from the highway bridge outside the city. But Periander, with the enterprise that characterized so many of the early tyrants, encouraged his engineers to develop their own ingenious solution. It was the *diolkos*, a stone road four miles long laid across the isthmus with two deep grooves for the wheels of the trolleys on which the ships were taken from one sea to another. Periander's engineers also created a hoist to lift the boats out of the water and on to the vehicles by which they were portaged. These inventions give the Corinthians credit for having built the first tramway in the world, the ancient precursor of modern railways.

Periander was concerned with public utilities as well as commercial advantages, and as Corinth developed under his rule he organized its water supply with a network of underground aqueducts with manholes for maintenance. He also encouraged visitors by operating what today would be called a wide open city. Thousands came to Corinth to take part in the pleasurable rites in the famous temple of Aphrodite on the peak of the mountain overlooking the city, and some of the women who worked there as sacred prostitutes, like the famous Lais, were among the celebrated courtesans of antiquity, as valued for their culture as for their beauty. Thousands of other travellers came to the Isthmian games, held close to Corinth; they were not so popular or prestigious as the Olympic or the

Pythian games, but enough athletes came to compete for the crowns of wild celery to make the four-yearly festival an important factor in the prosperity of Corinth, which profited not only from giving hospitality to the visitors but also from transporting many of them in its ships.

An even more celebrated member of the tyrant fraternity was Polycrates, who ruled the mountainous island of Samos. Polycrates was a violent combination of corsair, dictator and patron of the arts and sciences, of whom Herodotus, taking his tone from the accounts of the tyrant's contemporaries, wrote with a mixture of admiration and disgust.

In 538, with the support of a discontented populace, Polycrates seized the island from its reigning oligarchy; he was assisted by his two brothers, with whom at first he shared power. But soon he killed the elder and expelled the younger, and ruled Samos as his personal domain with a guard of a thousand Scythian archers. Like Periander in Corinth he became enough of a power in the Mediterranean for Ahmes II, whom the Greeks called Amasis, the last but one of the native Egyptian pharoahs, to conclude an alliance with him.

Polycrates was an adventurer who astonished all the Greeks, and even won the admiration of the Persians and the Egyptians, with a series of remarkable successes. For many years there was not a campaign he did not win, not a venture of his that did not succeed. He built a fleet of a hundred penteconters, swift narrow war galleys with fifty oars, and seized many of the islands, including sacred Delos, as well as some of the smaller Ionian towns on the Asian mainland. He was not afraid to go to war with the great trading city of Miletus. The Lesbians sent ships to the aid of Miletus, but Polycrates defeated them and used the prisoners in chaingangs; they dug the deep moat around the citadel in the city of Samos, which has now shrunk to tiny Pythagorion, named after the philosopher who was born there and who fled, it is said — though this is uncertain — because he feared Polycrates.

The citadel was a pioneer effort in the development of wall-fortification among the archaic Greeks, and altogether Samos was distinguished for its encouragement of the applied sciences, as distinct from the process of scientific enquiry and hypothesis that was developed in Miletus. Whatever Herodotus may have thought of the personality of Polycrates or his political inclinations, he admired his public works, which showed archaic Greek technology at its best. The great harbour of Samos, protected by a seawall running out to where the seabed was forty metres deep; the tunnel which Eupalinus drove through a mountain to bring water to the city; the great temple of Hera which, when the architect Theodorus began to build it, was the largest structure in the world, with 134 massive columns supporting its vast roof: these were all triumphs of the rapidly developing disciplines of engineering and architecture. The technical virtuosity of the Samians showed itself also in the great hollowcast bronze statues that versatile Theodorus made, and in the delicate gem carving of his nephew of the same name. With one gem in particular is linked one of the great moral stories of antiquity, a story the Greeks loved because it illustrated a theme that obsessed them, the idea that, whatever he wills, a man can never evade his fate.

Herodotus tells how the pharoah Ahmes II was troubled by the unfailing good fortune that marked all the enterprises undertaken by Polycrates. So Ahmes wrote a letter to his ally remarking on the gods' resentment of too much success: men whose luck was unbroken always seemed in the end to fall into ruin. He suggested Polycrates should choose what he valued most and get rid of it, and repeat the remedy whenever his good fortune seemed to be getting excessive. Polycrates took the advice to heart and decided the object he valued most was a ring with an emerald splendidly carved by Theodorus. He sailed out in his ceremonial barge and in the presence of many witnesses threw the jewel into the sea.

A few days later a fisherman caught an immense fish and brought it to the palace as a present to Polycrates. Polycrates, who like most tyrants had the democratic touch, accepted it and invited the fisherman to share the meal. But when the cook opened the fish, he found in its belly the ring Polycrates had thrown away. According to Herodotus, when Ahmes heard of this he decided Polycrates was destined for a wretched end, and terminated their treaty.

It may in fact have been Polycrates who abandoned the Egyptian alliance to curry favour with the Persians, for when Cambyses, son of Cyrus, invaded Egypt in 525, a contingent of ships from Samos sailed in his fleet. But Polycrates did come to a wretched end, at the hands of the very Persians he befriended. By playing on his greed, Oroetes, the satrap of Sardis, enticed him to the mainland and there tortured him to death and displayed his crucified and mutilated body at Magnesia.

During the years of his prosperity Polycrates invited to his court not only engineers and inventors, but also sculptors who executed the noble groups of deities in high relief that graced the temple of Hera, and some of the finest poets of the great age of Greek lyricism, notably Anacreon and Ibycus.

The sympathy between tyrants and artists was not peculiar to the sixth century; it existed in that equally creative setting, the Italy of the Renaissance, when the great *condottieri* like Sigismondo Malatesta protected and patronized the artists they admired. It was not the autocratic aspects of a tyrant's personality that dominated such exchanges; it was his highly developed individualism that found an echo in the poet's autonomous vision. Among the Greeks the sixth century was the first age of artistic individualism, when artists began to be appreciated as personalities rather than being treated as anonymous artisans. The relationship between creativity and personality was becoming recognized. In earlier times the names of men who commissioned and dedicated statues were recorded, but now it became the custom for sculptors to sign their work, and even the painters of vases began to record their names. The poets became the best known artists of all, since in those days before publishers or literary magazines they chanted their own poems before audiences or conducted their singing by choruses to the music of flutes. They depended on patrons to commission such poems. And in the sixth century the most consistent patrons, who provided the poets with bed

and board and gifts, were the tyrants of states as far scattered
as Samos, Athens and Syracuse. As the century drew to a close,
and tyrannies began to collapse everywhere but in Sicily, the
poets often found themselves unemployed and homeless. A
rich nest was destroyed when Polycrates was murdered, and
poets and other artists who found themselves in need of
wealthy friends, such as Anacreon and Simonides, crossed the
Aegean to Athens, where tyranny was still being maintained
by the sons of Peisistratus, Hippias and Hipparchus.

To return to the origins of the Athenian tyranny, it is not
entirely clear why the reforms initiated by Solon earlier in the
century had not survived by long his decade of wandering.
But it is certain that by the time Peisistratus first attempted
to assume power in 560 the old oligarchical families were
almost as powerful as ever. Enough resentment had developed
against them to enable Peisistratus eventually to conduct a
successful coup and set up a personal government so skillful
in catering to the wishes of Athenians that when he died in
527 it passed smoothly into the hands of his sons.

As absolute rulers go, Peisistratus was an enlightened one.
He observed the forms of the Athenian constitution and kept
in force the economic reforms Solon, who was his relative,
had made. He even went farther by establishing a fund to prevent small farmers from falling too deeply into debt. He made
justice more accessible by sending travelling magistrates to hear
cases and complaints in rural Attica, and himself went there
often to listen to the petitions of the poor, sometimes remit-
ting taxes and otherwise improving their lot. Once, accused
of infringing the code he upheld, he insisted on standing trial.
He was acquitted and must have known this would happen,
but the point of his action was to instil in the people the idea
of a universal obligation to keep the law in a society where
all men had access to the courts. Here he demonstrated the
difference between the best of the Greek tyrants and the best
of the despots who ruled outside the Hellenic world. Benevolent though they might be, one cannot imagine Croesus of
Lydia, or even wise Cyrus, subjecting himself in this way to
the law and its magistrates. In a different way from the pre-

Socratic philosophers of Miletus, Peisistratus was asserting the sixth-century emphasis on rational consistency.

Peisistratus was as great a patron of the arts as Polycrates, but his patronage was more public, in the sense that he encouraged and developed manifestations of the arts that, by involving all classes of the people, reflected not only the greatness but also the cohesion of Attic society. He developed the Panathenaic festival, with its splendid civic processions that celebrated both the city he ruled and its wise tutelary deity, the owl-attended Athene. He encouraged the cult of Demeter at Eleusis, with its teachings of redemption that anticipated Christian doctrines. But perhaps our greatest debt to him lies in his creation of the Great Dionysia, the festival for whose first celebration in 535 BC Thespis wrote the earliest of the Greek tragedies and initiated the dramatic tradition that still continues. So the stage was set for Aeschylus and his great successors; fifth-century Athenian drama flowered on a stem planted by a sixth-century tyrant.

Peisistratus was also a patron of the majestic Doric style of architecture that began to flourish in his time, and built the first great temple on the site of the Parthenon, to give greater glory to the cult of Athene. When the Persians destroyed this temple during their occupation of Athens in 480 BC, they also mutilated the archaic statues, the *kouroi* and *korai*, that stood in the building. The Athenians regarded these figures of youths and maidens as desecrated, and threw them into the foundations of the new temple they built in the age of Pericles. Recovered in recent years, these exquisite statues from the period of Peisistratus are among the most beautiful works of Greek sculpture; the enigmatic expressions on their pristine features eloquently convey the questing spirit of the archaic sixth century. Peisistratus also started construction on the great temple to Olympian Zeus, planned as the largest temple in the Hellenic world. Work on it was abandoned after the overthrow of his son Hippias in 510, and it stood half-finished for six centuries until the hellenophile Roman emperor Hadrian ordered its completion in the second century AD.

But neither Peisistratus nor his sons confined themselves

to erecting great monuments. They also carried out public works that benefited the populace, including the provision of abundant water. They established a modest and uniform tax on the land, much of which they redistributed to individual poor peasants by breaking up the estates of aristocrats who had exiled themselves because of their hostility to Peisistratus.

Finally, at the very time Jewish scholars were putting together in Babylon the Old Testament as we know it, Peisistratus gathered a group of Homeric rhapsodes in Athens and set scribes noting down their recitations of what each remembered of the *Iliad* and the *Odyssey*; these versions were collated into the written epics as we know them. Self-glorification and the glorification of Athens entered into the process. The public recitation of the epics became part of the Panathenaic festival, and the texts seem to have been tampered with to prove the prehistoric greatness of Athens by introducing an Attic contingent among the Greek ships that sailed for Troy. At the same period the Theseus myth was elaborated and the protagonist was turned into a national hero whose exploits exemplified the ancient greatness of Athens and reflected glory on his successor, Peisistratus. The Greek tyrants learnt early the value of image-making as an aid to retaining power.

Peisistratus died in 527, and Athens was now ruled by the tyrant's son Hippias, with the help of his brother Hipparchus. Like his father, Hippias exercised his authority through the republican office of archon, which had been established when the ancient kingdom came to an end in the eighth century, and ruled in his father's public-spirited and impartial manner according to the laws and reforms established by Solon and modified by Peisistratus.

No threat to his administration appeared among the populace. His principal enemies among the aristocracy were mostly banished from Athens, though a few had made their peace with Peisistratus and even held office under him. When a threat to the tyranny did appear in 514, it was, according to Thucydides, a conspiracy arising out of homosexual jealousy.

The tyrant's brother Hipparchus, the patron of Anacreon,

was attracted to the beautiful youth Harmodius, who rejected his advances since he already had a lover, Aristogeiton. In pique, Hipparchus insulted the family of Harmodius by refusing to let his sister take part in the great procession of the Panathenaic festival. Harmodius, Aristogeiton and some of their friends plotted revenge, and the two lovers slew Hipparchus. Harmodius was killed by the guards and Aristogeiton died under torture.

Later, after the overthrow of Hippias and the return of a democratic form of government, the two men were honoured as martyrs for liberty, and a bronze statue was dedicated to them. They were the subject of a popular Athenian song:

Your names will live for ever on earth,
Beloved Harmodius and Aristogeiton,
Because you slew the tyrant
And made Athens a city where all are equal.

Even Socrates (or Plato using his voice) expressed the same sentiment when he said that "the power of Aristogeiton's love and Harmodius's friendship brought the tyranny to an end."

But there is no evidence that the liberation of the Athenians was the aim of the assassins of Hipparchus, and it is doubtful if the regime's real political enemies, the Alcmaeonid clan, had any knowledge of the plot. But the cult of the two lovers, like the cult of Theseus, shows us how far sixth-century Athenians of all parties understood the value of creating martyrs and heroes as an aid to political propaganda. In fact, so little popular sympathy was shown for the assassins at the time of their act that the tyranny might have continued if Hippias had not reacted to his brother's death by becoming suspicious and vindictive. The open and expansive character which government had developed under Peisistratus was completely reversed. Hippias no longer troubled himself to serve the interests of the under-privileged, and so he lost his mass support, and the Alcmaeonids, aristocrats masquerading as democrats, returned with the help of the Spartans and the blessing of the Delphic oracle and easily expelled Hippias and the few followers who remained loyal to him.

What happened in Athens explains a great deal about the

way Hellenic attitudes were evolving during the sixth century. During the seventh century an oligarchy based on landholding power had emerged in Athens. But land was of dwindling importance, since Attica was rapidly turning into an industrial and trading society. Solon's reforms improved but did not radically change the system. He rectified some economic inequities and ensured that Athenians could never again use their financial power to enslave other Athenians; his actions implied no general opposition to slavery nor did they protect other Greeks from servitude to Athenians. He also opened the political system to involve the citizenry more directly and democratically. Yet even after his reforms Athenian society remained far from egalitarian, and much power was left to the landholding class. Peisistratus was able to take it from them with the open or covert support of less privileged groups, and during his reign he not only sustained Solon's laws but also interpreted them to the advantage of the poor.

In most sixth-century cities where tyrants took power, the citizens accepted them for relatively long periods; some hereditary tyrannies, like that of Corinth, lasted more than a century. When a tyrant kept the state prosperous and his people relatively content, there was neither any great inclination to rebel or any widespread tendency to emigrate. Those who fled from Athens under Peisistratus were not the poets, artists or thinkers; they were not the peasant farmers and especially not the artisans, who were largely metics or foreign workers who had come to Attica from choice. The fugitives were active political rivals of the tyrant, men who found it prudent to leave. A Greek tyrant was usually a citizen of the *polis* he ruled, and so the populace tended to regard him as one of their own, a man who understood and shared their beliefs and hopes. If, like Peisistratus or Periander, he made the city more splendid or prosperous, that went to show what a good citizen he was. The sense of cultural alienation from such a ruler never arose.

On the other hand, the sense of cultural alienation dominated the relations between Greeks and non-Hellenic rulers. Despite the tolerance of Cyrus and his successor Darius for the ways of life of subject peoples, Greeks did not feel they could live a full Hellenic life under a king whose culture was foreign. And so the very men — poets and thinkers — who gave Ionian Greek culture its special quality fled in considerable numbers and scattered over the distances of the Hellenic world when the Persians came. Xenophanes left Colophon and Anacreon left Teos, while the Phocaeans departed *en masse* in their penteconters to spread their settlements into the western Mediterranean. Many of those who remained, like the historian Hecataeus, became involved in the Ionian rebellion of 499 BC and after its failure joined the exiles. Clearly, provided he was a Greek, the rule of a tyrant supported by the populace fitted in with the Hellenic idea of good government in the sixth century BC, while a benevolent alien King of Kings who tolerated and even patronized the Greeks but had no feeling for their culture was unacceptable. Croesus had been accepted only because he became a kind of cultural convert, more Greek than many Greeks.

In retrospect, the tyrannies can be seen as part of a general social progression which by the end of the sixth century was moving away from them. By the early decades of the fifth century most of the tyrannies that had flourished within the preceding hundred years had come to an end. Even the Persians, sensing the trend of the times, withdrew their support after the Ionian revolt from the tyrants in the Greek cities under their control and allowed democracies to emerge. Only in Italy and especially Sicily did tyranny retain its vigour for a longer period, doubtless because of the tyrants' effective organization of resistance to the Carthaginians and the Etruscans, who were pressing on the Greek areas of trade and influence.

The tyrants had served their purpose by fostering trade, by cultivating foreign links that enriched Greek art, architecture and science, by enhancing with fine buildings and appropriate myths the standing of their cities, by providing needed public works which oligarchies might not have agreed upon, and by fostering the emergence of new classes of merchants and artisans to challenge the old landholding aristocracies. More surely than law-givers like Solon, who merely offered fragile codes, they prepared their cities for democracy by providing the economic and social foundations on which it could be based. So, in Athens, when Hippias had lost his popular support, the result was neither a return to the rule of an aristocratic oligarchy, nor the establishment of a military state like that of the Spartans, who participated so eagerly in the expulsion of the Peisistratids. Cleisthenes, the leader of the Alcmaenid clan, found it impossible to instal himself as a new tyrant. But the Spartans found it equally impossible to restore the oligarchy under Isagoras. The tyranny of Peisistratus, following on the reforms of Solon, had broken that pattern, making unthinkable a return to the old structures based on economic injustice between Athenians. In this way the rule of Peisistratus took its place in the evolution of Athenian political forms from monarchy through oligarchy and tyranny to the broad though male-dominated democracy that the reforms of Cleisthenes established by the late sixth century, a democracy that in all its vicissitudes proved more stable and more durable than Solon's reforms in the early years of the sixth century.

III

If the tyrannies often led Greek cities by indirect and culturally fruitful paths towards democracy, they did little to change the other striking characteristic of archaic Hellas, its expansive disunity. The Persians too were expansive, but the fundamental difference was that as imperialists the Persians created a unity embracing a diversity of cultures, whereas the Greeks were great colonizers, spreading their homogeneous culture over an even larger area than that over which the Persians established their empire, but remaining politically fragmented.

The motives of the Greek expansion, which began as early as the late eighth century, were partly demographic and partly commercial. Population pressures forced many Greek cities which had little arable land to send their surplus inhabitants abroad in search of places to settle. Most Greek cities became increasingly dependent on imported foodstuffs; Athens, for example, concentrated more and more on cultivating the vine and the olive, which suited its rocky ground, and bought vast quantities of foreign wheat to feed a population no longer content with the barley cakes of the past. As their scanty stands of timber were felled, the cities also had to import wood to build the ships needed for trading and warfare. The only economically important material readily available was the clay out of which Corinth and Athens built their great ceramic industries. Even stone had often to be brought from the islands, particularly the fine Paros marble which so many communities coveted as they became prosperous and anxious to enhance their civic images. Metals were even more difficult to obtain. Few cities had sources of their own like the silver mines at Laurium which the Athenians were just beginning to exploit at the end of the sixth century. Iron and copper had to be brought from the Balkans, and tin, an essential component of bronze, was carried by long inland routes from the North Sea or traded at ports like Tartessus, on the Atlantic shore beyond the Strait of Gibraltar.

These patterns were well established by the beginning of the sixth century, but they were given impetus when the kings of Lydia invented the standard coinage, which they used first to pay their Greek mercenaries. Its usefulness for trade was quickly recognized, and soon most Greek states, led by the highly commercial community of Aegina, had their own coinages. Only conservative Sparta continued to use such antique and cumbrous tokens of exchange as iron spits. With the introduction of portable money came the great increase in imports, which drew vast amounts of raw materials and foodstuffs to the cities of Ionia, the Greek mainland and Magna Graecia, and which was balanced by the export of Greek wine and olive oil and of manufactured goods like the pottery of Corinth and Athens, the fine woollens of Miletus, and the metalwork of Laconia and of the cities of southern Italy, notably Taras, the later Taranto.

Trade and colonization worked together. Many a place that

started as a mere emporium ended as a colony devoted to agriculture; Massalia with its vineyards and olive groves, its Rhône valley trade and its satellite centres of Antibes and Nice, Monaco and St. Rémy, fulfilled both functions. Trading voyages often by accident expanded the bounds of the known world and brought its people into the orbit of Greek culture. An example was that of the Samian trader Colaeus in the late seventh century. Sailing along the coast of Libya in the direction of the great Greek trading centre of Naucratis at the mouth of the Nile, Colaeus was blown by contrary winds westward across the Mediterranean and finally out through the Strait where he eventually reached Tartessus in western Spain. There he filled his craft with silver and other metals in which the Tartessians traded, made a greater profit on his cargo than any Greek merchant before him, and started a trade that scattered posts and settlements on its way all along the northern shores of the Mediterranean.

Another notable trader-navigator, celebrated by Herodotus, was Sostratus of Aegina, who traded extensively to Italy; a dedication made by him has been found in a Greek shrine at the port of Gravisca near the Etruscan city of Tarquinia, and vases that have been discovered bearing his mark suggest that he founded a considerable business in exporting Athenian black-figure ware to the towns of Etruria.

Colaeus and Sostratus were only the best known of the many Greeks who departed on trading voyages or loaded their ships with stock and seed and implements and set out to find a piece of land on shores inhabited by people less sophisticated and militarily adept. They travelled in every direction. The tale of the Golden Fleece narrates a mythical journey to the farthest end of the Black Sea, and certainly by the late sixth century the Greeks were trading for gold in colonies like Dioscurias in the shadow of the Caucasus, where seventy tribal languages could be heard in the market place. At Olbia near the mouth of the Dniester they traded fine silverware with the Royal Scyths in return for slaves and for the wheat that was already being grown on the steppes of the Ukraine. At smaller posts in Crimea they caught and dried fish for the cities of

Ionia and the Greek mainland. In Thrace on the western shore
of the Sea they mined and traded silver; on the south shore
Trebizond came into existence as Trapezus and dealt for metals
with the peoples of the Anatolian mountains.

Most of the Black Sea traders and colonists came from Miletus, which founded no less than forty-five colonies. But its
trading connections were far more extensive: it had close links
with Corinth and with Sybaris in southern Italy. Nor was the
Black Sea entirely a Milesian lake. Athenians occupied the
Chersonese, which we call Gallipoli, at the vital entry to the
Sea of Marmora, and Miltiades became its tyrant, while at
the entry to the Bosporus the people of Megara founded the
city of Byzantium, which long afterwards became the transmitter of Hellenic values to the modern western world.

Far to the west the Phocaeans had followed Colaeus in their
swift fifty-oared penteconters to Tartessus, which Ezekiel
called Tarshish, and between that far trading post and the
Ligurian coast they established a series of emporia and small
colonies on the shores of Spain and Provence. From Massalia, the centre of all this activity, which they founded in 600
'BC, the Phocaeans changed the whole character of Gallic
agriculture by introducing the grape and the olive and
encouraging a taste for wine among the Celts they encountered on the headwaters of the Rhône. Long before the first
local *crus* were gathered, Greek wine from Massalia was being
drunk by the people of what is now Burgundy. The Celts with
whom the Massaliot merchants traded belonged to the relatively sophisticated Iron Age culture centred on the Austrian
salt-mining centre of Hallstadt; they controlled a network of
trade routes by which the vital tin supplies were brought overland from Cornwall and Brittany. The Phocaeans even
founded a colony at Alalia in Corsica but were forced to abandon it because of the hostility of the Etruscans.

In southern Italy and Sicily, where colonists came from
every part of Hellas, there were so many Greek cities that the
region was known to the Romans as Magna Graecia — Great
Greece. Some of these places developed into major modern
cities, like Naples and Messina, Reggio di Calabria and Syra-

cuse. Cumae, of which only ruins remain, long exercised a civilizing influence over Etruscans and Romans, providing them with an alphabet and influencing their art; Cumae was the home of the famous oracular priestess known as the Sibyl, and the prophetic book she gave to one of the Tarquin kings of Rome, the Sibylline Leaves, was consulted for centuries after at times of crisis in Rome. Some cities of Magna Graecia, like notorious Sybaris, vanished without a trace, yet in this region the best relics of archaic Greek architecture have survived, such as the great temples at Paestum (Poseidonia) and Agrigento (Acragas), and to this day they give one a sense of the wealth that these far-flung Greek communities acquired in the sixth century and the vigour of the culture they transmitted from their homeland. Even in Africa, at Cyrene in Libya and Naucratis in Egypt, communities of Greeks sustained the common culture of the Hellenes, sharing gods and language, arts and literature, the cult of games and the Odyssean sense of venture.

Almost all these hundreds of Greek colonies lay on the shores of the Black Sea or the Mediterranean, and even the most agriculturally oriented, like Metapontum in Italy and Gela in Sicily, still engaged in seaborne trade. They allowed an increase in population that could never have been accommodated in mainland Greece with its rocky hinterland, and an upsurge in enterprise that could not have found satisfaction there. Except for Naucratis, which was a kind of ancient Shanghai, operated under the protection of the pharoahs by a consortium of trading cities that shared a common temple, the Hellenium, every one of the colonies was a city state, independent of the community from which the colonists had departed, and sometimes in conflict with it, as Corcyra was with Corinth. Hellas was a vast constellation of mutually independent polities, ranging from the simple pastoral communities of Arcadia to cities like Athens, Miletus and Syracuse, where a complex and vigorous civilization was developing. Whatever the political consequences of this fragmentation of the Hellenes, the cultural effects were extraordinary. Places we might regard as minor towns produced artistic movements and groups of philosophers and pioneer scientists that have given them a status in world history out of all proportion to their areas or their populations. Visiting the sites of the Greek archaic cities, one is always astonished by their smallness in comparison with their fame.

Compactness, civic pride and distance from each other resulted in the notable cities of the archaic age making unique contributions to the general Hellenic culture. We remember Athens for its drama, and the Lesbian city of Mytilene for the part it played in fostering lyric poetry. Miletus was the centre of the development of natural philosophy, though other Ionian cities produced notable thinkers, like Xenophanes of Colophon and Heraclitus of Ephesus, and by the end of our period Parmenides was making Italian Elea a new centre of philosophic speculation. Epidaurus maintained its repute as a healing centre owing to the ancient cult of Aesculapius, but Croton in Italy became a medical centre more experimental in its approach and produced many of the celebrated physicians of antiquity. Of science applied to architecture and engineering, the centres were Samos and Megara, whose engineers were famed for their expertise in providing public water supplies.

The archaic Greeks were highly conscious of the advantages of a relatively small community. Aristotle claimed generations afterwards that a city should not have an area larger than the eye could easily encompass from its acropolis; his sixth-century predecessors would have agreed with him. A small city was easy to administer, whether by direct democracy — provided the male adult population was small enough to assemble in a single space — or by a tyrant who moved as easily through the market place as the mayor of a small modern town, and who like Polycrates might ask fishermen to dinner or like Peisistratus might wander the back roads asking peasants about their personal grievances. Yet smallness was no bar to prosperity. Colonial cities that had sufficient land to feed their people, good craftsmen to create local industries, and an active trading system could become amazingly wealthy, as witness the remains of sixth-century communities like Acragas, Cyrene and Poseidonia, and the repute of others like Sybaris.

This was the period when the deliberate planning of cities

began. After Miletus was destroyed by the Persians in 494, it was rebuilt according to the design of Hippodamus on a regular gridiron system, like a modern North American town. But this kind of planning had already appeared in the new cities of Italy, which were built on virgin land portioned out in equal plots to the new settlers and restricted to manageable size. Some of the older cities remained irregular and even chaotic in their configurations; in Athens the embellishments of the Peisistratids affected mostly the acropolis and the area around the agora, and the rest of the city remained a swollen village with narrow and often muddy winding lanes. Sparta too, with deliberate rusticity, retained much of the character of the several closely-spaced villages out of which it had coalesced. And, though they were larger, more populous and more problem-ridden than most Hellenic cities, even Athens and Sparta long remained the kind of places where every man could feel, as he marched in the hoplite ranks or voted laws in the company of his neighbours, that he was a necessary part of a living community.

The archaic Greeks were patriots in the sense George Orwell used when he said, "By 'patriotism' I mean devotion to a particular place and a particular way of life, which one believes to be the best in the world but has no wish to force upon other people." The Greek cities warred with each other, mainly over trade and land; they might even enslave each other's citizens and sometimes massacre men capable of bearing arms. But the physical destruction of another Greek city was so unusual that the news of the levelling of Sybaris by the people of Croton, led by the Olympic wrestler Milo and egged on by Pythagoras, sent an agonized shudder through the Hellenic world. In general, in the sixth century at least, wars between Greeks were rarely fought to establish territorial domination, though Sparta, which was also exceptional in its devotion to the ideals of the military life, established a bullying hegemony, based on threats, over the other Dorian states of the Peloponnesus during the later years of the century; even then the constituent states retained their sovereignty, and there was no attempt at a federal administration. Cases like that of

Gelon, tyrant of Gela, who moved on from his own city to take power in Syracuse and unite a great deal of Sicily under a single rule, were quite exceptional.

IV

So, in the period ending in the decisive battles against the Persians in 480 and 479 BC, we see a Hellenic world consisting of hundreds of autonomous communities — oligarchies, tyrannies and democracies — bound together by language and culture but only in exceptional cases politically united. The occasions when the Hellenes came together were mainly ceremonial. Competitors and spectators from all over the Greek world gathered at Olympia and Delphi, at Nemea and Corinth, for the great games held once every four years at these sacred sites, dates in the sixth century being generally calculated by reference to the first Olympiad, which according to tradition took place in 776 BC. By tacit consent truces were established at the time of the games which allowed people to travel without hindrance or danger to these places, while at the games themselves athletes from cities that were mutually hostile competed in peace and fellowship under the protection of the gods.

Clearly there was no intrinsic inability to co-operate among the Greeks; they did it constantly on a civic level. The *polis* itself, even when operated by an oligarchy or a tyrant, presupposed a sense of community and a willingness to act together, particularly in the armies of citizen soldiers which the city states developed at this period, that had no parallel in the ancient empires of the Near East.

In specific instances Hellenic communities could co-operate just as effectively as individuals — in the Amphictyonic League, for example, that protected the shrine at Delphi and organized the Pythian games, and in the merchant community of Naucratis, where Greeks from a dozen cities shared in the administration.

But when it was a matter of a broader co-operation involving even a partial submergence of their local sovereignty, the

Greeks found it virtually impossible to unite. The case of the
Ionian cities is a particularly striking one. They had accepted
the suzerainty of the hellenophile Lydian kings, who had left
them largely to their own devices, so that when Croesus inter-
vened it was usually to perform some act of generous reverence to the Greek gods, like his giving subsidies towards the
building of the Artemesium at Ephesus. Miletus alone, thanks
to the adroit diplomacy of the tyrant Thrasybulus, had evaded
Lydian suzerainty and entered into treaty as an equal with the
Lydian kingdom.

When the Persians came in 546, Cyrus sent messengers
ahead to the Greek cities on the Asian shores of the Aegean
suggesting they transfer their allegiance to him. Enjoying the
easy yoke of Croesus, and preferring the congenial overlord
they knew to the unknown barbarian from the distant mountains, the Greeks ignored the Persian approaches. But when
Croesus was defeated, Cyrus automatically became the over-
lord of all the Asian Greek cities except for Miletus. The
Greeks hurriedly sent a delegation asking the King of Kings
to give them the same easy terms as Croesus had done. In his
best anecdotal style Herodotus recorded what happened:

Cyrus gave his answer in the form of a story. One day
a fluteplayer saw a shoal of fish swimming in the sea,
and he played his flute to them, hoping in this way to
tempt them on land. But when the fish took no notice,
he caught them in a net and hauled them on land. The
fish leapt about in the net, but the fluteplayer laughed
at them and said: "Now it is too late for you to dance;
you could have danced when I played to you, but you
did not want to."

At this time the Ionians had a kind of sacred league, and
a common temple to Poseidon, which they called the Pan-
ionium, on the cape of Mycale outside Priene. Here they met
to discuss the situation. For political reasons, the Spartans
refused them help. Then two of the Seven Sages offered their
advice. Thales, who knew something of military matters from
having served as a kind of consulting engineer for King
Alyattes of Lydia during his campaign against the Medes,

urged them not to fight singly but to form a confederation
for the purpose of common defence. Bias of Priene went even
further, suggesting that they pool their fleets, leave their cities,
and sail to the largely uninhabited island of Sardinia and there
establish a great Ionian republic.

The Ionians accepted neither sage's advice, nor did they
agree on a common plan. In two cities most of the people
decided to leave ahead of the Persian armies: the Phocaeans
went to join their fellow citizens in the western Mediterranean
and founded their short-lived city of Alalia on Corsica, while
the inhabitants of Teos, which Thales had suggested should
be the capital of the Ionian federation, set sail for the Black
Sea, with the young poet Anacreon among them, and founded
Abdera on the Thracian coast. Except for Miletus, which made
its own terms, the rest of the cities resisted the Persians singly,
and the invaders had no difficulty defeating them one by one,
occupying their territories and setting up puppet tyrants.

Many of the poets, artists and philosophers left the Ionian
cities, to the great cultural benefit of Athens and the cities
of Magna Graecia and Sicily. But the Persians were not in
fact bad masters by the standards of the ancient world. They
allowed the Greeks to follow their own customs and continue
their familiar trading practices, so long as they paid tribute
regularly. Yet the Ionians grew discontented with alien rule,
and in 499 they rose in rebellion with Miletus at their head,
and this time they gained the support of the Athenians, who
regarded themselves as the primal Ionian stock.

Politically, the forces aligned against the Persians were a
mixed group. The Athenians had thrown off their own tyrant
a decade ago and established a democracy, but in Ionia the
revolt was largely led by tyrants, including men like Histiaeus
and Aristagoras of Miletus, who only a few years before, in
513 when they accompanied Darius in his invasion of Scythia,
had rejected the suggestion of Miltiades that they break up
the bridge of boats across the Danube and leave the Persians
stranded in the Ukraine. With such men it is hard to distinguish personal from patriotic motives. But the alliance was
nevertheless a historic one, since for the first time a war was

being conducted on behalf of all Greeks, and it led directly
to the great conflict between the Persians and the Hellenes
with which our period ends.

But though they now had a common aim, the allies failed
to achieve any real unity of action. As we have seen in connection with his sacrilegious advice concerning the treasure
of the shrine at Didyma, Hecataeus suggested to them that
they develop a common navy, arguing that since they were
a maritime people they should fight at sea against the Persians, who were their military superiors on land.

The allies ignored him and paid for it. Instead of establishing a mobile seaborne force to defend their cities wherever
attacked, they took to the land and marched in from the coast
to burn the old Lydian capital of Sardis, where the Persians
had established a satrapy. But the weight of the Persian armies
defeated them, Athens withdrew its forces, and, for lack of
a rebel navy, the cities were again picked off one by one, and
Miletus was destroyed.

Neither the war nor the disunity among the Greeks ended
here. Once he had dealt with the rebel cities, Darius was eager
to take revenge on the Athenians. When they heard that the
Persian army was on its way, the Athenians asked the Spartans for help. But the Spartans were engaged in religious rites
and decided they could not march immediately to the aid of
their fellow Greeks. So when the Persians landed on Greek
soil with their great army recruited from the vast arc of
Achaemenian territory between India and Egypt, the Athenians could muster only their own ten thousand spearmen and
another thousand from the little city of Plataea.

What followed astonished the ancient world and radically
affected its history and ours. Herodotus describes vividly how
the Athenians surprised the Persians by advancing without the
support of cavalry or archers, relying merely on their spears
and their courage. The battle that had begun in a desperate
charge ended in victory as "the Athenians hounded the
defeated enemy down to the water's edge, slaying them as they
ran." The sense that Marathon had not only preserved Hellas
but had in some way elevated it gave the battle and its par-

ticipants a special place in Athenian esteem. Herodotus tells us, "The Athenians who fought at the battle were greatly honoured by their fellow citizens, and were distinguished for the rest of their lives by being called the Men of Marathon."

One of the Men of Marathon was Aeschylus, the dramatist, whose brother was killed in the battle. Nearly forty years later, when he was an old man living in Sicily, with a great dramatic career behind him, Aeschylus composed his own epitaph and did not even mention his plays. It was of the great battle that he wrote, with a clear sense of its historic importance:

Planted in the rich cornfields of Gela,
This stone shelters the body of Aeschylus,
Euphorion's son from Athens.
The glorious ground of Marathon
Can tell of his bravery;
The long-haired Persians felt its edge.

The Athenians not only ended the fear the Persians had inspired among the Greeks ever since the day they came in 546. They also showed that Greek hoplites drawn from their farms and workshops could be superior to the soldiers of the great Asian empires, and so when Persians invaded Greece again a decade later in 480 they found all the mainland cities united to fight against them at Salamis and Plataea.

It was the beginning of the long transition from tribalism through the city state to nationhood. But nothing resembling a modern nation state emerged during the archaic period in Greek history or during the classical age that followed it. Sometimes the cities formed leagues determined by common interests and usually dominated by a powerful state, like the Peloponnesian League under Sparta and the Delian League under Athens, but these were temporary arrangements, and there were no attempts to form a true and lasting confederation based in common interests. In later decades the cities fell under the control of imperial powers like Macedonia and Rome, yet even then they stubbornly maintained their individual polities. The self-governed and largely autonomous local community remained to the end of the classical period the nucleus of Hellenic society, and long into the Roman age the noble Greek cities of the sixth century, from Massalia and Cyrene and Syracuse in the west to Athens and Ephesus and the growing centre of Byzantium in the east, still continued as the focuses of culture.

Indeed, one has to set against the political disadvantages of city states in a world of imperial adventurers the encouragement such communities offered to a developing individualism, which paralleled the emergence of a historical as distinct from a mythical consciousness. Men and women had become more than mere members of the tribe fulfilling their ritual obligations to the collectivity. Within the invigorated Greek communities of the sixth century they burgeoned as personalities whose relation to the *polis* was a mutual rather than a subordinate one. A man might risk his life at Marathon so that Athens could be preserved, but this was because the freedoms of the city had allowed a way of life to emerge in which individuals could develop and in turn enrich the community with the fruits of that development. Nowhere in the world before that time did such a crop of highly differentiated personalities appear as emerged in the cities of archaic Greece — men and women who believed that not only their external achievements were important enough to record, but also their inner lives, their thoughts and emotions. Humanity strode the earth and the gods retreated.

This development was, perhaps naturally enough, most notable among the poets, who dealt with matters of mind and spirit and, above all, imagination. The tendency had begun to stir among them earlier on, at the dawn of the archaic age, and it can be seen very clearly in the way the character of Odysseus developed from one Homeric epic to the next. In the late ninth-century *Iliad* he is still the tribal chief, mainly distinguished by his pragmatic cunning, which contrasts with the passionate impetuosity of Achilles; his intelligence, so valued by the later Greeks, is represented as less admirable than the mindless courage of his fellow warriors. But the adventures of the eighth-century *Odyssey* reveal an individual who has his full share of encounters with mythical beings yet emerges out of this background as the first completely realized human being in literature, a man with whom we can identify as we can with no person in the *Iliad*, his character and his feelings so intricately presented that the *Odyssey* has often with some justice been described as the first novel.

From the *Odyssey* it was a relatively short step in time, beyond the mythological concerns of the Homeric hymns and of Hesiod's *Theogony*, to those extraordinary poems in which the seventh-century soldier from Paros, Archilochus, showed himself frankly in his courage and cowardice, and presented to the world for the first time an intelligence observing itself and its world with ironic clarity. When Archilochus mocked the heroic tradition by writing about how he left his shield and ran for his life and rejoiced in his survival, the emergence of realism in literature and in life was signified. From Archilochus it was only another brief step to the sixth-century poets who, in ways we shall discuss shortly, speak directly to twentieth-century men. In this way the first real windows into human minds were opened by poets in the Greek cities of the archaic era.

And just as those cities encouraged the flowering of individual personalities, so they encouraged the differentiation of thought and of its application, so that the philosophers of the time and the men who put philosophy to practical uses — as geometers, geographers, astronomers, engineers, architects — appeared in many places throughout the Hellenic world, and developed the amazing range of approaches that spans from Thales to Pythagoras, from Xenophanes to Heraclitus, from the physician Democedes to that Leonardo of archaic technology, Theodorus of Samos, all of whom we shall meet again in these pages. In the end the Greek cities were to die of their disunity, but that very disunity had produced a remarkable process of cultural variegation, and variegation, in the human as much as in the natural world, is the essence of creative evolution.

V

The disunity of the sixth-century world expressed itself not only in the presence of hundreds of city states, each of them a sovereign *polis*, but also in a basic division within the

Hellenic world, that between the Dorian and the Ionian races, which in political and cultural terms was projected in the historic rivalry between Sparta and Athens, between the city that during the sixth century degenerated into the world's first totalitarian state and the city that by the end of the same period was developing into the world's first real democracy.

Claiming descent from the god Heracles, the Dorian peoples occupied much of the Peloponnesus after the decline of the Mycenaean kingdoms towards the end of the second millenium BC. The Ionians had earlier settled Attica and emigrated in the beginning of the first millenium to found many Greek cities in Asia Minor and on the Aegean Islands. They also established most of the new cities on the shores of the Black Sea and the Mediterranean. Athens saw itself as the leading *polis* in the Ionian world, and with this in view exercised a protective role over the great Ionian sanctuary of Apollo on the island of Delos.

Sparta set itself up as the leading Dorian power, and claimed that its devotion to martial discipline came from the mythical connection with Heracles. However, the special characteristics and institutions of Sparta as it developed into a military state in the sixth century were not shared by other Dorian cities. The Peloponnesian League, as later historians call it (the Greeks preferred to say, "the Spartans and their allies"), was based on power rather than on cultural sympathies. Argos, an ancient Dorian city and Sparta's principal rival on the peninsula, did not join the league and allied itself with Ionian Athens, while Corinth joined because of its bitter commercial rivalry with Athens rather than because of any political sympathy for Sparta. Apart from a few small communities on Crete, none of the Dorian cities shared Sparta's military organization.

The great contest between Athens and Sparta and their respective leagues belongs to the fifth century, outside our period, but the seeds for it were sown by the different way the two cities developed during the sixth century. And here it must be emphasized that the history of Sparta introduces a cautionary note into our account of the period. It reminds

us that, if so many of the innovations of the age were beneficial, others were not, and left negative heritages.

Essentially what distinguished Athens and Ionia from Sparta
was a broad and flexible cultural receptiveness. Without los-
ing their essentially Hellenic outlook, the Ionians, including
the Athenians, were willing to adopt good ideas or useful
inventions that came from outside. Trading beside the Phoenicians, they saw the use of an alphabet; living beside the
Lydians, they adopted from them the idea of money and a
mode of music that was less stern than the Dorian mode. In
astronomy they borrowed from the Babylonians; in geome-
try, architecture and sculpture from the Egyptians. Even in
religion the new cults of Orpheus and Dionysus were Thracian, and out of one of them, as we have seen, Athenian drama
emerged. At the same time the Ionian Greeks gave as well as
receiving, projecting elements of their culture wherever they
traded or settled, so that art styles in regions as far apart as
Scythia and Etruria were influenced by Greek models; Ionian
sculptors introduced Greek motifs and skills into the Persian
palace complexes built by Cyrus and Darius; fortresses constructed by Celtic chieftains in Germany were designed by
Greek military architects; and the Romans derived their
alphabet from Cumae, which was settled by Greeks of Ionian
origin.

The spirit of Ionia, receptive and projective, spread to
Greeks of other origins, like the Aeolians, as Hellenic culture
spread outwards on the currents of trade and colonization,
until few communities were entirely unaffected. Even Dorian
Corinth exported its arts and its influence and adopted innovatory ideas from outside almost as readily as Ionian Miletus.

Sparta was the only major city state that deliberately refused
to join the movement of creative innovation, and, rather than
going forward, wilfully regressed into what, rightly or wrongly,
its citizens believed was their primal past. One of the most
significant decisions of the Spartans during this century was
to refuse to join the other cities of Greece in coining money.
In doing so they rejected as part of their way of existence the
commerce that was rapidly changing the lives of cities like

Athens and Aegina, Corinth and Miletus. Sparta would remain an agrarian and military community, its economy based on the labour of conquered serfs.

Why did Sparta break from the rest of the Hellenes to become the prototype of the modern totalitarian state? Both literary traditions and archaeological evidence suggest that during the seventh century and well into the sixth Sparta was moving in the same direction as other Greek cities. It was one of the leading centres of music and choral poetry. Not only were there fine native poets, but great lyricists were attracted from outside, including the early Lesbian poet Terpander, who is said to have invented the seven-stringed lyre, and the Hellenized Lydian Alcman, whose songs for choruses of maidens suggest a way of living and a style of music softer by far than those traditionally associated with Sparta.

Archaeological finds suggest that the artistic freedom represented by the seventh-century flowering of poetry and music in Sparta was accompanied by a great deal of richness and colour in an everyday life that by the late sixth century had become as drably austere as that of the citizens of Orwell's Oceania in *1984*. As Russell Meiggs remarks in his revision of J. B. Bury's *History of Greece*:

> Imports of ivory, often carved, amber, scarabs, gold and silver jewelry show that Sparta had wide contacts with the seventh century; and Laconian craftsmen in ivory, bone and pottery could compare with the best in Greece . . . . While other states developed industrial and artistic production, Sparta gradually lost the material refinements of living.

Meiggs as well links the decline in Sparta's artistic life with the failure to produce a silver coinage, a failure that automatically removed the state from the rapidly growing network of Hellenic commerce.

Undoubtedly the clue to Sparta's change lay in its increasing pursuit of war as a political means. By the end of the seventh century, through its two great wars with the Messenians, Sparta had conquered a great deal of territory in ancient Greek terms and was ruling it by turning its own people into a military caste governing a lower caste, mainly Messenian, who had no loyalty to the conquering state.

It was after the second Messenian war in the late seventh century — a great serf revolt that nearly succeeded — that the historic changes in the Spartan way of life began. The method of warfare which the Spartans perfected in winning that conflict was to use spearmen, the citizen hoplites, in well-drilled phalanxes that advanced with the relentlessness of tanks. The summit of military technology in its age, this form of warfare, unlike the earlier and essentially aristocratic cavalry warfare that still survived in backward Thessaly, demanded a large number of able-bodied men, and so the Spartan nation became an immense army, always in training and dedicated to keeping in order the helots who cultivated the land.

Everyone became involved in this reshaping of the nation into a military machine, and the technological talents that in the rest of Greece were being dedicated to engineering and architecture, to the arts and the crafts, were here devoted to evolving an efficient conscript army and to breeding and training a people to serve in it and service it. Once the military machine had been developed it acquired a secondary use in the conquest and intimidation of other states, so that Sparta soon became the dominant power in western Greece and later challenged Athens for the hegemony of the Hellenic heartland and temporarily won. But the Spartan citizen army's first and essential role was an internal one, to repress Messenian helots and disaffected Spartans, and this continued to be its primary function even in the days when the state was embarking on foreign adventures, so that the very heart of the system was a secret police, the Krypteia, that was the true ancestor of the Cheka and the Gestapo.

Along with their techniques of warfare and repression, the Spartans developed a system of social and genetic engineering aimed at providing recruits for the army. Women were expected to obey the dictates of the state in bearing children, even if this meant their being fathered outside the marriage tie; children, once born, were rigorously examined, and discarded if they were considered too weak to become sturdy soldiers or good breeding mothers. At the age of seven, boys were educated in training camps and subjected to severe and often humiliating disciplines that conditioned them to become unquestioning soldiers ready to die rather than retreat. Even in manhood, the male Spartans messed together and lived, in peacetime as in war, under military discipline, while the women too went through rigorous physical training and mental conditioning to make them fit to become the mothers of warriors.

In this way were bred the Spartan "virtues" — stubborn courage, unthinking obedience, physical hardiness, civic solidarity — that in later generations appealed to such a variety of authoritarians, from Plato to the stalwarts of the Jacobin Club, from the public school masters who trained the British rulers to the founders of Fascism and the pseudo-intellectuals of Nazism.

But the Spartan way of life, so praised for its simplicity and frugality, was in fact both complex and deprived. Until the advent of Alexander, the Spartan army was perhaps the most efficient and elaborately organized military machine in the ancient world, and the Krypteia was certainly its most efficient secret police. Nor was there anything simple — when one compares it with the fluent and easy Athenian life projected in Plato's dialogues and Xenophon's memorabilia — about the rules for living and the training techniques by which the Spartans became the flawless components in a machine for making war. As in most cultures dedicated to war, the quality of life suffered not merely because the arts and graces of contemporary Hellenic living were increasingly despised as luxuries unnecessary for the warrior, but also because the human resources of the state were increasingly dedicated to military service and the manufacture of arms. Hermann Goering's choice of guns or butter found its own terms in ancient Sparta, where the arts and crafts declined as commerce shrank and meaningful contacts with the outside world diminished.

In making a comparison between Sparta and Athens, one need not exaggerate the virtues of the Peisistratid tyranny, or of the democracy established by Cleisthenes, or of Periclean politics in the fifth century; the first degenerated into oppressive despotism, the second was full of corruption and intellectual intolerance — it sent Anaxagoras into exile and killed Socrates for expressing unpopular views — and the third led to unworthy expansionist ventures. Yet the fact remains that the age when the Spartan arts withered so far that we have no notable Spartan temple, no fine Spartan poem later than the early sixth century, and no remarkable Spartan dramatist or philosopher was also the age of the great Athenian achievements in drama, sculpture and the other arts, of the Artemesium and the great temples of Samos, Acragas and Poseidonia, and of the epoch-making achievements in the intellectual disciplines of the Ionian cities. And despite all the proud talk of heroes, whom the Spartans had to import the Ionian poet Simonides to celebrate, there was, significantly, no Laconian historian to match Hecataeus or, later, Herodotus. Like the republic imagined by Plato and like the world of the future imagined by Orwell, the Spartan state, monolithic and theoretically changeless, sought to live outside the flow and flux of history.

To modern man, with his experience of totalitarianism, the history of ancient Sparta, like the fiction of *1984*, can only be regarded as cautionary. Having taken notice of it to show the shadows as well as the highlights that must enter into any picture of the archaic age, I return in the chapters that follow to the examples that show the spread of the light of reason in its many moods across the Hellenic landscape.

Chapter 3

The Well-Used Lyre: An Age of Poets

The archaic age in Greece was the first period when men and women left their mark on history by creating works that, in fact or at least in style, bear their signatures and tell us how individuals felt and thought. The human mind began to find itself interesting, perhaps more interesting than the gods and their myths, and its manifestations were explored and exhibited in their various ways by poets and artists and philosophers seized with the new desire for self-expression that was brought about partly by the rise of literacy among the Hellenes and partly by that individualism, that sense of personal uniqueness, whose development we have already observed as a leading factor in the active as well as the contemplative lives of people in this period.

The best remembered are the poets. Literacy in Greece was born, as it were, into verse, for it emerged when the great oral epics not only made up the body of the poetry belonging to the early Greeks but also embodied such history and theology and rudimentary philosophic ideas as they then possessed.

It is in its emphasis on the ordinary world of men and women rather than the world of gods and heroes that the poetry of the sixth century differs from the traditional epics. The work that precedes it, in the dawn of literacy, is Hesiod's late eighth-century *Works and Days*, which really stands between two ages of poetry. A great deal of it is concerned with epic material, since it tells the mythical history of man's existence from the Golden Age in which men lived like gods down to the Iron Age, the brutal period in which it was Hesiod's fate to live. Essentially the purpose of the poem, like the works of many later archaic poets, is to instruct men in how to survive in such a dangerous age, and it becomes a song of praise to hard work and probity as ways to attain such happiness as man can gain in life. In this treatise on the art of survival Hesiod anticipates later poets by talking about his own life and discussing the practices of the farmer and their proper seasons, so that he is the first Greek poet who emerges as a distinct person living in the ordinary world, and in this modest way the autobiographical emerges into literature.

But though Hesiod's works, both the *Theogony* and *Works and Days*, were obviously well read throughout the archaic period, the most influential early poet in developing new attitudes was undoubtedly that loud and stormy man, Archilochus of Paros, who adopted the iambic metre of popular songs for his own poems, in which, as we have seen, he projected himself as the first true literary personality, telling of his loves, jealousies and resentments, of his courage and his cowardice. Iambics were a serviceable poetic form, with their simple rhythms, and they were used with malicious effectiveness by sixth-century satirical poets like Simonides and Hipponax, and also convincingly in argument, as by Solon. They also provided the metre which the dramatists adopted in the Athenian theatre for dialogue, and which eventually descended to Shakespeare in the blank verse pentameters favoured by the Elizabethan dramatists.

Other archaic poets developed different kinds of verse that have survived into later ages. There was the true lyric verse, sung to the lyre. It could be monodic, chanted by the poet to his own accompaniment, and this type, with its highly personal flavour, was developed during the sixth century by the Lesbian poets, Sappho, Alcaeus and Terpander, and by Anacreon of Teos. It could also be choral and might accompany dancing. The choral lyric reached its most complex development in the choral ode, composed for triumphal occasions like victories at the Olympic games. It became a convention that the choral ode be delivered in the Dorian dialect, though its most distinguished exponents in fact originated outside the Dorian-speaking area; Simonides and Bacchylides were Ionians, Pindar a Boeotian from Thebes (and proud of the fact) and Stesichorus (who took his name, meaning "arranger of the chorus," from his profession) a Sicilian.

Elegiac poetry was originally, as its name *elegos* suggests, a sad song, and this meaning has returned to it in the post-Renaissance world; for us an elegy is a lament. In this original form the elegy was accompanied by the *aulos*, a wind instrument of the recorder family, whose tone probably resembled that of the oboe. Fairly early in the sixth century the elegiac couplet became divorced from its musical accompaniment and even from its original elegiac mood and was used widely for all kinds of purposes. The Athenian Tyrtaeus, who emigrated to Laconia and became a kind of Spartan laureate, used it for songs intended to inspire men to fight more bravely; Simonides for concise and telling epigrams; Theognis for his pleas for an aristocratic order in a world that was progressing rapidly through tyranny towards democracy.

The vitality of sixth-century Greek poetry was shown not only in the range of experimentation, which in the case of poets like Sappho and Terpander went so far as the invention of new forms of lyre to suit their favoured style, but in the growing number of poets whose names and often works have come down to us, and in the broadening of their profession. Until the late seventh century, professional poetry was virtually confined to the rhapsodes, the descendants of the traditional bards who still, especially in Ionia and on the Aegean islands, recited not only the *Odyssey* and the *Iliad*, but also later epics and the so-called Homeric hymns composed by anonymous poets using the name of Homer. But during the sixth century the lyric and elegiac poets more than rivalled the rhapsodes in the range of their performances. The most professional of them, like Simonides and Pindar, wandered over the whole Hellenic world, from Ionia to the cities of Italy and Sicily and the African coast. They had a repertoire of poems they could render at private gatherings, accompanying themselves on the lyre, but they were also ready to accept commissions from patrons, either tyrants or cities, and many of them composed and conducted choral odes to be sung, to the accompaniment of the *aulos*, at civic festivals or in commemoration of victories at the games.

The best of these wandering poets became prosperous and respected figures wherever Greeks came together. They were the world's first professional writers, for they composed their poems on papyrus or on tablets even if recitation was their usual form of publication, and they included the first women writers, such as Sappho and the Tanagran poetess Corinna, who is said to have been Pindar's teacher, and to have told him to apply his mythological references by the handful rather than by the sack, as he first tended to do.

These poets have suffered from the ravages time has wrought on papyrus. Some of them we know only by name and others, like Corinna, by a few insubstantial fragments. Pindar and Theognis are unusual for the quantity of their poems that have survived. Other poets whose names are secure in the history of literature are often represented by scanty groups of poems. Anacreon is a striking example. He was so admired for centuries after his death that Hellenistic and Byzantine poets wrote lyrics in his manner, lyrics which in later years were passed off as his work, and which in turn gave rise to imitations of the imitations, so that English poets like Robert Herrick and Thomas Moore wrote verse in the manner and mood of Anacreon. In his long lifetime Anacreon composed enough poems to be made into five volumes about the transitory pleasures to be caught on the wing of time; now, among many fragments, some of them undoubtedly fakes, we have a mere handful of his short songs in their complete and original forms.

Yet despite the immense attrition to which it has been subjected by two-and-a-half millenia of natural decay, wars, civil disorders and cultural chance, the poetry that remains in such fragmentary form from the sixth century still speaks to us with a remarkable vigour and clarity, and in its very variety illustrates the rapid growth in individuality during this period and the way poetry developed into a well-adapted instrument for the expression of personal feelings.

Sappho was perhaps the most celebrated poet of her period, a woman around whom legends clustered, and her reputation has justly survived because her power to move us deeply has remained alive. We respond immediately to the feeling of loneliness, to the implication that a love is unrecognized and perhaps unexpressed, that is projected in a fragment such as this:

The moon has gone down
and the Pleiades have set.
The night is half over.
I hear the midnight watch go by
and I lie alone.

Sappho's feelings, which she seems to have cultivated as carefully and self-consciously as any lady of Victorian sensibility, emerge far less indirectly in other poems, which invert Anacreon's pattern in which a man speaks of his feelings for boys and instead overtly express a woman's love for girls, a love that in memory of Sappho now bears the name of Lesbian. It was the erotic emotion and its intensity rather than its object that seemed to matter to the archaic Greeks, and Sappho's piece which others have arbitrarily named "Ode to Anactoria" is one of the most frank poems of its period in detailing the symptoms of an unrequited and jealous passion:

A peer of the gods he seems to me,
that happy man who sits beside you
listening quietly to the sweet cadence
of your voice, and to your laughter
which sets my heart trembling in my breast.
I look at you now, just for a moment,
and I cannot speak. My eyes grow dim,
my ears are full of roaring,
the sweat pours down my trembling limbs.
I grow pale as the grass in winter
and swoon with love into a trance like death.

Anacreon wrote with as much charm as Sappho and a great

deal more sophistication, but his mood is more detached, and his hedonism finds expression in an easy and at times ironic celebration of pleasure. Yet he was capable of the projection of eloquent melancholy, and among his most appealing poems are those he wrote when he bowed like a sixth-century man of reason to the inevitabilities of existence and recorded, no longer carefree but still ironic, how pleasure must come to its end with the approach of age and death:

I am grey about the ears
and going thin on top.
What grace I had in youth
is rotting like my teeth.
I had sweet life before me.
Now it has passed me by.

Of course I lament it,
fearing what comes after.
It's a long way down to Hades
and the journey is frightful.
For him who has once gone down
there is never a climbing back.

Not all the poets were as private in the emotions they expressed as Sappho or as adept in evoking the ephemeral beauties of life as Anacreon. Men like Simonides were essentially public poets: Simonides spent most of his active life in writing choral poems that celebrated cities or their rulers and in leading the chorus when they were performed. Mary Renault aptly entitled the fine novel she wrote about Simonides *The Praise Singer*, for praise was his vocation. Yet Simonides was no mere public relations man writing in verse like some later Greek poets. He had a strain of thought that won him the admiration of philosophers like Plato, Socrates and Aristotle, and Plato paid him the compliment of using his definition of justice as a text in *The Republic*. His tributes were always dignified and deserved, and some of them, millenia afterwards, are still very moving, like that he wrote for the Spartans and other Greeks who in 480 died in the pass of Ther-

mopylae under the leadership of Leonidas in an unsuccessful
attempt to halt the Persians:

Splendid their fate who died here
and beautiful their death.
Their grave becomes an altar;
lamentation turns into memory
and grief into glory.
Decay will not darken their names
nor time that conquers all things.
This brave men's tomb contains
the glory of all Hellas.

Other poets of the time turned their verse to political themes
and often showed great polemical vigour. Both Theognis of
Megara and Alcaeus of Lesbos eloquently defended
aristocratic values against democracy and tyranny alike; they
were early examples of Orwell's contention that the best writers
are often political reactionaries. One of Alcaeus' most striking poems was called, though perhaps not by him, "The Ship
of State," and when we read these ambivalent verses, nominally about the difficulties of sailing a storm-tossed vessel,
we recognize that politics in ancient Mytilene was just as
chaotic as it has been ever since:

I am bewildered by conflicting winds.
One wind hits us to starboard,
another to port, and our dark ship
shudders between them,
fighting through the storm.
The bilge water is washing round the mast,
the sail is beginning to split and slacken,
the rudder is out of control.

A new wave is breaking over us.
It will fill us again and we must
bale hard and patch the planks
and run for a good harbour.
Keep up your courage. There are bigger
waves ahead. Just remember
we have been through all this before.

If every man keeps steady
we shall still be safe.

So many literary forms that we still use appeared during the sixth century that it is hard to decide which in the long run was the most important, but probably the choice would have to be between the prose developed by the historians and the natural scientists and the drama developed by the poets. We shall talk later about prose.

Drama actually arose from a form of choral poem, the dithyramb, devised in the seventh century in praise of Dionysus; it was sung with simulated frenzy by a chorus of fifty men dressed as satyrs to the accompaniment of flutes. The evolution of drama out of dithyramb actually began not in Athens but in Corinth, where it was developed by the poet Arion, from Lesbos, working under the patronage of the tyrant Periander. There are many tales about Arion, including the beautiful one about his being rescued by dolphins when he had been thrown into the sea by thieving sailors, but not a single fragment of his poetry has survived. Nevertheless, it seems to have been Arion who first introduced dialogue, the essential element of drama, by creating a discourse between the chorus and its leader.

From this time dithyramb had a double life. As a chorus of praise it continued to be written by Simonides, Bacchylides and Pindar, and was adapted to celebrate other gods, like Apollo, as well as Dionysus. As a dialogue it developed into drama, and the first dramatist appeared at the Great Dionysia which was organized under Peisistratus. He was Thespis, poet and actor, who introduced impersonation on the stage; in dialogue with the leader of the chorus a single actor played various parts in masks, which Thespis is also said to have introduced to the theatre. Classical tragedy developed quickly out of such beginnings, but another aspect of the original dithyrambic choruses survived in the satyr plays, which burlesqued the myths and of which each writer was expected to compose one to accompany the three serious tragedies he might contribute to a contest.

A tale which Plutarch tells about Thespis and Solon reveals

how early the division between the artist, who deals with imaginary things, and the politician, who deals with actual things, began to emerge. Solon, now an old man, went to see Thespis acting in one of his satyr plays, whose comic speeches lampooned with great exaggeration both people and events in Athens. Solon was appalled by these distortions of fact, as they seemed to him, and told Thespis that he should be ashamed of telling such lies for all Athens to hear. "Why, there's no harm in it," said Thespis; "It's only make-believe, after all." Solon stamped the ground with his staff and angrily answered, "And if we teach people to accept make-believe in the theatre, it will soon be creeping into our business affairs and ruining our public life!"

Thespis won the tragic competition in 535 BC. During the next quarter of a century the drama evolved, with the use of more actors and more roles, including female ones, which seem to have been introduced by Phrynichus, who won his first contest round about 511 BC.

It seems to have been with Phrynichus, celebrated for his choreography, rather than with Aeschylus, his younger and more famous contemporary, that Greek tragedy approached maturity. No play by Phrynichus has survived as a whole, and from the remaining fragments it is impossible to make a convincing reconstruction of any of them. But we do know some of their titles, and these suggest that Phrynichus was a pioneer in a revolutionary course that Aeschlyus followed — of regarding the misfortunes of contemporary human beings as equivalent to those of mythical heroes. True, Phrynichus wrote some plays on mythical themes, including *Alcestis*, *Troilus* and *Tantalus*. But he also wrote a famous play about contemporary events, *The Capture of Miletus*. It concerned the destruction of the city in 494 during the suppression of the Ionian revolt, in which the Athenians had played a less than heroic role, deserting the Asian cities after the first defeats and leaving the Ionians to face the revengeful Persians alone. Phrynichus was famous for his stirring laments, and the play had an extraordinary effect on the audience, who all wept. But instead of praising and rewarding the dramatist for his power to move them so deeply, the Athenians fined him a thousand drachma for "reminding them of a disaster that touched them so closely," and passed a law forbidding anyone ever to show the play on the stage again.

Phrynichus continued writing at least until the 470s, and in 476 he dealt in *The Phoenician Women* with another recent event, the defeat of Xerxes in Salamis a few years before; on this occasion Themistocles was his choregus, the patron responsible for providing and paying the chorus, and this suggests how highly the playwright was regarded even towards the end of his career.

Only a few short fragments remain of the text of *The Phoenician Women*, but enough is known of its plot to enable us to speculate on its importance in the tradition and its influence on *The Persian Women*, produced by Aeschylus four years later in 472. *The Phoenician Women* was set in Susa; there was a chorus of Phoenician women, and a prologue telling of the defeat at Salamis was spoken by a eunuch arranging seats for Persian noblemen. It seems impossible to avoid the conclusion drawn by H. D. F. Kitto that, apart from the eunuch, there must have been at least two actors, one who spoke for the Persian noblemen and received the news of the defeat at Salamis, and another, a messenger, who brought the news.

In other words, Aristotle may have been wrong when he suggested that Aeschylus introduced the second actor into Greek drama. The second actor must have been introduced by Phrynichus, in *The Phoenician Women* and possibly in *The Capture of Miletus*; this crucial change, which allowed dramatic rather than merely lyrical effects, belongs to the archaic rather than the classical era. By shifting the attention from the chorus to the dialogue between actors, Phrynichus heralded the end of the primitive phase of theatre in which the chorus was to all intents and purposes the protagonist.

Phrynichus, whose career spanned at least from 511 to 476, must be regarded as an archaic writer, and Aeschylus too had his roots in that era; his first plays were produced in the 490s, before he fought at Marathon, and he won his first prize in

484, before Salamis. That he was the pupil of Phrynichus is shown not merely by the fact that *The Persian Women* was much influenced by *The Phoenician Women*, but also by the compliment he paid the older dramatist by using the first verse of his play in opening *The Persian Women*.

Lacking the text of *The Phoenician Women*, we obviously cannot make a qualitative comparison between the plays Phrynichus and Aeschylus wrote around the same historical event. But *The Persian Women*, the earliest Greek play we can read in its entirety, suggests how far the historical events of this epoch, with their opportunities for human heroism, influenced the attitudes of early Greek playwrights towards the ancient myths of the Olympian deities and the heroic demigods. The series of events that ran from the Ionian revolt through the first invasion of mainland Greece and the Persian defeat at Marathon, followed by the Greek victories at Salamis and Plataea, must have given the Hellenes a sense that the intervention of Olympian gods or mythical heroes was not necessary for heroic acts.

When Aeschylus selected as the one event to be recorded on his tombstone the role he had played as a spearman at Marathon, he was making the existentialist statement which marks off his archaic age from its predecessors, that man's fate lies within his command; a man defines himself on those extreme occasions when he stands face to face with death, carries on despite his fear and trembling, and if he is fortunate survives. The darker side to this glorification of human courage appears in *The Persian Women*, where Aeschylus described the sea covered with wreckage, and the slaughter of men as the Greeks killed the Persians and their allies like tunny fish all day long while the light lasted. Aeschylus wrote with triumph, but also with a sense of the pity of it all that one does not find in the *Iliad* or even in the *Odyssey*, and that pity showed the new consciousness of a common humanity that was emerging among men during the sixth century BC.

How much of *The Persian Women* is derived from the lost *Phoenician Women* we do not know. Phrynichus' sense of a humanity uniting barbarian and Hellene in its compassionate sweep may not have been so developed as that of Aeschylus. But there seems no doubt, from what we have been told of *The Capture of Miletus* as well as of *The Phoenician Women*, that he stirred people's hearts by showing that the sorrows of ordinary men and women in one's own place and time can be as real and as wrenching as those of mythical heroes. This realization led to the humanization of the myths, and the presentation of Orestes by Aeschylus and of Oedipus by Sophocles not as heroic beings living in a haze of myth, but as characters with whom the audience can identify because their emotions are human rather than godlike.

Such a realization brings the dramatic poets who worked on the creation of Greek tragedy in the later decades of the sixth century into line with contemporary lyric and elegiac poets, who moved away from gods and heroes to show the erotic passions, the political angers, the jealousies and envies, the fears of age and poverty, that moved the ordinary men and women of their time.

Like the first philosophers and the first historians, these poets were involved in the task of bringing men out of the shadows of a mythical past, of making them aware and not ashamed of their humanity, and of subjecting the universe and its phenomena to objective examination and rational explanation. On the one side they were reducing the heroic to the human scale; on the other they were finding the universal in the particular, and paralleling the task of Xenophanes, who was both natural philosopher and poet, and who found his insights into the formation of the world by picking up fossils in the quarries of Syracuse.

Chapter 4

The Sons of Daedalus: Greek Archaic Art

Art for Art's Sake was a concept unknown among the archaic Greeks; Art for Life's Sake they would more easily have understood. No early Greek poet was a mere *littérateur*. The oral epic poets served as the remembrancers of the tribe, preserving history in mythic form. The later poets of the age of writing were clearly concerned with the technical aspects of their art, as the oral poets must have been, if one can judge from the elaborate conventions which the Homeric epics show they had developed. But they all wrote to present a view of life, whether it was Anacreon with his hedonism, or Solon with his social ethics, or Simonides with his civic idealism; whether it was Pindar with his notion that excellence must be strained after, or Xenophanes with his urge to discover the grandeur of God through a knowledge of the minutiae of creation.

In the case of the visual artists, the artist and the artisan were never far apart, and the skill of the maker verged, in legend at least, on the generative power of the creator. It is not inappropriate that Daedalus, whose name signifies "the cunning craftsman," should have been regarded by the Greeks as not merely the original artist but also the first inventor.

Whether there was a man actually called Daedalus is as uncertain as whether there was a man actually called Homer. One Daedalus was the magical artificer who created the wooden cow in which Pasiphaë presented herself to be impregnated by the bull; who created the Labyrinth to house the Minotaur, the offspring of that union; and who, with the artificial wings he constructed to escape from his enemies, appears in legend as the first of human aviators.

But the principal enemy from whom this Daedalus sought to escape was the Bronze Age king Minos of Crete, whose kingdom, if he ever ruled it, flourished round about 1500 BC. Yet there were Cretan sculptors working in the sixth century who claimed to be the apprentices of Daedalus, and who were even regarded by some as his physical offspring. Pausanias recorded the tradition that Diponius and Scyllis, two actual sixth-century sculptors whose works he found throughout Crete even in the second century AD, were the sons of Daedalus by a woman from Gortyn.

The appearance of Daedalus in the same place — Crete — in accounts relating to two periods so distant in time from each other as the Minoan age and the late seventh century suggests either that there was a succession of artist-artificers bearing the same name, as happens to this day among Japanese artist potters, or that "cunning craftsman" was a frequently given title of honour in the pre-archaic period, which lapsed after the individualizing trends of the sixth century led artists to take pride in their own styles and to work under their own names. Still, the traditional link between artist and inventor is important, because it demonstrates how far ancient artists were involved in the application of knowledge to practical ends, and in this way it anticipates the development of the applied sciences in archaic Greece in close association with the visual arts, particularly sculpture, and with the hybrid public art of architecture, with which the practical discipline of engineering is always associated.

The tradition of Daedalus the sculptor was strong enough not only to be associated with disciples whom we know to have lived, but also to be linked with tangible sculptural styles. In a loose way the archaic Greeks referred to all early wooden statues as Daedalic, but their primitive style also appears in stone figures and ivory figurines of the seventh century. It was

oriental in spirit, characterized by frontally seen heads with
wiglike hair, large eyes and prominent noses. However, the
Daedalus whom many scholars now believe really existed —
a sculptor from Crete, or perhaps from Athens, as the Athenians claimed — appears to have carried sculpture in the late
seventh century beyond the so-called Daedalic style to the more
lifelike style of the early archaic statues of young men known
as *kouroi*.

The legend claimed that the figures of Daedalus, like Pyg-
malion's image which Aphrodite miraculously animated, could
see, walk and talk. Diodorus Siculus, writing in the first century BC, reduced the myth to believable terms when he
remarked that the figures of Daedalus had open eyes, legs that
were separate and seemed to be walking, and arms free of the
body, which were exactly the characteristics archaic Greek
sculpture acquired when it was emerging from mere imitation
of Egyptian originals. Daedalus, the "cunning craftsman"
whose real name has not survived, may well have gone to
Egypt, for the mercenary and trading connections between the
cities of the Nile and the Hellenic world were being established
in his time. He was credited with introducing Egyptian styles
of furniture, including the folding stool, into the Hellenic
world, and this attribution gives a circumstantial touch to the
accounts of him, for the end of the seventh century was precisely the time when such luxuries began to spread among the
Greeks.

Even if it is impossible that the sculptor Daedalus and the
ingenious inventor employed by Minos of Crete were the same
person, their mythical identification is significant, for the link
between art, architecture and technological invention certainly
existed in archaic Greece, as it did in the Italian Renaissance.
The historic figure with whom it has been most closely
associated is Theodorus of Samos, a contemporary of the
tyrant Polycrates, who was among his many patrons and
employers.

Theodorus worked not only on his native island; he was
a true professional, willing to take commissions whenever and
wherever they were offered. His skills as architect and engineer

were put to work in both Ephesus and Sparta, while his workshop produced artifacts in precious metals for Croesus of Lydia and for Darius, the Persian King of Kings; one of his golden bowls stood in the palace at Susa. Theodorus was the son of Telecles, a famous Samian gem cutter, and he may have been the nephew of the architect and artificer Rhoecus, another man of many parts with whom he often worked.

Two projects in which they collaborated were the great temples built in the late sixth century to Hera on Samos and to Artemis at Ephesus — St. Paul's Diana of the Ephesians, the many-breasted goddess of fertility. An earlier temple had been built on Samos in the mid-sixth century and burnt down in 540, possibly in a Persian raid during the original subjugation of Ionia. Rhoecus alone was probably the architect of this first temple. He appears to have travelled in Egypt, for a Rhoecus dedicated an elaborate and graceful wine cup to Aphrodite in Naucratis at this period, and here he must have been impressed by the columned stone temples of the Egyptians, which had such an influence on the emergent Ionic style. When Polycrates commissioned a new Heraeum on the site of the burnt temple, Rhoecus and Theodorus worked together, and because of their experience in constructing it they were called in by Chesiphron, the Cretan architect of the new Artemesium which Croesus was helping to fund in Ephesus, because he needed their help in solving the technological problems he was encountering.

Both of these temples were, in Greek terms, immense — the largest buildings to date in the Hellenic world, as Herodotus remarked when he described the Heraeum with the 134 columns that supported its massive roof. Yet the sites of the temples in Ephesus and on Samos were as swampy as they were sacred, and the problem in both cases was to prevent the temples being pushed down by their own weight into the mud, particularly as their proximity to the sea resulted in constant tidal action, which made it impossible to drain away all the ground water.

Theodorus, technologically the more adventurous of the two partners, began on Samos by diverting the river Imbrasos.

Then, when he came to the actual building of the temple, he devised a solution he later repeated at the Artemision. He laid down many layers of charcoal, interleaved, as it were, with layers of sheeps' fleeces, and on this foundation he constructed his stone platform and covered it with marble. When the 134 columns of the Heraeum were erected on top of the platform, the vast raft of charcoal and fleeces did not yield perceptibly, and the temple seemed to float on the marsh, as did its sister temple to Artemis at Ephesus. The Heraeum floats to this day; the columns have mostly fallen and the stone has been taken away for other buildings or to be burnt for lime, but the stone platform is still there, with the bases of the columns and a few fluted drums, among which emerald green lizards bask and flit in the Aegean sunlight. At Ephesus, because of more persistent percolation of underground water, the temple sank, and all one sees is the oblong pond at whose bottom the platform lies, with a single column reconstructed by the archaeologists and rising up in the centre.

Theodorus is credited not only with such ingenious solutions to architectural problems, but also with the invention of some of the basic tools of the builder's craft — the square, the level and the lathe — and circumstantial considerations make us give some credit to these claims. The lathe was used in shaping the column drums of the Heraeum, and this is the first known example of such a process; the possibility that Theodorus invented it or at least adapted it to mason's purposes is too great to be ignored. At the same time it is hard to imagine so large a building as the Heraeum being built without the level and the square, and there is an even more striking contemporary example of Samian engineering that could not possibly have been carried out without the use of such instruments.

This is the tunnel hewn on Samos at approximately the same time as the Heraeum was being built. Like Periander and Peisistratus, Polycrates understood the importance of a plentiful supply of water in the effective functioning of a city, whether in peace or in war. Megara was well known for the efficiency of its water services, and Polycrates engaged an engineer from that city, Eupalinus, to drive an aqueduct tunnel, more than a kilometre long, two metres wide and two metres high, through a hill three hundred metres high. Eupalinus started his men digging from both sides of the mountain at once; his calculations were so accurate that there was less than a foot of error to be rectified when the two teams met under the hill. The tunnel contained a deep trench by which the water was led from a never-failing stream into the new city. It still exists, and venturesome people can break through the brambles at its entrance and make their way along it to the exit overlooking the bay where Polycrates ordered the construction of the third of the great sixth-century Samian works that Herodotus so much admired — the harbour protected by the great seawall running out to where the bed of the Aegean is forty metres deep.

It is tempting to see Theodorus as the originative genius at the centre of a whole technological revolution proceeding at this time on Samos. For there are other achievements credited to him. Like Telecles, he worked on the minute as well as the large scale and skilfully cut gems for fine gold settings. As well as his architectural activities, which led him as far afield as Sparta to built the Scias, a meeting hall for the Laconian assemblies, he ran a famous metal workshop where he made the great gold and silver craters which Croesus presented to the temple of Apollo in Delphi. The most important innovation he and Rhoecus developed was the perfecting of a method by which bronze statues, life-size and larger, which had formerly been made of sheets of metal attached to wooden armatures, could be hollowcast whole by an elaboration of the cire-perdue method, formerly used only for small solid sculptures. Pausanias saw some of their works many centuries later, but because metal is so easily recast, there was a steady loss of bronze statues, as opposed to stone ones, until connoisseurs during the Renaissance began to recognize their artistic and antiquarian value and to collect and preserve them. Few archaic bronzes are among the survivors, and none of them can be identified as the work of Theodorus.

He was as skilled a sculptor in stone as he was a caster in bronze and an architect. A story about him and Telecles tells

us a great deal about the arts in Hellas at this period. The
two Samians learnt in Egypt a method of plotting out a statue
in a grid of squares which enabled the key points to be determined before cutting even began. Using this method, they
carved independently the two halves of a single statue, Theodorus on Samos and Telecles across the strait in Ephesus,
and then put·them together; the fit was perfect.

The anecdote, told by Diodorus Siculus centuries later, may
not be strictly true, but it is in the spirit of the epoch. It illustrates how much the Greek sculptors and artists owed to their
Egyptian predecessors, and how artists from great trading
centres like Samos with links to Naucratis would travel so as
to learn at the source. But it also shows how much importance artists in those early days attached to the perfection of
techniques. The rapid progress Greeks made in both sculpture and architecture could have been achieved only by artists
sufficiently imbued with the enterprising spirit of that epoch
to use the new methods so imaginatively that they created a
vital new tradition whose products from the beginning were
sharply different in style from the increasingly remote Egyptian originals.

Innovation occurred in the other arts as well. Too few examples of Greek mural painting survive to allow us to judge
progress in that genre, though what we know of the Greco-
Etruscan paintings in the tombs of Etruria suggests that archaic
painting was as vital as archaic sculpture, an assumption
strengthened by the durable products of the ceramic artists
of sixth-century Greece.

Ceramic art went through notable technical developments.
The Corinthians perfected the clay figure sculpture they passed
on to the Etruscans, and the Athenians developed both the
black-figure and the red-figure styles, which they used not only
to portray the legends of the Hellenes, but also to record with
elegance and wit, and sometimes with a sharp satirical bite,
the daily lives of their contemporaries. Among potters, as
much as among sculptors, the individuality of artists became
recognized, and both painters and potters — often the same
people — began to sign their works. Potters like Exekias and

Onesimus are the most vital known painters of the archaic age and among the greatest potters of all time.

Some writers have suggested that the technological developments of the sixth century were directed mainly to religious ends, to the glory of the gods. It is true that architecture developed in the construction of temples, the most striking buildings of the era. Once they understood the techniques of construction in stone, the Greek architect-engineers quickly mastered the problems of magnitude as well as proportion; some of the largest Greek temples ever built were constructed at this early period, at Acragas and remote Selinunte in Sicily as well as on Samos and at Ephesus. Such buildings required not only the mason's and surveyor's devices whose invention is credited to Theodorus, and the claw chisel which Greek artificers invented at this time, but also devices to shift the large stone blocks and column drums that were now being used.

Building cranes and hoists, with lifting irons, rope slings and pulleys, were developed by the latter part of the century, and were used for stone blocks up to 20 tons in weight. An unsolved problem relates to the pieces weighing between 20 and 70 tons that were used often in the sixth century but seldom afterwards. There are no records telling us how they were put in place. But since the earliest of these great temples were in Ionia, and since the neighbouring Lydians used a siege technique that consisted of building great earthworks against the walls of a besieged city, as at Smyrna early in the century, it seems likely that the Ionian engineers learnt from them and used earth ramps to roll such colossal stones into place.

Most archaic sculpture as well was nominally religious, in the sense that it was made to be put in a temple or on a grave, or dedicated at games in honour of the gods at Olympia or Delphi. But here the edge of awakening Greek secularism breaks into the sacred, for the dedications at Delphi and Olympia glorify either individual winners in the games or cities that built treasuries in the holy centres, as well as ostensibly acknowledging the gods. Populist political fashions prevented the tyrants of the age from building splendid palace-fortresses

like their Mycenaean kingly predecessors, so they sought glory
with magnificent indirection, as Polycrates did in ordering the
construction of the Heraeum, as the Alcmaeonids did in
rebuilding the temple at Delphi, and as Peisistratus did in
beginning the vast temple of Zeus, which, if it had been completed, would have been the largest of all sixth-century structures. The rise of the *polis* and the subordination of the
Olympian deities to the role of personifying the cities, as
Athene did in Athens, made the borderline between the secular and the religious in Greek art and architecture very tenuous at this period; in some arts, like ceramic painting, the
sacred element is already virtually absent.

Nor were all the technological developments of the age used
for religious or even quasi-religious ends. Rulers sought glory
or power or mere commercial gain in large construction works
of an entirely secular kind, like the harbour at Samos or the
diolkos at Corinth, or the various waterworks, of which the
tunnel of Eupalinus was only the most spectacular, in cities
like Corinth, Athens and Megara, as well as Samos. These
works, of great public benefit, required the same surveying
devices as the temples, and the same kind of cranes and hoists.
Pumps were also developed at this period and used in clear-
ing waterlogged excavations.

There were also rapid improvements in navigation and shipbuilding that kept pace with the spread of trade. Specialized
fighting vessels, like the powerful trireme and the swift pen-
teconter, were developed, partly by Phoenicians and partly
by Greeks, and large trading vessels developed entirely for mercantile use began to ply the seas. Even the canal between the
Red Sea and the Nile, the ancient precursor of the Suez Canal,
may have been largely the work of Greeks. It was started at
Pharoah Necho II's orders and completed under those of
Darius, but Necho was in close contact with Periander and
probably had Corinthian advice, and it is likely that Darius
had the assistance of Greek engineers, since the Persians cultivated none of the technical skills and always employed artisans of other races for their constructions.

Other innovations improved the standard of living during

the archaic era. One example was the introduction of street planning to replace the dirty chaos of early Greek communities. It began in in Smyrna as early as the eighth century and characterized the new cities built in Magna Graecia during the sixth century. Other examples were the wine and olive presses, which not only added a convenience to daily life but also increased the output of oil and wine for export. A famous story told how the philosopher Thales proved his practical good sense to the citizens of Miletus by renting all the olive presses in a year when his observations told him there would be a good harvest and reaped a small fortune from the venture.

Technologically, in fact, the sixth century moved forward with a speed not to be repeated for centuries afterwards. A hundred years after the death of Polycrates, Herodotus was still speaking of the constructions the tyrant ordered on Samos as the greatest works of the Greeks, and long afterwards, in the Hellenistic age, the temple of Artemis at Ephesus was included among the Seven Wonders of the World.

Chapter 5

The Substance of the World: The Sages of Miletus

Myths arise even when myths are destroyed, and in archaic Greece, after the myths of the Olympian deities had been largely discredited by the philosophers, new myths arose about the philosophers themselves, portraying them as devotees of abstract thought endlessly pacing the paths of their academic groves or sitting in their epicurean gardens in earnest discourse.

In fact, few early Greek philosophers failed to engage themselves in the practical world; the ivory tower was the invention of later ages. Aristotle and Plato were closely involved in the political events of their times, and their interest went beyond theory; Aristotle as tutor of the young Alexander helped to shape his imperial visions, and Plato dabbled in the discreditable affairs of the tyrants of Syracuse. Pythagoras, for all the mystical pretensions of his later followers, was deeply involved in the even more discreditable business of the destruction of Sybaris.

All this was to be expected, since, as the inventors of the city state, the Greeks were the world's first truly politicized people, often compelled by the laws of their community to play an active role as oligarchs or democrats in its administration. Even tyrants, like Peisistratus, often left the democratic structure untouched, so that the citizen, whether a philosopher or a stonemason, or both as in the case of Socrates, inevitably became involved in practical affairs.

Thus Greek wisdom was largely worldly wisdom, the knowledge of how to live as a good citizen pursuing one's own interests and those of one's neighbours, which largely coincided. The famous Seven Sages, whom sixth-century Greece recognized as its wisest men, with one exception were not in later ages remembered as philosophers. They were men whose wisdom emerged in their practical achievements. Two were tyrants who ruled reasonably and benefited their peoples and their communities, Periander of Corinth and Cleobolus of Lindos on Rhodes. (Later on, as political fashions changed and tyrants became disreputable, Periander was sometimes dropped and the "noble savage" Scythian prince Anacharsis substituted.) Chilon was a statesmanlike Spartan magistrate. Pittacus took over the government of Mytilene at a difficult period — Aristotle described him as an "elective monarch" — and gave up his power after ten years lest habit should turn him into a tyrant. Solon, as we know, gave Athens its first moderately democratic constitution, reformed the landholding system, humanized the laws; he did the opposite of what Pittacus did by going away for ten years so that the Athenians could not get his consent to change the system he had given them. Bias of Priene excelled as a diplomat, working out the difficult relations between Lydia and the Ionian cities.

Thales alone we remember as a philosopher, yet in all the older accounts, of Herodotus, of Plato, of Aristotle, his practical side is emphasized. He appears not only as the sensible statesman whose good ideas were ignored by the Ionians at their cost, but also as the engineer who diverted part of the River Halys so that there were two fordable streams for King Alyattes' cavalry to cross instead of a single deep river. The tale of his cornering of the olive presses gives circumstantial support to the picture: here was a shrewd man with an eye to his own profit, a Milesian merchant who went off to Naucratis to make a little money as well as to satisfy his curiosity about the way other people did things, and who may even have found his way into Babylon, perhaps through Tyre or Sidon, for he is said to have been of Phoenician descent. His journeys were probably made in the first half of the sixth century, for the dating in 585 by modern astronomers of an eclipse he foretold suggests that he was born at the latest between 620 and 610 BC, and he must already have been an old man at the time of the Persian invasion in 546, the last public event with which his name is associated.

It was widely agreed in ancient times that Thales brought back from his journeys the knowledge that made him the earliest Greek geometer and something of an astronomer. He was the first to enunciate certain geometrical propositions among the Greeks, even if in doing so he was passing on knowledge picked up from the Egyptians. One of them — that a circle is bisected by its diameter — is a matter of observation that hardly needs demonstrating, though Thales may have pointed it out first. But he is also said to have shown that the angle in a semi-circle is a right angle, and to have been the first to propose the famous *pons asinorum* — that the angles at the base of an isosceles triangle are equal or, as he seems to have said, using Egyptian terminology, "similar." He also characteristically turned geometrical knowledge to practical ends. He found a way of calculating the height of the pyramids and a method of estimating the distance of a ship at sea, and so, like Theodorus with his level, he contributed to the development of surveying, that art so necessary for municipal development.

His prediction of the eclipse of the sun in 585 is probably the most famous of Thales' astronomical achievements. The eclipse coincided with the war between the Lydians and the Medes, and caused the war to end in peace and a blood-pact, because the darkening of the heavens was interpreted by the warring kings as a sign from the gods; Thales, of course, regarded it as a natural phenomenon to be rationally explained in the context of the known behaviour of the heavenly bodies. Eudemus, the fourth-century disciple of Aristotle, claimed that Thales also discovered the solstices and determined their cycles; and Callimachus, who in the early third century worked in the library of Alexandria, that great repository of ancient knowledge, remarked that Thales "was said to have measured the little stars of the Wain by which the Phoenicians sail."

These claims on behalf of Thales as astronomer deserve to be taken seriously. Herodotus, who talks very circumstantially about the eclipse of 585, was born only a century after this event and sixty years after Thales' death, while Xenophanes, who according to Eudemus praised Thales for his astronomical achievements, left Ionia while the older philosopher was still alive and may well have known him. Eudemus had access to Aristotle's notes on the Ionian natural philosophers, while Callimachus had vast archives at his disposal in Alexandria. These in their way were all privileged sources.

Thales seems to have been an oral teacher like Socrates and to have left no writings. His student Anaximander wrote enough for significant fragments to survive and to show that he was deeply involved in astronomical questions, and his interest, it is clear, was derived from Thales. Yet in all this Thales seems to have been less a discoverer than a transmitter and interpreter of ideas derived from elsewhere — from Babylonian priestly astronomers in the case of eclipses and solstices, and from Phoenician navigators in the case of "the little stars of the Wain," the Little Bear. It was Thales' inclination to follow up discoveries that might have practical uses, and the Little Bear was more useful than the Great Bear to those making long open-sea crossings; Thales' measurement doubtless saved Milesian navigators valuable time in sailing to Naucratis and the distant settlements of the Black Sea.

But, like Theodorus, Thales was much more than a versatile practical man. He was the kind of many-sided genius who emerges when the passing of old ways of perception and thought and action creates a mental flux in which men and women are forced into multiple awareness and become originative on many levels, ranging from the solution of mundane practical problems to the examination of the nature of the world. The secret of the versatility of men like Theodorus and Thales lay in their realization of the full extent of their capabilities as human beings. Like the rest of the Seven Sages, Thales had a special connection with the temple of Apollo at Delphi, where at least once these very practical wise men gathered and competed for a famous gold tripod which is said,

in a charming moral tale, to have been modestly declined by
Thales in favour of one of his fellows, and so on through the
seven, until in the end they decided to offer it to the god.
Thales was credited with suggesting on this occasion one of
the two great maxims written on the temple walls, "Know
yourself."

Whether he did so or not, there is a poetic truth in the
legend, for the kind of awareness that it seems to project
accords with Aristotle's definition of Thales, when he divided
the pre-Socratic thinkers into those he called *theologi*, who
like Hesiod described the world in terms of the mythological
and supernatural, and those who sought a rational explanation of it by the observation and description of natural
phenomena; these he called the *physiologi*, and among them
he classed Thales as "the first founder of this kind of
philosophy."

Aristotle does not mention any book by Thales, nor does
Theophrastus, Aristotle's disciple, who set out to be a historian
of Greek philosophy, and this is strong negative evidence that
he wrote none. But neither had any doubt that he speculated
on the nature of the universe, or that he was the first to put
the question, "What is the basic substance of which the
universe is made?" and to seek a natural explanation supported by reason rather than a mythological one. According
to Aristotle, who is supported by other early commentators,
Thales and the Ionian philosophers who followed him believed
that the original source of all existing things must be some
single substance which persisted but changed its qualities, and
from which all things first came into being and into which
they eventually dissolved; from this Aristotle concluded that
they believed the universe had neither beginning nor end, since,
change as it might, its original substance was preserved.

Thales believed that this elemental substance was water. He
declared that the world floats on water, and he went beyond
that curious view to conclude that the world also originated
from water and perhaps even was still constituted of water.
Aristotle suggests that he may have come to this conclusion
from observing that all living things are nurtured by moisture,

but the idea of the world floating on water and originating from it suggests the influence of similar notions of the world's origin evolved by the Babylonians, whose astronomical observations Thales had certainly absorbed.

Thales also concluded, from his observation of amber and other magnetic substances, that even inanimate things are in a sense alive and have "soul," a belief not unlike those being taught in India at the same time by the sage Mahavira and his Jain followers. According to Aristotle, Thales even asserted that "all things are full of gods"; with this assertion, he was perhaps, like Xenophanes, denying the anthropomorphic attributes of the Olympian gods, or perhaps evolving a kind of rational pantheism and seeing the whole world as animated by *psyche* — a ubiquitous life force or a moving intelligence or both combined.

The younger Milesian philosophers Anaximander and Anaximenes were associated with Thales, both in time and place of origin and also in their preoccupation with discovering the essential substance of the universe, but neither of them aroused so much curiosity among their successors or became the subject of so many revealing anecdotes.

We know that Anaximander was both the student and the friend of Thales, and that he led the contingent of Milesians who founded the colony of Apollonia on the Black Sea, facts suggesting that like Thales he belonged to one of the city's leading mercantile families. He returned to Miletus and went to Sparta to set up a gnomon for astronomical observations; while he was there he warned the Spartans of a coming earthquake. This journey suggests that he had a reputation in the archaic world as a student of the heavens, while his participation in the expedition to the Black Sea shows that, like his teacher Thales, he was a practical man as well as a speculative philosopher, a man active in the commercial and municipal affairs of Miletus.

Of Anaximenes we know even less, except that he was the youngest of the trio. He became active round about the time of the Persian invasion of Ionia in the mid-sixth century. Anaximander was his teacher and later his friend; certainly he was influenced by both the older philosophers. Unlike Thales and their other fellow Milesian, the historian Hecataeus, neither Anaximander nor Anaximenes seems to have taken any part in the political events of the times; because of the favoured status of Miletus they did not even depart from Ionia when the Persians came in 546. It is for their ideas, and the increasingly scientific nature of their speculations, that they are regarded as important figures in the development of Greek philosophy, which, with Thales, they liberated from the dominance of the *theologi*.

Anaximander showed a characteristic Milesian practicality by drawing up the first Greek map of the known world; his interests were geographical as well as astronomical. He invented the sundial by adapting the gnomon so that it could be used for measuring the hours of the day and the annual variations in the course of the sun, which is probably why he was invited to Sparta.

He also conceived and seems to have constructed a model of the heavens with the earth placed in the centre not as a sphere but as a disc whose height was one-third of its diameter, thus making an allowance for the obvious curvature to the horizon which strict flatearthism does not provide, but still not recognizing the globe's true shape. In doing so he anticipated Pythagoras by seeking to explain the universe in terms of mathematical relations. In his model the spacing of the celestial rings assigned to the stars, the moon and the sun were calculated at 9, 18 and 27 earth diameters respectively. There is something puzzling about his having assigned to the stars the ring nearest the earth, and it is possible that the account was distorted in its transmission through antiquity. But even if his view of the position and shape of the earth was wrong and his calculation of the spatial relationships of the heavenly bodies was false, that is less important than the fact that for the first time a philosopher had conceived the universe in which he lived in terms of rational concepts proceeding from the assumption that everything was ultimately in some way measurable. If Thales represented the beginning of scientific thought, Anaximander represented the beginning of its systematization.

Anaximander made the map and the celestial model in connection with his book, *On the Nature of Things*, which has survived not only in fragments of the text but also in accounts by later writers which give a fair idea of his general theories and of how they advanced on those of Thales in complexity and clarity.

On the Nature of Things might be described, according to one's inclination, as the first book of natural philosophy or the first true scientific treatise. Like Thales, Anaximander was concerned with the definition of a primary substance, and in searching for it he arrived at the notion of the four opposite qualities, which are hot and dry in perpetual conflict with cold and wet. If one accepts this concept (which ultimately evolved into the extremely durable notion of the four elements), then one cannot follow Thales in proposing as a primary substance something so limited in its attributes as water. Hot, represented by fire, cannot come out of wet, represented by water. So there must be something prior to either water or fire, and this Anaximander defined as *apeiron*, or "the unlimited," a primal substance without determinate qualities. From the "unlimited," at some point, separated off the primeval opposites of hot-dry and cold-wet. And so the earth emerged from a sphere of fire enclosing a moist mass, land (dry) and sea (wet) still combined but ultimately separating, while the heavenly bodies formed into disc-like compressed masses of air filled with fire.

Anaximander's theory of creation extended to the emergence of life, which he saw as also produced by the interaction of opposites, and in particular by the effect of the sun's heat on the cold and moist portions of the earth. The earliest creatures, he believed, developed to maturity within a protective membrane, rather like a chrysalis, out of which they emerged fully developed, and there is an eccentric anticipation of evolutionary thought in his idea that the original human beings must have been born from living creatures of another kind, since only man undergoes a prolonged period of helpless infancy.

Most striking about this whole scheme is that the gods have no place in it. It is a vision of autonomous cosmic process which even contains its own balancing mechanisms, for one surviving passage of Anaximander's great work clearly suggests a notion of justice operating in the cosmos so that the opposites balance each other; hot never burns out cold and dry never sops up wet. Nietzsche, among other commentators, suggested that Anaximander's cosmic justice implied that the opposites would eventually cancel each other out and all return to the "unlimited," but it is doubtful if this is what he really meant. What does seem certain is that Anaximander saw the "unlimited" as transcending and circumscribing the processes of creation, providing their motive power and energy, and extending beyond them into a timeless eternity. So that here, in the ideas of the second of the Ionian natural philosophers, we have not only a pioneer model of the worlds and their creation, but also, in the concept of the *apeiron*, the beginning of a new idea of divinity detached from the idea of a personal deity.

Anaximenes, the third of the great Ionians, is said to have been in his prime, which for ancient Greeks meant the age of forty, round about the time of the Persian invasion of 546 BC, and to have died between twenty and thirty years afterwards; he was therefore about two decades younger than Anaximander. There are no anecdotes about him, and he is credited neither with practical achievements like those that distinguished Thales nor with astronomical observations like those attributed to Anaximander. It is as a natural philosopher speculating on the operation of the universe that Anaximenes appears important to us now.

Like his master Anaximander, Anaximenes wrote a book (in "simple Ionic," as some of the commentators say — which may merely mean that it was in prose and not in verse) elaborating his theories of the nature of the universe and its moving forces. It seems to have been available to Aristotle and his disciple Theophrastus, and the ideas it contains were fairly widely summarized by commentators from the fourth century BC onwards, though only one sentence of it has survived in the form Anaximenes seems to have given it: "Just as our soul, which is air, controls us, so breath and air surround the whole world."

As will be evident from this quotation, Anaximenes had retreated from Anaximander's ideas in the direction of those of Thales, since he concluded that a primal substance could not be something so undefined as "the unlimited." It had to be a specific, recognizable substance, and for the water Thales had favoured he substituted air. The advantage was that he could associate with this substance an inherent process that did not depend on posing a conflict of opposites. The dialectical process by which the universe could be regarded as operating, Anaximenes saw as an attribute of changeable air alone. Air was elusive and invisible, yet concrete and material, and it exemplified the observable processes of condensation and rarefaction, by which, he suggested, the operation of the natural world could be explained.

According to Anaximenes, air rarefied became fire; air condensed became cloud, then water, then earth and rock and all other solid substances. Thus the four elements did not represent conflicting forces. They were manifestations of the same primary substance, and just as the material nature of the universe could be explained in these variant forms of air, so its processes could be explained by the behaviour of air within given spaces, and so, as W. K. C. Guthrie has said in *The Greeks and Their Gods*, "for the first time the idea enters science that qualitative differences are reducible to differences of quantity."

Anaximenes retained the ancient notion that breath (or air) and life are identical, and he saw the macrocosm as animated by the same principles as the microcosm. The operations of air become the all-embracing law of the universe, and air does not merely surround the world; it controls it as the breath controls bodily life. In this sense, Anaximenes as much as Anaximander contributed to a new concept of divinity detached from the myths and deities of the Homeric age, at the same time as he led Milesian thought nearer to the rational speculation based on observed phenomena which lies at the beginning of all scientific thought.

Certainly, before the Milesians, nobody among the Europeans had conceived that an intelligible order was concealed within the apparent chaos of the natural world and that this order could be explained by causes or laws operating within nature itself rather than by the caprices of the gods. From these early thinkers, whose statements were at best half-remembered, stems the whole western tradition of natural philosophy and its consequences in scientific discovery that have so changed not only our perceptions of the world, but also, for better or for worse, the world itself.

Chapter 6

The Guises of God: Xenophanes, Heraclitus, Pythagoras

"I searched within myself," said Heraclitus, and perhaps what most distinguished the three philosophers whom I now discuss is that, while the Milesian natural philosophers sought to present an objective view of the universe based on the observation of natural phenomena, Xenophanes, Heraclitus and Pythagoras all seem in their various ways to have considered the microcosm of the human mind a subject of examination as valid and fruitful as the great universe itself.

Perhaps that is what makes them more interesting as historical personalities. Xenophanes and Heraclitus have both come down to us as opinionated and intellectually combative men, not afraid to attack revered poets like Homer and Hesiod or to deride the gods as conceived by their predecessors. More is told us about Pythagoras, for he was a man about whom anecdotes clustered as they did about Thales, but less is known about him, partly because he never wrote down his teachings, and partly because, unlike Xenophanes, he never talked about himself or his ideas publicly, but created an order of disciples bound to secrecy like the initiates of Eleusis. Influential as his ideas clearly were, the way in which they were imparted meant that we are now rarely certain what teaching originated with Pythagoras himself and what developed among his followers later on and was conveniently attributed to him.

I begin with Xenophanes because in some respects his

thought comes very close to that of the Milesians, though his aim was not so much to give a comprehensive explanation of the natural world as to use the evidence that could be gathered from natural phenomena to create a concept of God that would be rationally acceptable.

Xenophanes was always the poet; he appears never to have written in prose. All his long life after he reached manhood he earned his bread wandering the Hellenic world and singing his elegiac poems. "Seven and sixty summers and winters," he said in what must have been one of his last pieces, "have wafted me and my thoughts this way and that in Hellas. I had already lived twenty-five years when my wanderings began, if I reckon the time correctly." Since he left his native city of Colophon in Ionia at the time of the Persian invasion, shortly after 546 BC, this means that he was born about 570, and since he must have been 92 when he wrote the poem I have quoted, he evidently lived well into the 470s. His own references to his contemporaries and theirs to him tend to confirm this. Heraclitus, writing in the fifth century, refers to him in a way which suggests that his ideas were then current and well known. He appears to have known Pythagoras, whose theories of metempsychosis he mocked, and Simonides, whose meanness he recorded, while a fourth-century historian, Timaeus, said that he was living when Hieron was tyrant of Syracuse; since Hieron's reign began in 478, this would confirm the supposition that Xenophanes lived well into his nineties.

He spent most of his years of exile in Sicily, where he lived at Zancle (later Messina) and Catana. He also spent some time at Elea in southern Italy, and the ancients regarded him as the progenitor of the Eleatic school of philosophy, which was represented with most distinction by Parmenides and Zeno of Elea. According to Plato he was the first of the "Eleatic tribe," which "explained in its myths that what we call all things are actually one," and Aristotle repeated the tradition that Parmenides had been his pupil. A resemblance to the thoughts of the Eleatics with their emphasis on the unchanging unity of things certainly appears in some of Xenophanes' famous attacks on anthropomorphic religion. But though Xenophanes offers the vision of a god who does not move and presumably does not change, this does not rule out the possibility of change in the universe. One could interpret his statements to mean that God, unchanging in himself, is the author of all change. There is no actual suggestion here, as there is with the Eleatics, that our perceptions of change are illusory.

That Xenophanes did influence the ideas of deity held by philosophic Greeks after his time there can be no doubt. In *The Literate Revolution in Greece and its Cultural Consequences* Eric Havelock justly remarks of Xenophanes,

Greek philosophers after him never used the old method of polytheistic narrative to describe phenomena. Many of them, like Xenophanes, were conservative enough to retain *theos* as a useful descriptive symbol, but only provided it was unified and stripped of concrete and pluralistic activities.

But there was more to Xenophanes than a philosopher rejecting outdated concepts. His very desire to find some way of describing, without offense to reason, the divine intelligence which he saw as keeping the universe in perpetual movement suggests that in his own way he was a deeply religious man, as well as a natural philosopher, conscious that the rational is more than the mechanical.

Xenophanes was a poet of considerable versatility. He is said to have written a poem in the epic manner on the founding of Colophon which ran to 2,000 lines, and another on the colonizing of Elea; neither has survived, but fragments of his other poems are numerous, which suggests that they were popular. Through his long years living as a wandering bard without patrons, he composed many pieces, elegiac and satirical, setting forth his philosophic principles and attacking anything he thought false or pretentious. Unlike Alcaeus and Theognis, he avoided merely political themes, and unlike Sappho and Anacreon he wrote no love lyrics. (Apparently he had sons who died before him and whom in his grief he insisted on burying with his own hands, but we know little else of his

emotional life.) But he could celebrate with warmth the good
things of existence that he knew, as in this song with which
we can imagine him opening some banquet of congenial
friends:

Now we have swept the floor and washed our hands
we put fresh fragrant garlands on our heads,
and there the bowl stands waiting, brimmed with wine
scented like flowers and dulcet in its flavour.
The smoke of incense sanctifies the air,
and here the water's clean and cold as ice.
White bread and cheese and honey are to eat,
and there's a flower-strewn altar, and we sing.
We praise the god with pious words,
pour our libations, and we pray for strength
to act in righteousness and duty.
Then we can drink our fill, tell of fine deeds
and sing our jocund songs.
So long as we can keep from quarreling
and safely find our pathways home
the gods will know that we remember them.

From such a poem one gains the impression of a genial man,
willing to be at peace with the world, willing even to make
a gesture towards gods whose existence he doubts, because
he seeks to sustain the Apollonian virtue of moderation in all
things. He is said to have carried the cult of moderation so
far that when his fellow poet Lasus of Hermione once invited
him to gamble when they were drinking wine, he refused, and,
upon Lasus calling him a coward for not being willing to take
a chance, he replied that indeed he was a coward when it came
to doing ill.

Yet Xenophanes was not a timid man, and seems to have
been distinguished among his contemporaries for the out-
spokenness and the lack of concern for personal advantage
with which he would attack accepted attitudes. He discarded
a good source of patronage when he attacked the cult of games
by which Pindar and many other wandering poets profited.
Indeed, it is refreshing to encounter a Greek philosopher-poet
criticizing the reverence his contemporaries showed for phys-

ical achievement, and comparing the feats of the athlete unfavourably with the pursuit of wisdom and the establishment of social virtues:

> If a man wins by fleetness of foot in the races
> beside the Pisan river at Olympia, or triumphs
> in wrestling or the painful art of boxing,
> or conquers in that dread bout, the pentathlon,
> then he is honoured by his fellow townsmen.
> He merits the best place in public gatherings,
> he is feasted at the cost of his fellow citizens
> and a purse will always be provided for him.
> If he wins with horses it is just the same,
> though he deserves it less than I do, for my wisdom
> is worth far more than strength of men or horses.

Xenophanes also spoke out against the official wisdom of the age, when the poems of Homer were honoured by recitation at the great public festivals, by denouncing the old poets for portraying the gods of Olympus as less moral than human beings were expected to be: "Homer and Hesiod have credited the gods with all those acts that are subjected to blame and reproach among men, such as stealing, adultery and deceit." In rejecting this idea that gods were like men but more powerful and less worthy, he came to his own deistic concept of a God having none of the special characteristics of the beings who are his creatures.

Xenophanes emerges as a rather puritanical social critic when he writes vividly of the degenerate love of luxury that had corrupted the people of his native Colophon even before the Persians came in 546. The Colophonians had once been a forthright, even somewhat uncouth people, but in the reign of Croesus they developed friendly relations with the Lydians, and so, in Xenophanes' view, became corrupted:

> Even while they were still free of the Persian despot's
> yoke, they went off to the agora in purple robes, decked
> out in the useless finery of their Lydian neighbours, a
> thousand men displaying gilded ornaments in their hair
> and doused in costly perfumes.

The thousand men were the citizens with full voting rights,

allowed by Ionian custom to wear their hair long to show their rank. For Xenophanes the display of useless luxury was no more consistent with citizenly responsibility than the cult of sportsmanly achievement, and he may well have been thinking, as he wrote this passage, that these ornamented fellow citizens had quickly accepted the domination of the Persian conquerors while he and a few hardy fellow spirits chose the uncertainties of a wandering exile.

If Xenophanes was sharply critical of the social attitudes current in his time, he also displayed a true scientific spirit by renouncing any hope that man would ever understand the universe completely: "The gods have not granted to man the gift of knowing all things from the beginning; he seeks and little by little he finds." He showed the same empirical attitude when he wrote the passage which may have been the opening to his major poem on the nature of things:

No man has direct knowledge of the gods or of everything I treat of, for even if one speaks the truth about matters beyond the senses, one cannot know it to be so.
And thus all I say beyond my observation is based on no more than plausible inference. Only God knows all things.

Human knowledge, as far as it can be certain, is based on experience and therefore is relative. As Xenophanes put it, "Imagine that God had never created honey; we would think figs far sweeter than they now taste."

Yet, despite the cautions he addressed to his audience and himself, Xenophanes did fall into the succession of Ionian natural philosophers by speculating on the operation of the universe as well as on the nature of God, and in the process he hit upon some notions that modern scientists share.

He envisaged a world that, moved by the thought of an unmoving god, had no space for manlike deities or the activities with which the myths had credited them. He went against the grain of his time by denying the validity of oracles, which trespassed on the knowledge only God could possess. Like the Milesian physiologues, he sought the primordial substances, and found them in the two elements of earth and water. Air he saw as a product of the rarefication of water. Clouds and rain he explained as emanations from the sea; beyond earth and water he envisaged only the boundless. The existence of anything resembling heaven he denied.

Xenophanes developed geological insights that showed a genuine scientific ability to generalize from observed fact to plausible hypothesis. He was particularly interested in the phenomenon Darwin discussed in *The Voyage of the Beagle*, the presence of fossil shell beds in the mountains. He observed the impressions of fishes and seaweed in the quarries of Syracuse; deep in the rocks on Paros he had seen the impression of what he thought were bay leaves, and in Malta he had observed "flat shapes of all marine objects." One gets the sense of a man of infinite curiosity, an antique version of Gilbert White of Selborne, interested in all manner of curious things and anxious to fit them into a system that would offer some kind of coherent explanation of the world he inhabited. From his observations of fossils, which he interpreted as the relics of once living animals or plants, he concluded correctly that at certain times and places the earth had been submerged under the sea. He went on to the idea of a cyclic pattern of great inundations in which life was destroyed and afterwards built up from the start through the fruitful interaction of water and earth.

This suggestion, with its early anticipation of evolutionary theory, was not an unreasonable hypothesis, given the facts Xenophanes had observed in his wanderings, and its reasonableness makes rather surprising the more bizarre astronomical theories attributed to him by Aetius in the second century AD. According to Aetius, Xenophanes taught that the sun was recreated every day out of little particles of fire generated like lightning out of moisture, that it and the moon moved close to the earth, and that there were in fact different suns and moons for different regions. Given the good sense Xenophanes displayed in most of his statements, and especially in his geological speculations, it is hard to believe that he could seriously have advanced such theories. And since, as G. S. Kirk and J. E. Raven remark in *The Pre-Socratic*

Philosophers, he was "a critic rather than an original dog-
matic" and a man of notable wit, one may reasonably assume
that, if the statement paraphrased by Aetius was ever uttered
by Xenophanes, he spoke in mockery of the more naive cos-
mographers who were his contemporaries. To take seriously
what he is supposed to have said in this context is like believ-
ing that Swift intended his *Modest Proposal* as a literal guide
to action.

When Xenophanes and Heraclitus agreed, it was usually in
the targets of their attack, among whom Pythagoras was
prominent. Heraclitus mocked him for "learning of many
things" rather than concentrating his reason on important
truths, and Xenophanes for his teaching of metempsychosis.
Xenophanes recounted how, when Pythagoras was out walking one day, he came upon a man beating a dog, and when
he heard the animal's yelps and howls he agitatedly strode up
to the man. "Stop!" he cried. "Don't keep on beating him!
When he howls I cannot help hearing the voice of an old
friend."

Little is really known about Heraclitus for, unlike
Xenophanes, he was resolutely unautobiographical in such
fragments of his writing as have survived. He too was an
Ionian, born of the royal line of Ephesus and a descendant
of the founder Androclus. He even held the ceremonial title
of *basileus* or king, but set so little store by it that he surren-
dered the honour to his brother. He does not seem to have
left Ephesus, for there are no records of his journeyings, and
he did not share the kind of celebrity and influence the wandering life brought to Xenophanes and Pythagoras. He played
some part in the politics of Ephesus, and persuaded a certain
Melancomas to give up his plan to establish a tyranny; he
denounced the Ephesians for their lack of a sense of freedom
when they expelled his friend Mermodorus the lawgiver.

What does seem certain is that by his intellectual arrogance,
which prevented him from acknowledging the merits of other
philosophers, Heraclitus also made himself unpopular among
his fellow citizens, and in later centuries legends grew up about
his reclusiveness and his eccentricity which, if all the tales are

true, must have verged on madness. According to Diogenes
Laërtius,

> He finally became a misanthrope, withdrew from the soci-
> ety of men and went to live in the mountains, where he
> kept body and soul together by eating herbs and grasses.
> As a result of this regime he fell into a dropsy and
> returned to the city, where he put a riddle to the doctors:
> could they make a drought out of rainy weather? When
> they did not understand that by this he was referring to
> his condition, he buried himself in a cow-stall, hoping
> that the heat of the manure would cause the dropsy to
> evaporate; nothing came of this attempted cure, and so
> he died at the age of sixty.

This account of his end may be fanciful, but we have no other,
and his philosophy certainly suggests that he was a fanciful
man.

The fragments of his writing that have come down to us
derive from a volume he deposited in the temple of Artemis
at Ephesus, and now they take the form of detached aphorisms
rather than of continuous argument. The book itself may have
been destroyed during the great fire that burnt the temple in
the fourth century BC, for even early commentators like
Aristotle and his disciple Theophrastus seem to have been
working from fragments. Theophrastus complained that the
pronouncements of Heraclitus to which he had access were
either incomplete or inconsistent, and Socrates regarded him
as so obscure in his statements that "one had to be a sponge-
diver to go down to depths like that." Whether this was due
to a corruption of the texts by the fourth century, or to their
intrinsic difficulty, is now virtually impossible to decide, but
Heraclitus seems to have seen himself as presenting an eso-
teric doctrine that could not be understood by ordinary men.
At the beginning of his book he is traditionally said to have
spoken of the Logos, or principle of the universe, in terms
that displayed his contempt for the understandings of his fellow men:

> Men can never understand this eternal Logos of which
> I speak, either before or after they have heard it. For

though all things happen in accordance with this Logos, men act as if they had never known it, even when they encounter such expositions as mine, in which I treat of everything according to its nature and to its relationship with other things; most men fail to observe even what they themselves are doing when they are awake, in the same way as they forget their actions when they go to sleep.

But despite the undoubted obscurities in his teachings and his deliberately oracular ambiguity of expression, Heraclitus has caught the imagination of the centuries and has influenced philosophers and poets alike from his day to our own, so that the echoes of his thoughts are to be found not only in ancient thinkers like Plato and Zeno the Stoic, but also in the declarations of unorthodox modern philosophers like Nietzsche and vatic modern poets like W. B. Yeats. Almost everyone who has adopted or adapted the thoughts of Heraclitus has been accused of misinterpreting him, and this shows how far we are from a general understanding of his teachings, but it also demonstrates what an extraordinary range of minds his striking aphorisms have ignited; he was a revolutionary thinker in his time and continues to be one twenty-five centuries afterwards.

Heraclitus stands firmly in the archaic Ionian tradition by rejecting mythical explanations of the nature and origin of the universe and seeking natural laws to explain its order and its functioning. In contrast to later philosophers like Parmenides, who proposed an unchanging reality behind the deceptive appearance of change in the phenomenal world, Heraclitus saw the very principle of the world's life as change and struggle. The Logos is the unifying principle by which all this operates; it is both symbolized by and embodied in fire, which Heraclitus regarded as the purest and therefore the most primal element: "Fire is the underlying element; the world is an ever-living fire." Fire is the constant presence in the unending process of flux by which the other elements of water, earth and air are always changing into each other, never retaining a constant form yet maintaining the same proportions according to the Logos. This everlasting metamorphosis of the elements resembles similar processes in the systems proposed by Anaximenes and Xenophanes, and the presence of the Logos and of constant proportions if not constant form suggests that the Heraclitean system is not so innovatory as has often been assumed; the desire to relate the process of change evident in nature and in the lives of men to a constant ground is present in the Milesian philosophers as well, and even the idea of a creative tension produced by the struggle of opposites, "like that of a bow or a lyre," to use Heraclitus' own image, reminds one of Anaximander's similar proposition.

Perhaps the great originality of Heraclitus lay in his power, even greater than that of the professional poet Xenophanes, of clothing his thoughts in images that still seem fresh and striking after two-and-a-half millenia. Who can fail to listen to the inventor of a phrase like "the world is an ever-living fire," or to respond to the insight embodied in the philosopher's other famous aphorism, "You cannot step twice in the same river," where the image of a flow ever renewed really embodies two truths: what seems constant is always changing, but the change takes place between the banks of a Logos (or governing intelligence, if one wishes to use that word) which guarantees the ultimate stability of the world in flux — another pair of opposites in tension.

Heraclitus claimed that he reached his philosophic conclusions by "searching within myself" — in other words, by rational introspection. However, as I have suggested, the likelihood of influence by the Milesian physiologues and by Xenophanes is strong, and it may have some significance that Heraclitus wrote while Ephesus was under the domination of the Persians. He could hardly have avoided contact with this people whose dominating philosophy, propounded by Zoroaster, saw the world operating in a dualistic pattern of everlasting struggle and treated fire as both the purifying and transforming element and the centre of ceremony.

With Pythagoras we are on even more doubtful ground than with Heraclitus, since we have no certain knowledge of any of his teachings. Only two of his contemporaries, Xenophanes and Heraclitus, mention him, and then in derision. The secrecy which he and his followers sustained about their beliefs makes it difficult to determine how much of the body of doctrine that had come to be regarded as Pythagorean by the fourth century in fact derived from Pythagoras, and how much was developed by others in the order of initiates he founded.

From near contemporary sources we can establish a few facts about the life of Pythagoras. He was born on Samos, probably near the middle of the sixth century, and was the son of a gem cutter, which would place him in the same circle as Theodorus the artist and architect and perhaps explain his concern for mathematical proportions. Some time in the 520s he left Samos; he is said to have incurred the hostility of the tyrant Polycrates, but this is by no means certain, and he may have left, like Anacreon, during the disorder that followed the tyrant's death in 523 BC. He went to Croton in the heel of Italy, from which a famous physician, Democedes, had shortly beforehand arrived at the court of Polycrates; Democedes may well have sung to Pythagoras the praises of his city as a centre of scientific enquiry.

The brotherhood Pythagoras founded at Croton was devoted to *philosophia*, the love and pursuit of knowledge — a term Pythagoras is said to have invented. Its affairs were kept secret and we know as little about them as about the rituals of Eleusis, but there is no doubt that the group, and Pythagoras in consequence, acquired political influence and was largely responsible for the expedition led by the wrestler Milo that with puritanical zeal destroyed the hedonistic city of Sybaris — one of the more dramatic examples which teach us that philosophers should never be trusted as kings. By this time Pythagoras seems to have acquired a reputation as a charlatan, for Herodotus in the next generation followed the example of Heraclitus by talking of him as a swindler who imposed on the credulous; there seems no doubt that he claimed powers of divination and prophecy under the direct inspiration of Apollo. Not long after the destruction of Sybaris, the citizens of Croton began to resent the influence of the Pythagoreans and some kind of disturbance led by a certain Cylon forced Pythagoras to flee to the neighbouring city of Metapontum, where he died. His order seems to have revived in Croton after his death, and the city remained a centre of Pythagorean teachings until the middle of the fifth century, when there was a second upsurge of hostility, and some of the Pythagoreans were killed while the remainder scattered among the other cities of Magna Graecia.

Pythagoras is credited, like many Greek teachers of the time, with going to Egypt; it is likely he did, as Samos had close commercial links with Naucratis. He is also said to have reached India, which is less likely though not impossible, given the easing of communications created by the Persian Empire; certainly it would fit in with the ideas about reincarnation which he shared with the Hindus.

What went on in the brotherhood is only vaguely known; most of what has come down to us are comic rules of behaviour, like the ban Pythagoras is said to have imposed on eating beans because he regarded them as likely vehicles for souls awaiting rebirth. It is possible that the traditions which represent the brotherhood as a great centre of philosophic, mathematical and astronomical enquiry were developed later under Platonic influence. Hostile accounts suggest it may have been like the cults of modern California, where obedient disciples accept without discussion the revelations of an "inspired" leader; a situation of this kind, in which real enquiry and debate were impossible, might explain the hostility of men like Xenophanes and Herodotus, who were in the Ionian tradition of open discussion and free speculation. Nevertheless, other traditions do point to the contribution of the Pythagoreans and Pythagoras himself to mathematical knowledge, and it is reasonably certain that his experiments with the monochord led him to the momentous discovery of concordant musical intervals corresponding to simple numerical ratios, and that this discovery inspired him — or perhaps only his followers — to seek an explanation for the universe in terms of mathematical proportions, a pseudo-scientific approach that led eventually to the Platonic obsession with form rather than substance.

In fact we know so little about Pythagoras, despite the legends that have gathered around his name (including the tale that he possessed a thigh of pure gold), that it is hard to place him clearly in the sixth-century tradition, and we can perhaps best see him as bridging two tendencies of the time, both of which represented an advance beyond the past dominated by the cults of the Olympian gods. One was the trend towards new religious cults, more popularly based, which stressed congregational participation and offered assurance of a meaningful life after death; there seems to have been a close link between the Pythagoreans and the Orphics, and some historians have regarded Orphism, with all its mystical connotations, as a Pythagorean invention. The other was the rational trend represented by the Milesians, though, in the case of the mathematical theories developed by the Pythagoreans and perhaps by Pythagoras himself, the reasoning seems to have been deductive rather than inductive like that of the Milesians and Xenophanes, who tried to generalize from observed phenomena. The Pythagoreans seem to have sought the instances — as Pythagoras did when playing with the monochord — that would prove an already established view of a universe based on numerical ratios. Yet the most famous, and perhaps the greatest, of the Pythagoreans, the physician Alcmaeon, seems to have reached his revolutionary conclusions in the fifth century (such as the recognition that the brain is the receptacle of all sense-impressions) through a process of reasoning from observation that was very Milesian in character and probably owed most to the tradition of experimentation among the doctors of Croton like Democedes rather than to the teachings of Pythagoras.

Perhaps most of all Pythagoras is important less for his ideas, whatever they were, than as an illustration of the intellectual flexibility of the archaic age, whose growing tendency towards independent thinking produced philosophers, as well as poets and artists, who fitted into no single mould, so that we see all the later philosophic developments of antiquity in some way or another prefigured in the sixth century.

Chapter 7

The Uses of Wisdom: Solon and Hecataeus

If the sixth century extended beyond the more purely scientific speculations of the Ionian philosophers into the brilliantly applied science of architects like Theodorus and engineers like Eupalinus, it also developed out of its philosophical thought the beginnings of social sciences, represented in the great lawgivers and the pioneer historians of the period. Perhaps the best representatives of these trends were the two men with whom I deal principally in this chapter, the lawgiver Solon and the historian Hecataeus.

For all its largeness of achievement and of geographical extent, the Hellenic world of the sixth century was in many ways a small one, and the Greek inclination to wander in search of knowledge meant that the men we remember from that time were often acquainted with each other even if their homes were on opposite sides of the Aegean or even the Mediterranean. Thus we can perhaps give credence to the story that is told of Solon's visit to Thales in Ionia on the great journey which the former made after presenting the Athenians with his code of laws.

Thales was unmarried and had no children, and, according to Plutarch's account of their meeting, Solon expressed surprise that he had shown no desire to raise a family. Thales did not answer immediately but contrived a curious and rather cruel lesson for his fellow sage. He arranged for a man Solon

did not know to come to his house announcing that he had
just arrived from Athens. By this time Solon had been away
for a long time, and he asked eagerly for news. The stranger
answered that he had been present at the funeral of a young
man much mourned by the whole city because he was the son
of a wise and respected citizen who had been long abroad.
Solon asked more questions, to which the stranger, briefed
by Thales, answered in such circumstantial detail that Solon
finally told him his name and asked him if it were his son who
had died. The stranger replied that indeed it was so, and Solon
burst into tears. Thales took him by the arm, and assured him
that what the stranger said was in fact untrue: ''Now you can
understand why I have not married and had children. The sorrows it may involve are clearly too much even for a dauntless
man like you to bear.''

Even if the story is apocryphal, its implied teaching (so similar to the Buddha's at the same period) of the virtues of non-
attachment to other persons does reveal an important distinction between Thales and Solon in the way they projected their
insights. Thales was mainly directed towards the world of
things. He studied the stars and the nature of the universe.
He applied his knowledge practically to the measuring of
things, in terms of height or distance, or to their manipula-
tion, whether it meant diverting rivers or cornering olive oil.
His attention and that of his Ionian followers was directed
to the processes of the universe, and to human life only in
so far as it was an emanation of such processes. His disciple
Anaximander evidently speculated on the origins of man as
a species but there is no evidence that he speculated on the
nature and origins of human societies.

But in the Athenian Solon and the Milesian Hecataeus we
have men whose interests led them to direct the rational way
of thought that emerged in their period towards the human
societies to which they belonged, Solon as a political
philosopher and Hecataeus as a historian.

Solon, of course, was known as the great Athenian lawgiver, and his reputation as a poet — though he was the first
distinguished Attic elegist — has always been subordinate to

that of his political achievements. He was not the first Athenian lawgiver to appear in that age of rapid social change. He had been preceded in the late seventh century by Dracon, who devised a code so severe that people said his laws were written "in blood, not iron." Dracon's laws were supposed to protect ordinary men from the capricious administration of the customary law that had survived from the tribal and myth-ridden past, and they did represent an improvement in one area. For the first time they distinguished deliberate murder from justifiable or accidental homicide, but Dracon retained the barbarity if not the capriciousness of the past, and the death penalty still applied to a multitude of offences, including petty theft. Dracon was also responsible for important constitutional changes. He was aware of the shifting power relations of the time brought about by the emergence of citizen armies whose members constituted a middle class of foot soldiers prosperous enough to buy their arms and light armour, patriotic enough to fight for their cities, and powerful enough to challenge the existing oligarchies of landholding aristocrats; to meet this situation he created the hoplite franchise, by which the obligation to fight for the city carried with it the right to vote in its affairs.

But Dracon did nothing to ease the situation created by economic difficulties in a society where the prosperous had the right to make slaves of the poor who could not pay their debts. The invention of coinage and the breakdown of the traditional barter system aggravated the situation; poor farmers became virtual serfs to their rich neighbours, their lands were mortgaged, and eventually their persons and those of their families were sold into slavery.

By now the development of hoplite service had given the less prosperous ranks of society more power, and even the oligarchs feared a rebellion that might play into the hands of potential tyrants like Cylon, who tried to seize power late in the seventh century. In a situation of mounting crisis, Solon, who had already distinguished himself by urging the Athenians to seize from Megara the strategically important island of Salamis, was appointed "sole archon." This gave him the temporary powers of a dictator with a mandate to reform the laws. In the spirit of the Delphic dictum "Nothing to excess," Solon gave in neither to the rich who wanted things to remain as they had been nor to the poor who wanted radical political changes:

> I gave the common folk such concessions as were proper for them and I made sure that the powerful who were admired for their riches did not suffer unduly. I thrust a strong shield between the two sides and ensured that neither should prevail unrighteously over the other.

One thing Solon found intolerable was that an Athenian should be able to sell a fellow citizen as a slave; he abolished the practice of enslavement for the non-payment of debts and freed those who were in bondage, though he was not opposed to the institution of slavery as such and even tolerated other Greeks being kept as slaves by the Athenians. According to his own boasts, he seems to have arranged for many Athenians who had been sold abroad to be redeemed and brought home. At the same time, he revised the Draconian laws, retaining the death penalty only for murder: "And laws I made that gave impartial justice to all men, the good and the bad alike."

Finally, Solon reformed the constitution, retaining some of its oligarchic features but introducing democratic elements. He perpetuated the divisions based on property qualifications, with their varying responsibilities. The high ranks of archon and treasurer of Athens were reserved for members of the highest class; members of the three upper classes could hold a variety of other offices and were eligible to be elected to the Council of Four Hundred, whose main function was to prepare the agenda for the meetings of the Ecclesia, the full assembly of all the adult males of Athens, to which members of the lowest, labouring class were admitted. The whole of the citizenry was eligible for juror service.

Solon had these laws inscribed on wooden tablets set in revolving frames in a public building. He called the citizens to take an oath to obey them and decreed that they should remain in force for a hundred years. Then he set off on his travels, visiting Lydia, Egypt and Cyprus, and perhaps Magna

Graecia. He lived long enough to see his intentions subverted when his relative Peisistratus established his tyranny, and seems to have died round about 558 BC. But his work was not entirely lost, for Peisistratus observed the forms of his constitution and worked scrupulously within his laws, while Solon's work came eventually to fruition when the Peisistratid tyranny collapsed at the end of the sixth century and Cleisthenes created a democratic Athenian constitution.

Solon's reforms fit well into the general movement of society and of thought during the archaic period. Just as the Milesian philosophers abandoned authority in the realm of thought when they sought to explain the universe by reasoning rather than by myth and priestly lore, so Solon abandoned the authority of tribal custom and the remnants of sacred monarchy. He sought to arrange political relationships according to a rational consideration of rights and duties and a respect for the dignity of individual men, represented by fellow Athenians threatened, often through no fault of their own, by the wretched fate of enslavement.

Solon was not alone at this time in his endeavours to create rational structures of law that would ensure the stability of societies. The new Hellenic colonies of the Mediterranean seem to have created systems of laws, just as they instituted regular town planning, even before the cities of the Greek mainland, and doubtless they ventured into these areas because it was easier to start with a clean slate in newly founded colonies than in old established cities. Zaleucus is credited with having elaborated at Locri in southern Italy the first Greek code of laws, and he may have done so as early as 650 BC; Charondas, who performed the same service for Catana in Sicily, was probably Solon's contemporary. They were obviously meeting a deeply felt need among the western Greeks, for both of them were invited to visit other cities in Sicily and Italy to devise appropriate constitutions. Not long afterwards the Cretan city of Gortyn inscribed on stone an elaborate code that was discovered more or less intact at the end of the nineteenth century; it shows how carefully and how sensibly the communities of that time must often have provided for their political needs as they emerged out of the age of tribal kingship.

Such concern for the rationalization of laws and political arrangements was related to the development during the sixth century of a critical historical awareness. It is not accidental that the first of the true historians, Hecataeus of Miletus, should, as we have seen, show such notable political wisdom in the acute political crisis caused by the Ionian revolt of 499 BC.

This event helps us to date Hecataeus. Obviously by the end of the sixth century he was a figure whose views could command audience if not acceptance. Details about India in his geographical treatise, *Periegesis*, suggest he was familiar with the account the explorer Scylax brought back from his journey to the Indus in about 514 BC, while early in the fifth century Heraclitus talked of him, in the disparaging tones he used towards most contemporary thinkers, as if he were still living. The Byzantine lexicon, *Suda*, dates his birth from as late as 520 BC, but this is a tenth-century AD compilation based on sources in the sixth century AD, and the earlier evidence certainly suggests that Hecataeus was born considerably earlier than 529 and was at his prime a generation before his great follower Herodotus, who does not appear to have known him personally, though he tells some fresh-sounding anecdotes about him.

The earliest Greek historical writings were local chronologies which tried to make sense out of the founding myths of communities, and genealogies which sought to establish family or community lines of descent, usually from gods or heroes. Miletus seems to have been an early centre of such writing, for a certain Cadmus of that city, whose name suggests Phoenician descent, wrote at the beginning of the sixth century an account of the founding of Miletus and the settling of Ionia.

Cadmus seems to have been an early prose writer, and Hecataeus followed his example. But he may have gained more from another pioneer Milesian prose writer, Anaximander, whom he almost certainly knew. Hecataeus, reputed to have been a "much-travelled man," drew a map that was an improvement on Anaximander's because it incorporated not only his own observations but also later accounts like those of Scylax in India and those of the Phocaean mariners who went beyond the Strait of Gibraltar — the *Periegesis* refers to the kingdom of Tartessus and to the Atlantic coast of what is now Morocco. The fragments that survive of this work show that Hecataeus attempted to present an objective account of the world in his time. He not only lists peoples and places but is at pains to describe customs, dress and vegetation in the various regions, and he must have been impressed by phenomena like the Nile flood, for he once described Egypt as "the gift of the river." He had all the urges of a true geographer, even though he seems to have clung to some ancient beliefs, such as that of the "river of Ocean" which was held to encircle the earth. Indeed, his map appears to have been circular "as though drawn by a compass," for which Herodotus mocked him.

But there was nothing in Hecataeus' experience to disprove the idea of a circumambient ocean, and for this reason he continued to accept it, perhaps no more irrationally than Thales accepted that the world floated on water. In his other role, as a historian, he also examined the myths critically without wholly rejecting them. He opened his *Genealogies* with the bold proclamation, "Thus speaks Hecataeus of Miletus: I write such things as seem to be true, for many and foolish — I believe — are the tales told by the Greeks." But he may not have been as sweepingly critical as these remarks suggest, if we are to believe a tale Herodotus told about him. On his visit to Egypt Hecataeus conversed with the priests of one of the temples at Thebes and made the claim that his ancestor sixteen generations before had been a god. Thereupon the Egyptian priests showed him the great wooden statues which each high priest ordered to be made during his life and which were later preserved to commemorate the succession. There were 345 statues, representing more than twenty times the generations of human ancestry to which Hecataeus laid claim, and there was not a god among them.

What Hecataeus, who was certainly of aristocratic descent,

made of this we are not told directly. But we do know that
he set out to maintain the Hellenic myths as a basis for history while seeking to find rational explanations for their more
unlikely aspects. He believed that what Homer asserted contained the germs of history and that, rather than rejecting these
ancient tales outright, we should read them critically, seeking
the core of fact. For many centuries, while historians regarded
Homer's works as mere romantic invention, Hecataeus seemed
discredited. But the finds of archaeology, from Schliemann
at Troy and Mycenae onwards, have changed our views of
prehistory in Greece to something much nearer what the
archaic Hellenes believed. We now know that the Trojan and
the Theban wars must have taken place, that the High King
who ruled in Mycenae, whether or not he was called Agamemnon, was the *primus inter pares* among a cluster of Achaean
chieftains very like the heroes of the *Iliad*, and that the command of the Dardanelles was even then crucial to the politics
of trade, since Greek merchants had already begun to penetrate the Black Sea.

So Hecataeus takes his place as the first critical historian
whose works we know, and it was evidently thus that Herodotus, for all his jesting asides, regarded him; on several occasions, after all, he paid him the compliment of extensive
borrowing. The critical examination of myth and legend,
which is now a respectable branch of history and at times the
only means we have of making sense of archaeological discoveries, began with him, for he was not seeking to establish
a theogony, but to discover the roots of human society by
bringing the myths — the only history the Greeks had before
his day — down to the earth of probability.

Hecataeus was not merely a pioneer in the critical examination of the heritage of myth and legend. He was also the
first recognizable ethnographer, extending geography beyond
mere topography to a consideration of the manners and customs of peoples. The fragments that survive of his works show
a concern for accurate detail mingled with a sense of wonder
at the exotic, both of them qualities that make for good history. Perhaps he can best be compared, if one seeks a recent

parallel, to a scholar like James Frazer, who was much more a myth-oriented historian than an anthropologist in the ordinary sense, and who, like Hecataeus, sought the configurations of our remote past in myth and custom, and found as many clues in the behaviour of the strange peoples who were his contemporaries as he did in analysing the legends of antiquity.

We must never lose sight of the fact that Hecataeus came from Miletus. He was perhaps still a boy when Thales died, but it is virtually certain that, moving in the same patrician circles, he knew both Anaximander and Anaximenes. As a geographer he accepted the same approach as the natural philosophers, and his ideas owe something to Anaximander, whom he imitated and apparently improved on when he made his world map. His *Periegesis* is an empirical compendium of facts about the known world gathered by him and his contemporaries on their journeys motivated by trade and curiosity. Even the tall tales, including his classic account, which Herodotus copied, of the strange life cycle of the phoenix, are part of the lore gathered by men on journeys and are presented as something told the stranger rather than as proven fact. The two aims most evident in his geographical writing are to base what he tells as far as possible on first- or at most second-hand experience, and to offer what does not come directly from such experience tentatively and critically.

If the historical writing of Hecataeus seems different from his geographies, the difference lies in the material rather than the approach. The material of geography is the earth as it exists, and the authenticity of information is relatively easily established so long as the regions described are open to travellers; it is the forbidden and the remote lands that are the abodes of monsters and marvels. But the material of history, which deals with what is past, is either in the written record, which in the archaic age hardly existed, or in the oral memory, which after two or three generations becomes diffused into myth. In the absence of the objective history he himself was in the process of creating, Hecataeus had to proceed from mythical history and reshape it as he went by criticism. In this sense, seeking to give order to the unordered past, by reason rather than by blind faith, and on the assumption that tradition and authority were subject to critical examination, Hecataeus was closely paralleling the efforts of his Milesian contemporaries to find an ordered structure in a universe about which their exact knowledge was as scanty as his of what had happened in Hellas three centuries before. Given their lack of the apparatus — archives and instruments — available to modern scholars, the advances made by all these great Ionian scholars towards a rational view of the nature of the universe and the history of man are among the most remarkable manifestations of the sixth century's questing and critical spirit.

PART III

THE MIDDLE EAST IN TRANSITION

Chapter 8

The Kings of Kings and the Prophet of Progress

I

The Greeks resented the Persian domination of Ionia and drove the Achaemenian army away from their European heartland, yet they retained an extraordinary admiration for the two great Kings-of-Kings, Cyrus the Great and Darius, even though neither was a hellenophile like the Lydian king Croesus. Cyrus became the subject of an exemplary biography by Xenophon, the soldier disciple of Socrates, and Alexander the Great took him as the model of a wise conqueror. Even before that, when the memories of the wars between the Hellenes and the Persians were still fresh in men's minds, Herodotus wrote with admiration of these early Achaemenid rulers, not only recognizing their abilities but also perceiving how their actions had shaped the world in which he lived and wrote his *History*.

To trace the circumstances of the Persian rise to power and their retention of it is one way of drawing the political map of the sixth century over the whole vast area that lay between the Greek world and the confines of farther Asia, an area reaching from the plains of the Punjab to the deserts of Libya and the windswept grasslands of the Ukraine.

The origins of Persian power are inseparable from the rise of the kingdom of Media which consolidated into a single mobile army the mountain tribes of northern Iran. In the last

117

decades of the seventh century, adopting the Scythian cavalry tactics of troops of elusive mounted archers, King Cyaxares extended the Median realm until it covered the whole area from Bactria, now Afghanistan, to the verges of eastern Anatolia.

During the same period the revival of Babylonian power under the Chaldean king Nabopollassar shifted the balance of power in the valley of the Euphrates; an alliance between Media and Babylon led to the destruction of the once powerful and irresistible empire of Assyria, long the dominant Middle Eastern power, and the fall of the Assyrian capital of Nineveh in 612 opened the way for more flexible kinds of imperialism than those of the ancient hieratic realms of the great river valleys, the Euphrates and the Nile.

As they consolidated their realm, the Medes came into contact and potential conflict with the powerful Anatolian kingdom of Lydia, which had risen to prominence after the decline of Phrygia in the early seventh century, and had established its suzerainty over the Greek city states scattered along the Aegean coast of Asia Minor. In 585 BC the westward movement of the Medes brought the two states to the point of war, which, as we have seen, was averted by an event that marked the emergence of science as a factor in determining human affairs. At this time Thales of Miletus was already a Greek institution respected by a succession of Lydian kings who called upon his knowledge and advice. Accompanying the forces of the Lydian king Alyattes, he evidently predicted an eclipse of the sun at the time the Medes and the Lydians would clash with each other, and he was proved right. In the midst of battle day seemed to turn into night and, whatever Thales may have said in explanation, both sides took the phenomenon as a warning from the gods. They stopped fighting and promptly concluded peace, Alyattes and the Median king Astyages cutting their arms with their swords and licking each other's blood, and afterwards sealing the pact with a dynastic marriage between the Lydian prince Croesus and the daughter of the Median king. The researches of modern astronomers give an actual date to at least one of the key events of the archaic world: the Medians and the Lydians ceased fighting and became allies on the 28th May, 585 BC.

The unsteady balance of power between Babylonians, Medes and Lydians lasted for a long generation. During this period the Lydians reconstituted commerce by inventing coined money, and the Ionian Greeks under their suzerainty embarked on the long journey of scientific enquiry. Nebuchadnezzar made Babylon into a great kingdom once again and rebuilt his city on an imperial scale that aroused the admiration of the ancients. An attempt by Pharoah Necho II to re-establish Egyptian power in Palestine was foiled; the kingdom of Judah, making the wrong alliances, was destroyed and its people were sent into their historic exile beside the waters of Babylon; and the powerful and prosperous Phoenicians and Philistines were reduced by Babylonian invasions into minor actors in Middle Eastern power games.

In the middle of the sixth century this equilibrium was destroyed by the emergence of an unknown prince, Cyrus the Persian, who ruled a little Iranian realm called Anshan, near where Shiraz now stands. At the head of his tough nomadic horsemen, Cyrus revolted and seized the empire of Media from Astyages, his maternal grandfather. And so in 550 Cyrus became King of Kings and the Achaemenian Empire was born. Cyrus treated his defeated enemies with such clemency that the Medes willingly joined the Persians in the avalanche of conquest that followed. In Biblical tradition the Achaemenian Empire was always a matter of the Medes *and* Persians.

With the happenings of 546 BC this chain of events moved out of what might otherwise have remained the realm of archaeology into that of written history, for this was the year "the Persians came," as Xenophanes remembered, and encountered a people who were beginning to see the fates of men and peoples not as matters of myth or even chronicle, but as the subjects of philosophic reflection and ordered record. These were the Greeks, who under Alexander would eventually become the nemesis of the Achaemenian Empire, but who also would eventually preserve it in the clear amber of historical recollection through the writings of Herodotus and Xenophon.

But the Persians came into contact with the Greeks only because of their war with Lydia, that ancient nation of shop-keepers, whose coins, the first in history, bore stamped on them the image of a lion fighting with a bull. Croesus, now king of Lydia, meant the lion to represent himself and his house, and it is possible that the bull may have represented some ancient conflict with the kings of Crete. But it was no Cretan bull that brought Lydia to its end.

Croesus had been troubled for many years by the course of events that was to lead to the deposition of his father-in-law Astyages by the upstart chieftain Cyrus. But Astyages had been removed from his throne and Cyrus had ruled for some years before in 547 BC Croesus decided that he should take action against the increasingly powerful empire on his eastern border. It is possible, if we are to accept the account in Herodotus of the emissaries sent to the Ionian Greeks, that Cyrus was trying to subvert his realm, and Croesus decided to act before it was too late.

He received his equivocal oracle from Delphi, and made his preparations, which seem to have been elaborate, including the diversion of the Halys River under the supervision of Thales to facilitate the passage of his Lydian cavalry, reputed to be the best in Asia. The first battle was indecisive because Cyrus was using mounted archers who shot and rode away rather than face the weight of a charge of heavily armed horse-men. Croesus went back to Sardis and, as was then the cus-tom in Middle Eastern warfare, disbanded his infantry levies for the winter. Like all Lydian rulers, he was accustomed to campaigning only in good weather. But that was not the way of the Persians. Later they might become soft and rotted by luxury like other warrior peoples who settle down to enjoy the fruits of their conquests, but in the beginning they were men from the mountains who possessed only their horses and their weapons, and winter meant nothing to them. So Cyrus pushed on and arrived, to the Lydians' astonishment, on the plain outside Sardis in 546. Croesus rode out to meet him at the head of his cavalry, the only troops on whom he could now call. Even now, the issue was doubtful, since Cyrus' men and their horses were exhausted by a long march. But the Great King mounted his men in camels, which horses detest, and when the mounts of the Lydian cavalry smelt their stench, they bolted, the Persians gained an easy victory, Croesus was captured, and the Lydian kingdom became another satrapy in the Achaemenian Empire, with the Ionian Greek cities, once they had been suppressed, as its tributaries.

Now the Persians commanded the Iranian and Anatolian highlands from the Hindu Kush to the Aegean, and their attention turned to the great valleys that were the cradles of Middle Eastern civilization. Eight years after conquering Lydia, in 539, Cyrus invaded Babylon, where Nebuchadnezzar had been succeeded by the weak and unpopular Nabonidus, and the country's great capital fell to him virtually without resistance. Cyrus himself was killed in 529 when he headed an expedition against the Massagetae, a Scythian people encroaching on his northern frontiers, but in 525 his son Cambyses, having entered into agreements with the Bedouin chieftains of Arabia to give his armies free passage and water, invaded Egypt. Despite the hard fight put up by the Greek and Carian mercenaries whom the pharoahs were now employing, Psamtik III, the last king of the 26th dynasty, was defeated at Pelusium, and Egypt ceased to be an independent country for almost 2,500 years, until Nasser seized the Suez Canal and effectively ended foreign domination in 1956 AD. A decade or so after Pelusium, Darius, the successor to Cambyses, sent his armies over the Hindu Kush and occupied Gandhara and the Punjab, including the Indian holy city of Taxila.

The Libyan desert and the Scythian steppes, the lengthening of lines of communication and perhaps a softening of the Persian fibre with success, put an end to further expansion. The Persians were a terrestrial people, relying on Phoenician and Ionian ships and mariners when they needed navies, and their empire was essentially land-based, an empire that armies could control. They despised trade and never competed with the Greeks or the Phoenicians in establishing far-spread sea-linked networks of colonies and trading depots, and clearly they never conceived the kind of hybrid empire that the British finally established.

Still, the empire Cyrus initiated and Darius consolidated was different from earlier empires in being at once more tolerant and more efficient. Cyrus conceived the idea of a great multicultural empire to which Alexander gave dramatic expression later on when he tried to remove the barriers between Greeks and barbarians by intermarriages leading to closer contacts between peoples. There is no sign that Cyrus or Darius conceived any experiment as universalist as Alexander's, for, like the Hellenes, they regarded themselves as a superior people, and what they sought was not homogenization, but a community of peoples, each following its own customs, worshipping its own gods, even following its own patterns of local government, but united in a lasting Pax Persica and governed by a great bureaucracy with an intelligence network manned by officials called "the ears of the King," who watched over the actions of local satraps and reported irregularities. The general aim of this overriding organization was not merely to guarantee that tribute flowed in regularly and to anticipate rebellion, but also to ensure that an even standard of justice prevailed, that the "laws of the Medes and Persians" should be seen to be impartial and unalterable, and that the king's promises should be kept to the word.

A classic case was that of the Temple at Jerusalem. In 520 the Jews of the city complained to Darius that the satrap of Syria had curtailed work on the Temple authorized by Cyrus in a decree of 534. Darius ordered the archives to be searched for the edict; when it was found he ordered it to be immediately honoured and reprimanded the erring satrap. Though in general Persians and Medes held the highest offices in the empire, this was not a universal rule; there were Lydian and Babylonian satraps, and Greeks were often entrusted with important missions, as Scylax was when he commanded an expedition to explore the approaches to India as a prelude to the Persian invasion.

The efficiency and pervasiveness of the administrative system Darius created was matched by the completeness of the road network by which, in anticipation of the Romans, he linked his realm from one end to the other. The greatest of the royal roads began at Sardis, the old capital of Lydia, and ended in Susa, the former Elamite capital, which the Persians took over as a winter capital to balance their summer capital of Ecbatana, the old Median centre in the Iranian highlands. Later the road was extended to the new capital of Persepolis, which Darius founded near Cyrus' simpler palace complex at Pasargadae in the old Persian homeland near Shiraz. Finally, it was extended over the mountains through Bactria into Gandhara and the Punjab, where it terminated at the ancient scholarly centre of Taxila, headquarters of the satrapy of India, one of the wealthiest provinces of the Persian Empire. India meant essentially the Punjab. Persian power did not extend into the valley of the Ganges, where native kingdoms were arising, though the example of the Persian ruling system had a lasting effect on Indian styles of government that is perceptible in Delhi even to this day.

The Achaemenian roads were used by the Persian armies, by the wandering "ears of the King," and by the mounted couriers who in all weathers carried the royal messages in relays riding night and day. But perhaps the most important feature of the great road system was that it was used freely and in all security by merchants, by ordinary travellers and by foreign visitors satisfying their curiosity like Herodotus, who followed it without hindrance to Babylon and Susa even after the Persian wars had marked the historic rift between Hellenes and Iranians. Journeying was facilitated by the presence of a post house inn every twenty miles, which made easy and convenient stages for the man who decided to take a leisurely journey on foot with three months to spare on the way from Sardis to Susa.

The safety of the great road was proverbial, continuing century after century and preserved so long that as late as the first century AD, four centuries after the Persian Empire had faded away, the Greek thaumaturge Appolonius of Tyana travelled along it unharmed all the way from the Aegean to

India, as St. Thomas also may have done at about the same time. Certainly when it was new in the later part of the sixth century BC the royal road of the Kings of Kings was the foremost artery for the transmission of cultures.

That process was perhaps most strikingly, because most enduringly, embodied in the great palaces, with their synthesis of art styles, which Darius and his son Xerxes built at Persepolis in the old Persian heartland of Anshan and at the former Elamite capital of Susa. Unlike the royal structures of earlier empires, they were built not by slave labour but by paid artisans gathered from among all the peoples of the empire. The tall sixty-foot columns were carved and raised by Egyptians and Babylonians accustomed to such massive masonry. Phoenician carpenters made the roofs and ceilings from the cedar wood they had brought from Lebanon, as centuries before they had made the ceilings of Solomon's great temple in Jerusalem. The delicate friezes of stone carved in low relief at Persepolis, showing the people of twenty nations in their characteristic costumes bearing tribute to the King of Kings, were done by Ionian and Lydian sculptors, among whom the name of the Phocaean Telephanes has come down to us.

The great palaces were monuments to all-embracing might, but they also embodied the idea — strongly enough for Alexander to be moved by its vibrations two centuries later — that with wise and just leadership peoples of many races and nations could live beside each other and retain their customs and traditions without being constantly, as the Greeks were even among themselves, in the shadow of war. And behind this concept lay the universalist beliefs developed by Zoroaster in the Bactrian highlands, beliefs that undoubtedly influenced the Persian kings and that went beyond monotheism into eschatological doctrines of the end of things and the destruction of evil and the eventual renewal of the world.

The influence of sixth-century Zoroastrianism on major world religions, which I shall discuss later, was part of the great heritage which the Achaemenian Empire left to subsequent ages in the western and the eastern worlds alike. Equally important was the concept of a wise and benevolent universal rule, a concept that survived long after those first austere years when the simple Persian mountaineers destroyed the decadent realms of the old Middle East. Despite the Persian wars, which extended into their own Greek heartland, the Hellenes still found in the idea of a great well-governed assemblage of peoples a concept that challenged their own failure of unity. Even those among them who had no desire to remain under Persian rule were willing to grant Cyrus an esteem which included something more than mere admiration — the desire to imitate.

This warmth of feeling can be seen emerging in Herodotus, writing about half a century after Marathon and telling us how Cyrus, in the kindness of his heart, was constantly concerned for the welfare of his peoples. By the fourth century, when the terrible internecine wars between Athens and Sparta, and Sparta and Thebes, had tarnished the memory of their resistance to the Persian invaders, Cyrus had become, for many of the Greeks, an exemplary ruler, not far removed from Plato's philosopher king. They admired him and the unspoilt Persians of his day for the discipline and unity they themselves lacked, and one of the ironies in which history abounds is that Alexander, the ruler who temporarily united the Greeks and led them into Persia on a great expedition of revenge that destroyed the Achaemenid dynasty, should have taken with him on his campaigns Xenophon's *Cyropaedia* — *The Education of Cyrus* — to remind him of that model of wise kingliness.

The Hellenistic period, when Alexander's successors ruled over the whole of the Middle East as well as Greece, really represented, in its combination of Persian-style imperial organization and Greek culture, a late culmination of the sixth century. Similarly, the Mauryan emperors, who in the third and second centuries united much of India under their rule, modelled the organization of their realm on the Achaemenian Empire, and the *Artha-shastra*, the classic manual of Indian statesmanship, written by Kautilya, minister of the first Mauryan emperor Chandragupta, reads in passages remarkably like the descriptions of Darius' methods by Herodotus. The Mauryan combination of Persian political organization and Brahminical culture was modified under Ashoka by Buddhism, another sixth-century development, and the wisdom and tolerance of Ashoka's rule suggests that, in a different way from Alexander, he too learnt from the legend of Cyrus the Great.

II

In terms of the ancient world, Cyrus was a wise ruler who conquered but did not annihilate. The imperial government defended and drew tribute from the heterogeneous assembly of peoples it ruled, but abstained from proselytization. Yet there was a static quality in the Persian form of imperialism as practised by the Achaemenids which ultimately made it incapable of resisting Alexander's dynamic assault. Even its principal virtue, tolerance, slipped too easily and often into indifference and, as happened under the rulers who followed Darius, it tended to encourage inertia rather than to stimulate development. If the splendid organization of the Achaemenian Empire, and even its great road system that opened communications between Europe and Asia, were all that the Iranian civilization contributed to the great changes of the archaic world, its role would have to be dismissed as instrumental rather than inspirational.

But the dynamism of the early Achaemenian Empire, which enabled it to overthrow the old semi-sacred kingdoms of the Middle East and establish a new and more secular kind of imperialism, was linked with the emergence of a current of belief and thought which, though it seems to have stemmed from the same source as Hinduism, developed a sense of progress and purpose in the working of the universe and in the history of the world that was very different from the cyclic and unprogressive patterns in which the older civilizations of the Middle East and India saw the temporal world revolving.

That current of thought is linked with the name of Zoroaster, one of those figures of the archaic age about whom we have little verifiable knowledge. Even his date has long been in dispute. Some historians have placed him in the middle of the second millenium BC, though a doctrine that had shaken itself so notably free from mythological trappings as that which he preached could hardly have appeared so early, and there are good reasons for accepting a much later date, not the least of them the fact that the traditions of the Parsees, which preserve an unbroken continuity from the Achaemenian age, declare that he lived between 660 and 583, the period in which the great Iranian cosmology, the *Zend Avesta*, was rendered into its present form.

Zoroaster's name is associated with that of King Vishtaspa, who was the early sixth-century ruler of a small kingdom in Bactria which was eventually absorbed into the empire of Darius, and this would fit him into the pattern suggested by the Parsee tradition, while the fact that Zoroaster is said to have originated in eastern Iran and to have done much of his preaching in what is now Afghanistan, makes this identification all the more likely. A final reason for accepting the end of the seventh and the beginning of the sixth century as the period when Zoroaster was most probably active is that his thought reveals an intellectual daring, a power of generalization and a desire to present a rationally acceptable view of the universe and its processes that fits admirably with the spirit of the sixth century BC. He was clearly of the same mental company as the Ionian philosophers and the heretical preachers of the Ganges valley. Putting the matter simply, he had quite obviously a mind that belonged to the sixth century and no other.

Yet, like those philosophers, he emerged out of his own special tradition, and if they were reacting against an unquestioning acceptance of the ancient Greek theogonies and against the Vedic teachings of the Brahmins, he appears to have been intent on changing the traditional religion of the Iranians, which was associated with the Magi, an order of priests in origin doubtless similar to the Brahmins who formed the priesthood of the other great branch of the Aryan peoples, which had migrated a millenium or more ago across the mountains into India. The original gods of the Magi, which became the official deities of Iranian rulers, were personifications of natural forces very similar to the gods of sun and sky and earth that dominated the Vedic pantheon of the invaders of India. The links between the religion of the Magi and that of the Vedas are shown most clearly by the importance both of them attached to the cult of fire, which in the Vedas was associated with the god Agni, and which, even when he had evolved what was to all intents and purposes a monotheistic religion, Zoroaster still retained for its ceremonial and symbolic value.

The two elements of Zoroastrianism that made it so influential in later times were its virtual monotheism and a paradoxical dualism which saw cosmic process in terms of a dialectical struggle between the powers of good and evil that must eventually end in the victory of Ahura Mazda, the principle of good, over Ahriman, the principle of evil, or, to use more Zoroastrian terms, truth and the lie. In this vision the eschatological principle first enters into religious thinking and into man's view of the process of history, for the struggle was seen by Zoroaster as ending in a final battle and a cosmic conflagration in which the lord of darkness, the prince of lies, would ultimately be defeated. Light would triumph, the process of history would end, and the kingdom of Ahura Mazda, of truth and goodness, would continue unchanged for ever. In that struggle each man must make his free choice, whether to ally himself with the true god or to serve the prince of lies.

Described in this way, the teaching of Zoroaster seems to overleap the ages, for there is no doubt that the process by which Yahweh was changed in the eyes of the Jews from an exclusive and jealous tribal deity to a universal One God began at the end of the Babylonian captivity when they came into contact with their Persian liberators. At the same time, the imaginative and highly original eschatological model which Zoroaster developed became the pattern not only for the Judaic but also for the Christian and the Islamic visions of world history, terminating in the last of the great eschatologies, that of Marxism, with its dialectical progression towards the earthly paradise of utopia, where all struggle ends and all progress withers away with the state. In this sense Zoroaster was without doubt the most ultimately influential of all the great teachers of the sixth century, and thus there emerged from the East the concepts that would mould the world of the West over twenty-five centuries and distinguish its dynamic ways of thought, with their manifestations in action, from the cyclic, unprogressive and destinationless concepts of cosmic change that survived in the farther East of India and China.

The basic ideas that Zoroaster incorporated into his eschatological vision were not unknown to Greek thinkers. Xenophanes presented a vision of the One God even more uncompromisingly monotheistic than that of Zoroaster, while both Anaximander and Heraclitus saw the interaction of opposing forces or elements as essential to the cosmic process. The fact that the Ionian historian Xanthus and some of his contemporaries spoke of Zoroaster early in the fifth century leaves little room to doubt that the Greeks who stayed in the Aegean cities after the fall of Lydia in 546 learnt from their conquerors some of the basic elements of Zoroastrianism, and one is tempted to think that the imagination of Heraclitus was stirred by the Iranian cult of fire when he made that element dominant in his vision of the cosmic process. But none of the pre-Socratic Greek philosophers developed anything resembling the eschatological vision that Zoroaster presented of a progression terminating in the conflagratory end of the world of change and the triumph of the principle of good and light. Among the legends of the Pythagoreans was one that their master had discourse with Zoroaster in Babylon, but there is nothing in what we know of Pythagorean beliefs that resembles the teachings of the Persian master.

Zoroaster seems himself to have been one of the Magi, and it is likely his teachings represented a reform widely accepted among his fellows in the order. Ahura Mazda, to whom the Achaemenid monarchs paid deference, was already a Magian deity, and it is not certain how far Zoroastrianism actually became a state church endorsed by the dynasty. If one can reason from the benevolent tolerance the Persians showed to the religions of the people they conquered, and if one can draw analogies from the other Indo-Iranian tradition of Hinduism, which has tended to be not only tolerant but also absorptive of new trends, the likelihood is that even if Zoroaster's ideas were regarded with distrust by some of the more conservative of the Magi, the Achaemenian ruling class recognized the imperial value of their universalizing tendency and adopted them for this reason.

If Ahura Mazda ruled over the lesser spiritual beings, Cyrus and his successors ruled over all the lesser kings. And so, while prudently continuing to worship their dynastic gods, the Achaemenids doubtless accepted as much as they needed of the cosmology of the new prophet who had providentially appeared at the time their dynasty was moving into the position where it would seize power and unite all the Iranians — Medes and Bactrians as well as Persians — in its great imperial venture. The fact that by the Greeks who encountered the conquering Persians Zoroaster was regarded as the leading Persian prophet and "master of the Magi" suggests that his teachings were already accepted widely among the Iranian ruling class, and that his eschatological dynamic, which would carry those teachings into the great religious movements of the post-classical world, also helped to create visions of an empire where all peoples would eventually come together under a single benevolent ruler — visions that inspired Cyrus and, later, Alexander, long before they were taken over by Jewish messianists, Christian chiliasts and Marxist secular millenarians, all of whom saw the struggle of good and evil forces ending in a New Heaven and a New Earth as Zoroaster first imagined.

Chapter 9

Departing Glories: Egypt and Babylon

The rise of the Iranian peoples, like the later incursions out of the heart of Asia into the civilized world, acted as a great historic catharsis in which many old realms and cultures were eliminated. Some, like the Assyrian Empire and the Caspian kingdom of Urartu, which the Medes seem to have destroyed at the same time as they overthrew the Assyrian kingdom, left little heritage and therefore played a scanty part in the events of the sixth century. On the other hand, Babylon, which did not fall to the Persians until 539, played a considerable role in the international politics of the century, and also, by the transmission of knowledge and styles, contributed notably to the cultural developments of this period.

While Persia was busily creating a new kind of empire and the Greeks were passing through tyranny towards democracy, both Babylon and Egypt were reactionary realms seeking to maintain their stability in an unsure and shifting world by preserving and even reviving the values, the institutions and the styles of life and art of eras of past greatness.

Already under its later rulers Assyria had shown a tendency to counter change by strengthening the traditional framework, at least in symbolic ways. Ashurbanipal, the last great Assyrian king, who brought about a fleeting rebirth of his kingdom before its final collapse at the end of the seventh century, was exceptional in his time because of his interest in antiquities and his sense of the importance of preserving traditions through establishing permanent records and collecting memorabilia. His vast library of clay tablets, preserving the records and the literature of ancient Babylon as well as Assyria, was a true precursor of the library in Alexandria, and more durable, since in the destruction of Nineveh the baked tablets were — unlike papyrus — resistant to fire, so that almost all we know of the ancient realm of Mesopotamia before the sixth century BC is derived from the assiduous chronicling and collecting initiated by this remarkable king.

When Assyria was destroyed, and Nabopollassar absorbed his share of its remnants into a new Babylonian Empire, the desire to establish continuity with the earlier Babylon, the one which flourished before the Assyrian interregnum, led to even more complex revivals of the past. While he built a new city larger and more splendid than the original Babylon, his son Nebuchadnezzar continued to honour the traditional gods and to preserve the ancient styles of art and architecture, enlivened with a touch of Assyrian floridity.

Babylon, and notably the Chaldean region from which the new kings came, had been for centuries a centre of mathematical speculation and of astronomy carried out with simple instruments but amazingly careful observations. Under Nebuchadnezzar there was a resurgence of these sciences, which located myriads of stars, charted the motions of the moon, established the plan of the zodiac which is used by astrologers to this day, and eventually, by the sixth century, successfully predicted eclipses of the moon and later of the sun. To the Babylonians of this age we owe practices we take for granted even in our daily lives. It was they who first divided the circle into degrees and decided that the day should have twenty-four hours of sixty minutes each, the minutes in their turn being composed of sixty seconds. Thus, long before clocks were invented, the shapes their dials would assume were ordained by ancient Babylonian astronomers.

The Babylonian links with Greece were more tenuous than the political ones Egypt cultivated. But trading connections existed. Al-Mina, the early Greek trading post on the coast of Syria, may have been destroyed by the Babylonians when

Nebuchadnezzar attacked the Phoenicians, but another post, Tell Sukas, continued trade in this region throughout the sixth century. However, Babylonian artifacts are not so commonly found in archaic Greek sites as Egyptian ones, and trading seems to have been slight in comparison with the commerce carried on at Naucratis on the Nile. Yet if one can judge from the example of the Mytilenian Antimenidas, brother of the poet Alcaeus, Greeks sold their services as mercenary soldiers to the Babylonian kings as freely as they did to the Lydians, the Egyptians or, later, the Persians, while the range of astronomical knowledge shown by the Milesian philosophers like Thales and Anaximander suggests that Babylonian learning was already finding its way to Greece, as it did increasingly in subsequent centuries. At the same time there is no evidence of any aesthetic influence emanating from Babylon that affected the work of archaic Greek artists or architects, and at such a receptive period in Hellenic culture this suggests a relative remoteness of contact.

The Persians clearly found much to learn from Babylonian and Assyrian methods of administration and adapted Babylonian architecture to their own uses; in these ways they perpetuated the heritage of the older empires, to whose authoritarian style they were sympathetic. The attitudes of the Greeks to Babylon seem to have varied considerably. Herodotus, who saw Babylon and first wrote of it, admired its splendour and vastness. But Aristotle, champion of the compact city state, recorded with disapproving wonder that Babylon was so immense that it took two days for the news of its capture by Cyrus to reach some parts of it, and found this contrary to Hellenic ideals of moderation and due proportion. Alexander, Aristotle's pupil, was more of Herodotus' mind, and it was largely through his successors, the Seleucid rulers of Mesopotamia, that the contribution of sixth-century Babylon to science and mathematics was preserved and found its way into the general stream of classical knowledge.

Egypt and Babylon came into inevitable conflict in the sixth century as the Saite pharoahs sought to create a buffer state in Palestine to protect their country from Mesopotamian incursions. The Saite dynasty began in the early seventh century when Ashurbanipal of Assyria drove out the Ethiopian kings of the 25th dynasty, who had usurped power in Egypt, and made the governor of Sais a puppet ruler as Necho I. Necho's son Psamtik I rebelled against the failing Assyrian power and in 663 established the native 26th dynasty. His successors waged war unsuccessfully against the rising Babylonian power. Necho II sought to take advantage of the fall of Assyria to establish an Egyptian hegemony over Palestine and Syria; at first he was successful, but he was heavily defeated at Carchemish in 605 by Nebuchadnezzar, who ascended the Babylonian throne immediately afterwards. A later pharoah, Apries, encouraged Zedekiah, the king of Judah, to rebel in 588 against the Babylonians, who had established control over the country after the original fall of Jerusalem in 597. The Egyptians moved into Palestine in support of the Jews but were easily pushed back by the Babylonians. This was their last attempt to establish control over the lands east of the Red Sea.

With the Babylonian domination of the Phoenician cities, which in the past had provided Egypt with ships whenever they were needed, and its subjection of buffer states like Judah and the Philistine communities, Egypt had become more isolated than in the past, and it was natural that its rulers should now look beyond the Asian and North African mainlands. In doing so they made their most important contributions to the pattern of change that characterized the sixth century.

Necho II, after his defeat at Carchemish, began to seek an expansion of Egyptian influence by sea rather than, in the customary way, by land. He conceived the idea of cutting a canal from the Nile to the Red Sea, the earliest precursor of the Suez Canal; for reasons which are not quite clear, the work was not finished, and it was left for Darius to open the canal to navigation almost a century later.

Necho also organized, round about 600 BC, an expedition of Phoenician ships that seems successfully to have circumnavigated Africa approximately two millenia before Vasco da Gama. Some historians, even in the archaic world, cast doubts on the authenticity of the exploit, but the very reason that

Herodotus gave for his scepticism actually serves to authenticate the story of the voyage.

He tells how the Phoenician ships were two years on their voyage, south from the Red Sea and around the tip of Africa, which he called Libya, until they reached the Pillars of Hercules and entered the Mediterranean. Herodotus accepted as credible that on their long voyage they stopped for a while every few months to sow and reap a crop of grain. But he repeats with evident incredulity the mariners' statement that when they sailed around the tip of Africa they saw the sun at noon on the starboard side, to the north of them. That of course is precisely what they would see in the southern hemisphere, and it makes completely plausible the claim that Necho's expedition indeed sailed all the way around Africa two-and-a-half millenia ago.

Yet Africa south of the Mediterranean played hardly any role in the important events of the sixth century, though its own life was changed in significant ways through the influence of Egypt, transmitted by land rather than sea. In about 715 BC Egypt had been invaded by Kushite kings of Ethiopian origin based in the Sudan, who reigned for fifty years until they were expelled by the Assyrians shortly before the establishment of the native Saite dynasty. The Kushites retreated to their original capital of Napata, just below the fourth cataract, and established a new capital at Meroe near present-day Khartoum, where they survived until the Ethiopians from Axum overwhelmed them in the fourth century AD. The culture the Kushites created in sixth-century Sudan was a prime example of the conquest of the conquerors, for it was greatly influenced by Egyptian customs and styles; the rulers of Meroe became god-kings like the pharoahs and built pyramids to commemorate themselves.

They also maintained closer links with the rest of Africa than the Egyptians. Meroe in fact became a trading intermediary between Egypt and the rest of the continent, and its most important role in the sixth century was the establishment of an Iron Age in the African hinterland; the huge slag heaps that still exist there testify to the great industrial activity that must have made it an important exporter not only of iron but also of the skills of the iron-worker to tribal Africa.

Egypt's own important approaches to the outer world were directed towards the Greek communities around the Aegean, and though in the end they did not greatly benefit Egypt, they had wide-reaching effects on Greek civilization. The links between Egypt and the Hellenic world were established in three ways: by the employment of Greeks as mercenary soldiers; by the establishment of trade on a limited basis; and by the development of relations between the Egyptian pharoahs and the Greek states, notably those ruled by tyrants.

It was as mercenaries that the Greeks first became involved with Egypt; their earliest appearance there is commemorated in the story of how Psamtik I, the real founder of the Saite dynasty, secured his throne with the help of "men of bronze" who came out of the sea. These were Ionian and Carian soldiers in bronze armour whom Psamtik used to defeat his rivals and retained as the reliable nucleus of his army. They may have been wandering bands of warriors seeking employment who had come by chance to the Egyptian seacoast, but it has also been suggested that they were sent to the aid of the Egyptian leader by Gyges, then king of Lydia, with whom the Saite rulers established a loose alliance.

Psamtik I established his Greek soldiers in camps beside the Nile, and later they were stationed at Daphnae, to guard the eastern approaches to Egypt. Necho II used them in his campaigns in Palestine, and in 608 BC, in gratitude for the local service of the Ionians, he dedicated a suit of armour at the temple of Didyma near Miletus. Psamtik II incorporated Greek soldiers into his expedition against the Nubians in 591 BC, and some of them left graffiti scratched into the leg of a statue at Abu Simbel. They gave their places of origin as well as their names, and all of them were from the Aegean coast or the islands — places like Teos, Colophon and Rhodes.

Apries, the next pharoah, used his Ionian troops to less effect when he invaded the Greek colony of Cyrene and was defeated in the Libyan desert; perhaps the mercenaries did not fight happily against their fellow Hellenes. Shortly afterwards Apries was deposed by Ahmes II, whom the Greeks called

Amasis. Ahmes II reigned for forty years and despite the Persian menace kept Egypt independent and out of serious wars.

Ahmes kept on the 30,000 Ionian and Carian mercenaries whom Apries had employed, shifting them from Daphnae to Memphis, his capital, where he used them as bodyguards, trusting them more than his fellow Egyptians. The mercenaries remained after the death of Ahmes until the end of the Saite kingdom, when they fought well against the Persians at Pelusium in 525.

The presence of the mercenaries encouraged trade between the Greeks and Egypt, for the soldiers were customarily paid in silver, which Egypt had to import since it lacked natural sources. Trade began quite early in the seventh century, for Egyptian bronze statuettes of that period have been found in abundance both on Crete and in the Heraeum on Samos. Samos may have been the first of the Greek states to start regular trading, for Colaeus the Samian mariner was on an Egyptian trade run round about 640 when he was blown off course and found his way to Tartessus. But the merchants of Miletus established the first actual trading post, known as "the Milesian fort," on one of the branches of the Nile. This happened about 630, during the reign of Psamtik I; about ten years later, to judge from the pottery found there by Flinders Petrie, the *emporion* of Naucratis was founded on the Canopic branch.

Naucratis was not a Greek colony in the ordinary sense of being a new independent state hived off from a parent city, and there were, in the strict sense, no citizens of Naucratis. It was a community under the rigorous supervision of the Egyptians so far as its relations with the country as a whole were concerned, and was internally ruled by a consortium of the various Greek states whose merchants operated there. Twelve cities were involved. Nine of thcm, all from Asia, came together in the shared sanctuary of the Hellenium: these were Chios, Teos, Phocaea, Clazomenae, Rhodes, Cnidos, Halicarnassus, Phaselis and Mytilene. These, however, seem to have been the minor trading powers; the major ones were those with sanctuaries of their own: Aegina, Samos and Miletus.

Like the Romans later, the Greeks were most interested in

buying the grain which the Egyptians then grew in exportable
quantities, but there was also a trade in statuettes, scarabs,
faience work of various kinds and other luxuries, and also
in certain minerals like alum. The Egyptians largely bought
silver, not merely in coin for paying off the mercenaries but
also in bullion to be hoarded by rich Egyptians. Oil was
brought into Naucratis and so was wine; one of the merchants
who imported Lesbian wine was Charoxas, brother of the poet
Sappho. But whether the wine was sold to the Egyptians or
imported merely for the use of the inhabitants of Naucratis
and the Greek mercenaries is uncertain.

Like the twentieth-century international settlement of
Shanghai, which it anticipated in so many ways, Naucratis
seems to have been a city largely devoted to pleasure. Herodotus remarked that "attractive courtesans tend to flourish in
Naucratis," and this applied as much in the sixth century,
when the local temple of Aphrodite was famous, as it did in
his day. Sappho chided her brother for his attachment to the
slave prostitute Doriche, whom he purchased and set free.
Rhodopis, another Naucratic courtesan, was one of the most
celebrated and desired *grandes horizontales* of the ancient
world; she was a beautiful Thracian slave who once belonged
to the slave master on Samos who owned, and also freed, the
fabulist Aesop. By selling her favours in Naucratis, Rhodopis
bought freedom and made a fortune afterwards; retiring early
from the profession, she made a pilgrimage to Delphi, where
she made an offering of iron spits for which her dedication,
carved in stone, has survived.

One can hardly separate these matters of mercenaries and
merchants from the links which the Egyptian kings established
with states and rulers in the Hellenic world, since trade and
military reinforcements were obviously important matters in
international relations. Necho II was in contact with both
Thrasybulus, the tyrant of Miletus, and his friend Periander
of Corinth, and the latter link seems to have been a cordial
and lasting one, since Periander's nephew and successor was
named after the pharoah Psamtik II. It is likely that the basis
of this relationship was a nautical one. During the reign of

Periander, the Corinthians began to imitate the Phoenicians and build triremes, and about this time Necho II also ordered triremes to be made for use in the Mediterranean and the Red Sea. Since the Egyptians were not expert in shipbuilding, and since there are Egyptian inscriptions describing an admiral named Hor as "commander of the foreigners and Greeks," it seems likely that Necho used the services of Corinthian shipbuilders and later of mariners from Corinth or the Ionian cities. Rather surprisingly, Corinth is not recorded as one of the cities sharing in the control of Naucratis, though much Corinthian pottery was found on the site.

Ahmes II was the pharoah who developed the closest links with the Greek world. He has been described as a hellenophile, but it is doubtful if he fell under the influence of Greek culture in the same way as Croesus of Lydia did. Like all the Saite kings, he sought to revive and observe strictly the old forms of traditional Egyptian life. He found it to his advantage to rely on Greek soldiers and to encourage Greek merchants, but he was careful to keep them segregated from the Egyptian people, who seem always to have resented their presence. We can probably gain a more realistic view of his overtures to Greek states and his offerings to Greek temples if we regard them as acts intended to attract useful international allies in an unsure world rather than assuming, as the Greeks in their vanity tended to do, that he was paying deference to their civilization and their gods.

To protect his western flank, he reversed the hostile policy that Apries had developed towards Cyrene and concluded a treaty with the state, accepting its princess Laodice as a wife and presenting the Greeks of the colony with gilded statues of Athene and of himself. He asserted his suzerainty over Cyprus, which on and off for centuries had been an Egyptian dependency, and he courted both Sparta and Lydia when the Persian threat became evident, in the hope of forging a defensive alliance with them and Babylon. Among his gifts to the Spartan kings, one that gained celebrity in antiquity was a splendid corselet of linen wonderfully decorated with many figures of animals wrought in fine gold thread; Samian pirates intercepted the gift so that it never reached Sparta. Ahmes sent a contingent of Egyptian soldiers to aid Croesus when war began between him and Cyrus, preferring to keep the Greek mercenaries for his own protection, and according to Xenophon these men, after the fall of Lydia, were settled by Cyrus at a place near Cyme which was afterwards known generally as Egyptian Larisa.

When Croesus was defeated Ahmes persisted in cultivating the friendship of the Greeks. He entered into some kind of agreement with the people of Rhodes and dedicated two stone statues in the temple of Lindos on their island. To keep on the right side of the influential priests of Delphi, he contributed to the restoration fund for the temple of Apollo after its burning in 548 BC a donation of a thousand talents of alum, or, according to the Attic measure of 59 pounds to the talent, almost thirty tons — a gift of considerable value at the period.

The closest Greek alliance into which Ahmes entered was with Polycrates, and from it comes the story of the tyrant's ring. With his efficient fleet and apparently impregnable island fortress, Polycrates was a notable power in the eastern Mediterranean after the fall of the Lydian kingdom, and he could be a useful ally as long as it served his interests. Yet the writers of antiquity, including Herodotus, seem to have magnified into a friendship what was almost certainly a relationship of convenience between Ahmes and Polycrates. There is no evidence that the two men ever met, but some formal connection did exist, sealed by gifts like the two wooden portrait statues of Ahmes that Herodotus saw in the Heraeum when he visited the island in 460 BC, a mere seventy years after they were dedicated. The excavations of the Heraeum have been particularly rich in Egyptian figurines from this period, mostly in bronze but including two small statues in wood which the marshy ground has preserved.

None of these alliances saved the Saite dynasty from eventual destruction by the Persians, and Egyptian trust in the Greeks ended in betrayal, for Polycrates, as we have seen, offered ships to Cambyses for his invasion of Egypt, and the Persians received the information they needed to cross the desert from a certain Phanes of Halicarnassus, who had been a mercenary of Ahmes.

It is unlikely that ordinary Egyptians were in any real way influenced by Hellenic civilization. Desperately as the Saite kings sought to sustain the alliances that might protect their independence, they were engaged internally in a process of restoring the glory of their country's past, but through commemoration rather than emulation. As in Babylon at the same period, an archaicist trend developed: old records were carefully studied, temples and other historic buildings were restored meticulously to their ancient forms, and the artistic styles of earlier dynasties were imitated sedulously. The form was preserved but the spirit of the great ages of Egyptian civilization had vanished. Yet the very desire to continue the past by endlessly repeating its forms made the Egyptians impervious to the revitalization of their culture by the introduction of new elements from outside.

The situation of the Greeks was quite different. They came as enquiring and open-minded men into a world that was strange and interesting even when it awed them by the magnitude of its past achievements and the length of its history. The story of Hecataeus and the Egyptian priests is indicative. The important thing about it is that though Hecataeus may have been abashed by the low value the priests set on his own claims to descent from the gods in comparison with their long human genealogies, he seems to have accepted the criticism of his own pretensions, for he decided that Greek stories — as he once said — might be absurd and began to look beyond them.

Herodotus once remarked that of the Greeks who went in growing numbers to Egypt as the sixth century wore on, "some, as one might expect, went there for trade, some to serve in the army, and others, no doubt, out of mere curiosity, to see what they could see." Herodotus himself, and Hecataeus and Solon, belonged to the last category, but one cannot assume that either the traders or the mercenaries failed to share the intellectual interests of their time. There was nothing dishonourable in archaic Greece about hiring out one's military skills as a mercenary, and those who fought in the Greek corps for various Asian rulers were often more than mere men-at-arms. The most famous scholar soldier in antiquity was Xenophon, the disciple of Socrates, who became a commander in the forces Cyrus the Younger raised at the end of the fifth century to displace Artaxerxes from the Persian throne, and who led the ten thousand Greek survivors of the battle of Cunaxa on their great march to the Black Sea in 401 BC, afterwards settling down to write, largely out of what he had learnt in his mercenary years, some of the most important prose works of classical antiquity. If there was no mercenary soldier in early generations quite so erudite as Xenophon, we must not forget that the fine elegist Archilochus sold his services as a soldier, and that Alcaeus the aristocratic poet of Mytilene had a mercenary brother who, he claimed, slew on behalf of the Babylonian king a giant enemy eight feet tall.

Serving long periods in Egypt, the mercenaries must have taken home not only tales of the strange country they had come to know and of the vast buildings and colossal statues where they carved their names, but also souvenirs in the form of Egyptian artifacts. The merchants of Naucratis exported such objects to Greece, and when one also remembers the statues sent out by the Egyptian kings as diplomatic gifts, it seems evident that in some areas of the Hellenic world the people were aware of Egyptian art in the same way as Europeans became aware of Japanese art in the nineteenth century, as the product of an alien, exotic and fascinating world from which something might be learnt.

The Greeks were skilful and selective borrowers, taking from various cultures what might be most helpful to them. For example, having acquired from the Phoenicians such a practical instrument of writing as the alphabet, they made no attempt to adapt or adopt either Egyptian hieroglyphs or the variant of cuneiform which the Persians had borrowed from the Babylonians. What the Greeks derived of science and mathematics from the Egyptians it is hard to determine in precise terms, and it is possible that the example of a disciplined approach to observation was more important than any facts or methods actually transmitted. As R. J. Hopper remarks in *The Early Greeks*, "In the main it was more the stimulus than the matter which produced the physical ideas of a Thales as an alternative to the mythological Theogony of a Hesiod."

In the area of art and architecture one is on more solid ground because the objects with which one deals are concrete, visible and to a large extent surviving. The influence of Egypt on Greek archaic buildings and sculpture was broad and creative, and changed the whole character of Hellenic architecture. Until the seventh century the Greeks had built either in the rough massive stonework of the Mycenaeans or in wood and mudbrick. In Egypt they saw great buildings constructed of carefully dressed stone and supported by columns with carved capitals and bases. By the seventh century they had produced their own adaptations of Egyptian originals, transformed to meet local ceremonial and social needs, the Doric order on the Greek mainland and the Ionic order among the Asian Greeks. It is significant that the greatest temples of sixth-century Hellas, on Samos and in Ephesus, were designed by or in co-operation with architects from Samos, whose links with sixth-century Egypt were close. In the sixth century there was also a tendency to plan sanctuaries in the Egyptian manner, with processional avenues lined with series of similar sculptures, like the lions of Delos that remind one so strongly of the lines of rams leading up to the great temple at Karnak.

In sculpture also the influence of Egypt was rapid and dramatic. From carving small figures in soft stone the Greeks turned to monumental figures in hard stone, life-sized or larger. The early *kouroi* were very close in proportions as well as stance to Egyptian standing figures. The Greeks quickly found their own style, replacing the draped Egyptian figures with the familiar naked athletes; by the end of the sixth century the connection between the two types of statuary survives, but it is their differences that catch the eye.

In all these areas the influence is present in terms of concept rather than in the details of working out the concept, and this suggests a considerable degree of indirection. There are no records of Greek craftsmen having undergone apprenticeships in Egypt or of Egyptian sculptors or architects working among the Greeks, though in Athens there was a painter of pottery who signed himself Amasis and may have been a metic who found his way from Egypt or an Egyptian slave captured on some piratical raid on the Nile delta. If Greek architects or sculptors did wander to Egypt, it would take months or years before they began translating their observations into Greek terms, time for plenty of afterthought, and many were probably interpreting the descriptions of travellers such as Hecataeus, who recorded what he saw on his journeys. Nevertheless, no matter how indirect the transmission, the main innovative contribution of Egypt in the sixth-century world was the influence its ancient artistic forms had on the new architecture and arts of the Hellenes, and later, at Susa and Persepolis, on those of the Persians. The revelation it offered was comparable to that of primitive art in the modern world, an ancient conservative form producing an innovative and revolutionary effect.

Chapter 10

The Struggle with God:
Judaism, Jeremiah and Isaiah

One of the ironic processes of history is the way subsequent events act as a filter to modify our view of a particular period—a filter that often diminishes peoples who at the time appeared great, and that brings forward to our attention others whom their contemporaries regarded as insignificant, if they were even aware of their existence. In our view of the sixth century, as of other periods, this exaltation of the humble has taken place.

The peoples who then really seemed to count, in their own eyes and those of their contemporaries, were Greeks and Persians, Indians and Chinese; by the end of the century the Assyrians were hardly remembered, and the Egyptians and Babylonians were powerless and respected merely for the great antiquity of their cultures. But nowhere in Herodotus or in the inscriptions of the Persian Kings of Kings is there any mention of the tiny kingdom of Judah. By the same token nobody anticipated the strange destiny that would make what happened to the Jews in the sixth century so important to that vast section of humanity we call the Peoples of the Book, adherents of the world religions of Judaism, Christianity and Islam, all of which derive their basic traditions from the Old Testament in the form it attained, by editing rather than by revelation, during the sixth century BC.

Central to the history of all the religions of the Book is the

Babylonian captivity, which transformed the Jews from the inhabitants of an insignificant Palestinian kingdom into a "chosen" people guided by a prophetic elite and creating out of defeat and nostalgia not only a great religious tradition but also a poetic tradition as powerful in its influence on world literature as that bequeathed by Homer, Sappho and Aeschylus.

"By the waters of Babylon, there we sat down, yes, we wept, when we remembered Zion," lamented the writer of the 137th Psalm, who seems himself to have been an exile. His song has become a part not only of the Christian tradition but also of English literature through the Jacobean translation made at a time when English prose was in the process of formation, as Greek and Hebrew prose had been in the sixth century. But the 137th Psalm has not survived merely as a borrowing incorporated into English literature or as part of the Bible still used devotionally by twentieth-century Christians. It is also a historical record, an authentic cry from the heart of an exiled people, a sign of the difficulties of living in the ancient world as a small nation becoming conscious of its special destiny.

The kingdom of Judah, by the sixth century, was the mere remnant of King Solomon's tenth-century realm. The larger part, the kingdom of Israel, had been so thoroughly dispersed by the Assyrians in 722 that the fate of its ten lost tribes is still a matter of active conjecture. When the sixth century dawned, Judah still maintained a precarious independence. It had recently gone through a religious reformation. The Phoenician and Babylonian cults that so attractively competed with the worship of Yahweh had been suppressed, though pagan tendencies lingered and a genuine monotheism did not emerge until the Jews had undergone the experience of exile, had reacted against the circumambient polytheism of Babylon, and had come under the influence of the Zoroastrian teachings that Cyrus and his warriors brought with them into the valley of the Euphrates.

Despite the internal consolidation the reformation had brought about, Judah at the beginning of the sixth century still remained at the mercy of the shifting power currents of the Middle East, and its kings made the mistake of backing Egypt against the rising power of Babylon.

Almost the only man who foresaw the fate the Jews were preparing for themselves was the prophet Jeremiah. Whether he spoke from revelation or from good common sense, Jeremiah was one of the great polemical poets of the period, and he cloaked what were clearly meant to be urgent political warnings, and were probably heard as such by his people, in the rhetoric of religious prophecy, attributing his own native perspicacity to the prescience of God:

> For thus has the Lord said, the whole land shall be desolate; yet I will not make a full end.

> For this shall the earth mourn, and the heavens above be black, for I have spoken it, I have purposed it, and will not repent, neither will I turn back from it.

> The whole city shall flee from the noise of the horsemen and bowmen; they shall go into thickets and climb up among the rocks; every city shall be forsaken and not a man dwell therein.

Jeremiah's warnings came true when Nebuchadnezzar laid siege to Jerusalem, and in 587 the city was captured and its fortifications and temple were destroyed. In the next year, 586, many, though not all, of the Jews were taken into captivity in Babylon. There they doubtless helped in the vast building programme as Nebuchadnezzar constructed the great towered gates and processional ways and temples that were the glory of the new sixth-century Babylon, including the Hanging Gardens and the House of the Creation of Heaven and Earth, which we know as the Tower of Babel, and which was still standing, despite the Biblical story of its fall, as one of the greatest buildings of the ancient world when Herodotus visited the city in the fifth century.

It would be wrong to see the Jews in Babylon merely as exploited helots. They were like exiles everywhere, some adapting admirably to their new circumstances and even prospering, others longing to go home and restart their interrupted lives. Compared with that of modern political prisoners, their lot seems to have been reasonably easy. When the captivity ended many of them stayed on to establish a long-lasting Jewish community beside the Euphrates. Yet for all these Jews in Babylon, whether in the end they departed or stayed, the captivity was a period of intense return to the fundamentals of their religion, of re-examining it in the light of the alien Babylonian and Iranian creeds with which they had come into close contact and reshaping it into the Judaism we know today.

The scattered writings of the Jews were now edited, rewritten in so-called Classical Hebrew, which developed at this period, and assembled into something very like the Old Testament of the Christian Bible. The Psalms and the Pentateuch, the basic five books of the Old Testament, were given their definitive form at this time, and the historical books were either revised or rewritten. The dominant tendency was in keeping with the spirit of the sixth century everywhere, the rejection of polytheistic myth in favour of the more rational concept of a single creating and sustaining First Cause or deity.

At the same time, the religious centralization that had been associated with Judaism from Solomon's day down to the exile was replaced by a decentralist arrangement of local congregations or synagogues, a pattern that was to continue from one *diaspora* to the next. Thus the religion's organizational pattern today also derives from the circumstances of the Babylonian exile in the sixth century.

Judaism at last shed the final remnants of Palestinian paganism and emerged as a monotheistic religion. Yahweh, the tribal deity, had been progressively transformed into the Jehovah we know, the one and universal creator and ruler of the universe, but at the same time Satan grew in stature as a principle of evil, and so the underlying dualism of Persian religion came to be echoed, even if it was often denied, in the religions of the Book.

At the same time the special relationship between the Jewish people and their God continued, so that Judaism became both a tribal religion, deeply involved in the fate of a single small people, and a universal religion whose offshoots, Christianity and Islam, became world creeds with hundreds of millions of adherents. At times of crisis the tribal side of Judaism emerged, as it has continued to do over the ages. When Cyrus the Great, the King of Kings, destroyed the realm of Babylon and encouraged the Jews to return to Jerusalem and rebuild their temple, they saw history centring on themselves, and regarded Cyrus as the instrument of Yahweh, their own special god:

Who raised up the righteous man from the east, called him to his foot, gave the nations before him, and made him rule over kings? He gave them as the dust to his sword, and as driven stubble to his bow.

He pursued them, and passed safely; even by the way that he had not gone with his feet.

Who hath wrought and done it, calling the generations from the beginning? I the Lord, the first and last; I am he.

The islands saw it and feared; the ends of the earth were afraid, drew near, and came.

Those were the words of the Hebrew prophet we know as the Deutero-Isaiah, the Second Isaiah. The early chapters of the book of Isaiah were written by a man living in the eighth century, when the Jews were being persecuted by the Assyrians; the later ones, as we shall see, were the work of another man living at the end of the Babylonian captivity. The message of this second Isaiah is one of joy and confidence, the joy of returning exiles, the confidence of a people that finally senses it is stepping on to the stage of history.

The sixth century was a time of great importance not only in the development of Jewish (and by inheritance of Christain and Islamic) beliefs but also in the flowering of a Jewish literature, for the emergence at this time of the Old Testament as we know it involved not only the editing of the earlier narratives and the insertion of passages intended to make them seem more consistent; it involved also much new historical writing, as well as the composition of many of the Psalms, the writing of the Book of Job, and the declarations of the later prophets, of whom Jeremiah and the Second Isaiah were only the most important — and important they were, as sixth-century men who gave expression within their own beleaguered culture to the spirit of the age.

The Book of Jeremiah is not an easy text to read, largely

because, though he wrote when the sense of history as a chronological progression was appearing among Jews and Greeks alike, his thought was too insistently chaotic to be set down in smooth sequential order. As Michael Grant has remarked in *The History of Ancient Israel*, the book is as varied in its forms as it is uncouth in its ordering: "it provides a mixture of the most diverse literary forms—prose and poetry, taunt and lamentation, biography, autobiography, history and acted parable."

It can be viewed in two ways, according to both of which it is important in terms of its age. First, despite its unchronological form it is deeply involved in history, in the great events that were changing the destiny not only of Jeremiah's homeland of Judah but also of the whole known world. Jeremiah struggles throughout his life to see God's purpose in creating and allowing such disasters, and he attributes them time and again to the failure of the Jews to fulfil the divine will. In this aspect of his teaching he sought to liberate belief from convention. He taught that it was more important to believe sincerely than to follow the law meticulously, that attendance at the Temple was meaningless if it were not accompanied by a personal search for God.

Jeremiah seems to have been born about 550 and began to prophesy in the reign of Josiah. This was a time of relief and relative prosperity for Judah. The power of Assyria was declining; the last great invasion by the rulers of Nineveh had taken place in 701, when Sennacherib suddenly retreated for reasons that have never been explained. Whether through his visions or because of his good sense, Jeremiah was fully aware that his people were living in a state of illusory calm, and during the 620s he began to prophesy, mingling denunciations of the priests and the official cult of the Temple in Jerusalem with forecasts of a foe who would come down from the north and cause great destruction. Trouble certainly came, but it came from all directions. The alliance of resurgent Babylon and the Medes finally destroyed Assyrian power. The allies captured and destroyed Nineveh in 612, but Ashuruballit, the last Assyrian king, fought on for a while in his western territories, and in 609 pharoah Necho II, concerned over the Middle Eastern balance of power, marched north through Palestine to his aid. Josiah, who had profited territorially from the fall of Assyria, tried to intercept him but was killed at Megiddo. Necho had some initial success and continued to dominate Palestine until 605, when he was defeated at Carchemish, together with the last remnants of the Assyrians, by Nebuchadnezzar. Nebuchadnezzar came down into Palestine and expelled the Egyptians, so that the region fell under what at first appeared to be his benevolent suzerainty.

Whether from his prophetic faculties or from shrewd political insight, Jeremiah realized that the destruction of Assyria and the expulsion of the Egyptians from Palestine created a new regional situation, and he warned that those who appeared as the friends of Judah might become its enemies. When King Jehoiakim in about 601 withheld tribute from the Babylonians, Jeremiah realized that, with Assyria destroyed and the Egyptians expelled, the tiny kingdom of Judah would stand alone in rebellion; he warned of the dangers of such a course. Jehoiakim persisted, and Nebuchadnezzar invaded, laying siege to Jerusalem and taking large numbers of Jews into exile.

Throughout these events and the later invasion after Zedekiah in his turn rebelled against Babylon, Jeremiah persisted in declaring that the misfortunes of the Jews were visited on them as a result of their impieties, and in advocating submission to Yahweh, which in political terms meant submission to Babylon as God's instrument. His treason, as it seemed to the anti-Babylon faction, led to his being imprisoned and thrown into a cistern where he would have been left to die if it had not been for the intervention of the Ethiopian eunuch Ebed-melech; he was released by the Babylonians after Jerusalem fell for a second time in 587, and was offered a safe conduct to Babylon, but though he advised those already in exile to settle peacefully in their new homes, he refused to follow them. Later he was taken against his will to Egypt, where tradition asserts that the Jews stoned him to death because they were exasperated by his continued denunciations. This is said to have happened in about 570.

The combination of his reformatory zeal, his defiance of

religious hierarchy, his advocacy of non-resistance to evil
strongly resembling that of Tolstoy, and his realistic political
analysis shows the public Jeremiah as, under his prophetic
guise, an innovative thinker with a strong historical sense. But
some of his prophecies go beyond the world situation of his
time. This is especially so with the prophecy of the "new
covenant," in which both Christians and Zionists were to see
a foretelling of the realization of their respective visions:

> Behold, the days come, saith the Lord, that I will make
> a new covenant with the house of Israel, and with the
> house of Judah:
> Not according to the covenant that I made with their
> fathers in the day that I took them by the hand to bring
> them out of the land of Egypt, which my covenant they
> broke, although I was a husband unto them, saith the
> Lord:
> But this shall be the covenant I will make with the house
> of Israel; after these days, saith the Lord, I will put my
> law in their inward parts, and write in their hearts; and
> will be their God and they shall be my people.
> And they shall teach no more, every man his neigh-
> bour, and every man his brother, saying, Know the Lord;
> for they shall all know me, from the least of them unto
> the greatest of them, saith the Lord; for I will forgive
> their iniquity, and I will remember their sin no more.

Whether or not Jeremiah was foretelling the rise of Christianity six centuries later or the recreation of an Israeli state
twenty-five centuries later, we can also see in this passage the
second important way in which the Book of Jeremiah
manifests its era. For Jeremiah presents himself as a man
aware not only of the historical realities of his own period but
also of himself and his personal relation to God and the
universe. Like such Greeks as Xenophanes, he emerges as a
vividly realized personality, cultivating his idiosyncracies and
anxious to tell people, through his scribe Baruch, all about
his life, his misfortunes, and his struggles not only with the
world but also with God.

The Book of Jeremiah is in fact one of the world's first

experiments in autobiography, and it is so because Jeremiah himself had insistently emerged from the tribe and claimed the right to be valued for himself, as an individual. This sense of an individuality ready to break with the collectivity where necessary emerges in his defiance of priestly religion and of the centralized cult of the great Temple, in his disrespect for the forms of Judaism, and even in his refusal to support those who sought, it seemed to him unrealistically, to resist Babylonian power instead of repenting and reforming their attitudes and their behaviour.

Jeremiah stood aside from his society while he spoke as its conscience; he never married, and when he said "I am alone," it was with a profound sense of having no one but God on whom he could rely. Even God he sometimes accused of deceiving him, and at times his Book rivals that of Job in emphasizing that God's ways cannot be judged by human morality or even common decency. Yet he also hears the word of God as "a joy and the delight of my heart," and he denounces his fellow Jews for failing to obey God, for showing "the stubbornness of the evil heart."

Instead of putting his faith in a complex of tribal rites aimed at the preservation of the group, Jeremiah began to see religion as really an individual choice, a matter of personal searching, as it was becoming for many men in many places in his time — for the Greek philosophers, for the Indian heretical teachers, for the followers of Lao-tzu. And this is the immediate meaning of his "new covenant." It is not, like the covenant of Moses, a matter of laws written on stone to be obeyed without thought. It is a matter of law "in their inward parts," and therefore of personal faith, of personal relationship with a deity who speaks in each man's soul yet whose power is infinite, for we can be certain that Jeremiah, ahead of most of his fellow Jews at the beginning of the sixth century, had already arrived at a monotheism as thoroughgoing as Zoroaster's. The whole long struggle between personal and institutional religion, between the mystic and the hierarchy, is prefigured in the complaints of Jeremiah.

Jeremiah's emphatic personalism contrasts strikingly with

the complete impersonality of the other great Jewish prophetic voice of the sixth century, that of the Second Isaiah. The original Isaiah, who flourished in Judah during the late eighth century, from the reign of Ahaz to that of Hezekiah, was an active and identifiable historical figure, even though he did not indulge in the autobiographical excursions that make Jeremiah so vivid and interesting a historical character. Like Jeremiah, he was a fierce moralist, and just as acutely conscious of the political perils of his time, advising the kings of the vulnerable little Jewish state to trust in God rather than in precarious alliances. For him the Assyrians—as the Babylonians later for Jeremiah—were the instruments of God's wrath. He too distrusted the religious establishment, and spoke for the poor and the rejected; just as Jeremiah looked forward to a New Covenant, he looked forward to a time when the remnant of the Jewish people, having survived the troubles that beset a small nation in the ancient world, would take their place in the golden age of a renewed Eden, where "The wolf also shall dwell with the lamb, and the leopard shall lie down with the kid; and the calf and the young lion and the fatling together; and a little child shall lead them." In anticipation of the universalism of later Judaic, Christian and Islamic thought, he looked forward to the time when "the earth shall be full of the knowledge of the Lord, as the waters cover the sea."

In the Bible as it has come down to us from the sixth century, the words of this Isaiah occupy most of the first 39 chapters of the book that bears his name, but the remaining 27 chapters, as their references to the Babylonian exile and the conquest of Babylon by Cyrus make quite clear, are the work of a later unnamed hand or hands. There is no internal evidence as to how or why the additions were made, but they may have been the work of a brotherhood like the Pythagoreans that kept its activities secret. It is significant in this connection that the most spectacular find among the manuscripts of the supposedly Essene community at Qumran was the earliest scroll of the Book of Isaiah in existence. "Seal the teaching among my disciples," the original Isaiah said, and it is possible that a group of them did keep alive his words, polishing and editing and, as time went on, modifying and adding to them to suit the changing historical conditions and to sustain the hope of the people in a world where survival for a small and beleaguered nation was precarious, and where the kind of liberation the Persians brought was so surprising as to appear a miraculous intervention of God, using Cyrus as his instrument. If such a brotherhood of Isaiah's followers did exist, it is possible that the Essenes, who four centuries later were to echo in so many ways the aspirations of the Isaiah literature, were its remote successors.

The final chapters of the Book of Isaiah are more polished and more eloquently poetic than the original 39, and so are good examples of the sophistication of thought and writing which the detachment of exile and the contact with Babylonian and Zoroastrian examples developed among the Jewish scholars who worked in Babylon. These writings are not the spontaneous utterances of men in prophetic frenzy; they are deliberate compositions, and some of them are among the greatest passages of Jewish poetry and also, in the King James version, of English prose.

Here, at last, one encounters an absolute and unlimited monotheism even more certain and uncompromising than Jeremiah's. The possibility of any other god than Yahweh is denied. Yahweh is not just a better god; he is the only God, sole creator and univeral ruler. To his will man must make willing submission; the free choice of obedience is clearly implied, as in Zoroaster's exhortations to choose voluntarily the side of the great god Ahura Mazda in the struggle against the powers of darkness. Given the eagerness with which the Second Isaiah welcomes Cyrus as the instrument of God's purpose, one realizes that he must have been sophisticated enough to accept Ahura Mazda as Yahweh under another name and that the example of Persian monotheism strengthened him.

The most striking passages of the Second Isaiah, and those most familiar to Christians, concern the suffering Servant of God, who has been variously envisaged in later generations

as Israel collectively and, by Christians, as Jesus of Nazareth.
His sufferings are described in poignant words that inspired
Handel to some of his most sublime music:

> He was despised and rejected of men; a man of sor-
> rows, and acquainted with grief: and we hid as it were
> our faces from him; he was despised, and we esteemed
> him not.

That the Servant is made to suffer not for his own sins but
for those of others—that he is performing or suffering an
atonement—is also made clear:

> All we like sheep have gone astray; we have turned
> away every one to his own way; and the Lord hath laid
> on him the iniquity of us all.

> He was oppressed and he was afflicted, yet he opened
> not his mouth; he is brought as a lamb to the slaughter,
> and as a sheep before her shearers is dumb, so he openeth
> not his mouth.

> . . . he bare the sin of many, and made intercession
> for the transgressors.

When we look at such statements in relation to their time,
it seems best to relegate to theology the explanation that the
Suffering Servant is meant to be Christ, and to agree that there
is too much of the personal tone, too strong a sense that this
has happened or is about to happen to an individual human
being, for us easily to accept these passages as referring collectively to the people of Israel, genuine though in recent centuries their sufferings have been. And if we remember the
autobiographical passages of Jeremiah and look forward to
the references to the sufferings of the Teacher of Righteousness in the Essene scrolls from Qumran, a different picture
begins to emerge — of the sufferings of those who by election rather than choice become the prophets of Yahweh.

The sense of a prophetic succession was strong among the
Jews, and from Samuel onwards there seems to have been a
community or order, however loosely organized, of those who
recognized each other as in this way possessed. In the case
of Elijah and Elisha a succession is clear enough, and so it
seems to have been with Isaiah and those who over the centu-

ries revised and expanded his prophecies. Is it not possible that the Suffering Servant, instead of being the people of Israel considered collectively, represents the prophets considered as a succession and personified as a single being? They were men elected arbitrarily, possessed—often unwillingly—by the spirit of God, whose servants in this way they were, and because of the statements they were impelled to make they often endured persecution both from those in authority, to whom they addressed unwelcome rebukes, and from the general population, whose sins they felt compelled to denounce. Though the Bible says nothing of it, there are traditions that Isaiah as well as Jeremiah died as a result of his prophetic profession, executed, as the Talmud asserts, at the orders of Manasseh, king of Judah. A tradition may well have developed that certain men were destined to suffering for the sake of others, a tradition related to Jeremiah's suggestion that the law whereby the children suffered for the sins of the fathers— the law of Original Sin—would henceforward be superseded. A consciousness of this role may in turn have led men to shape their actions to it, seeking, even provoking, the fate that went with the prophetic role, as both the Essene Teacher of Righteousness and Christ appear to have done with some deliberation.

Underlying this acceptance of the suffering role, there is a questioning, even a critical, stance that shows among the Jewish thinkers of this period the same kind of awakening rationality in the face of accepted myths and traditions that we encounter in this era everywhere else in the literate world, from Greece to China. The acts and commands of Jehovah are seen as arbitrary and not in accordance with human concepts of justice. The great gap between what is and what, according to human reason, should be, which more than two thousand years later would haunt the Christian existentialists, now appears for the first time in the Judaic consciousness. Jeremiah shows all the pangs of it, and in the Book of Job it is presented fictionally, even dramatically — the drama of the man who does everything that the human mind can think might be pleasing to God, yet who is visited with endless misfortune and who calls God to account. The same ambivalence is evident here as in Aeschylus, another man of the sixth century, who must have put into the obliquities of art the thoughts of many of his Greek contemporaries when in *Prometheus Bound*, written not long after the century ended, he presented the tragedy of the good being, Prometheus, whose very compassion for mankind places him in opposition to the will of Zeus and earns him the god's inescapable punishment. Thus, each in his different way, the Jew and the Greek challenged the ancient acceptances, and declared that, even if God's will is ineluctable, man has the right and perhaps, being human, the duty to challenge it. Before the sixth century nobody had put the case for human protest against the workings of the universe so explicitly as Jeremiah, Aeschylus and the unknown author of the Book of Job.

PART IV

BEYOND THE DESERTS

Chapter 11

The Shadowy Frontiers

Herodotus talked of the Indians as "the most easterly people in Asia about whom we have any reliable knowledge," and the Greeks had seen them in their white cotton garments marching in the great armies that Darius and Xerxes had assembled for the conquest of Europe. One Greek, Scylax, had led the expedition of Darius to the Indus, and although unlike him they did not leave narratives, it is likely that other Greek travellers made the journey through the Hindu Kush. Some of the Greeks were in fact settled in that range after the Ionian rebellion as part of the Persian policy of exiling malcontents; they formed the community of Nysa, which Alexander encountered on his way to India. Near Samarkand he found another colony of Greeks whose very name, the Branchidae, was that of the priestly clan of the temple of Didyma near Miletus.

But long before Darius or Alexander the links between India and the West had been established. As early as 1500 BC there had been trade between the cities of the Euphrates and the cities of the Indus. Even when the great centres of that early Indian civilization, Harappa and Mohenjo-Daro, were destroyed by invading Aryans in about 1000 BC, the trade did not entirely cease. The dhows still edged from the Persian Gulf and Hadhramaut along the shores of the Arabian Sea, as they continued to do within living memory, transporting goods and later the Islamic faith as far south as the Malabar Coast.

When Scylax in the sixth century went by the overland route

he was the pioneer of a different connection, political rather than commercial. He crossed the mountains, and on the farther side he and his men constructed boats to take them down the rivers of India to the Arabian Sea. They launched their craft into the Kabul River, following the valley which is now arid but was then dense with forest, and finally entered the Indus and passed through the terrible gorge at Attock, where the Great Moghul Akbar later built his massive fortress. Thence they sailed through the deserts of Sind down to the sea, and as a small party they do not seem to have encountered the hostility that Alexander met when he took his army through this territory two hundred years later. They sailed around the southern shores of Iran and Arabia and home by way of the Red Sea and Necho's canal, which had recently been completed by Darius' orders, to the Nile. The Persian army followed the mountain way pioneered by Scylax to the city of Taxila, which became the capital of their province of India, and where the merchants learnt from their new overlords the use of coinage which the Achaemenians in their turn had learnt from the Lydian kings and the Ionian cities.

Indian rulers learnt other lessons from the Persians, who for a couple of centuries ruled the northwestern part of the subcontinent, incorporating Indian contingents into their gigantic armies and levying a tribute that made India the most profitable satrapy in the whole of their empire. Early Indian administrative scripts, like Kharosti, were adapted from the Aramaic used by the Persians at this period, and this borrowing explains why Indian languages are alphabetic. Indian official architecture imitated the Persian; the great lion capitols of Ashoka's time might have been made for Persepolis. Indian kings borrowed their administrative structures from those developed by Darius and adapted by Alexander.

Records of all this are scanty, for words, except for the rare occasions when they were engraved on stone, were as perishable as the papyrus or parchment or paper on which they were written, and they stood even less chance of survival in the humid heat of India than in the dryness of the Nile valley. But the roads, the trade, the advance-guard explorers, the marching armies, the common rulers and presumably the shared sense of a civilization in transition were all there. Thus the question of the sixth-century links between India and the West is fairly clear. We know the physical and especially the political and economic connections that existed, given which it is unlikely that mental connections were lacking.

The matter of China is different and more puzzling. There is no literary evidence that the Greeks, the Persians or the Indians in the sixth century knew anything about China or that the Chinese knew anything about them. The Himalayas and the jungles of Burma formidably divided the Indians from the Chinese, and the Greeks and Persians were separated from them by a Central Asian complex of mountain ranges and high desolate plateaus and deserts at least as formidable as the Himalayas. Yet it was in this region that the destinations of the legendary Golden Journey of later centuries lay—Samarkand and Ferghana—and here in historic times the roads of the East and the West knotted in the Silk Road. Thus towards this mysterious region high among the spurs of the Hindu Kush and the Pamirs a great deal of our speculation regarding events in the sixth century is bound to direct itself. For one cannot ignore the possibility that connections between East and West were already created by the sixth century, even if only in a tenuous and indirect way, through the links between the Asian nomadic peoples who wandered over the vast area between the Gobi desert and the Black Sea, some at least of whom were in contact with Greek merchants and travellers.

Among these Asian nomads the best known to the Greeks during the sixth century were the Scythians. People with a high pre-literate culture, they had come from the heights of the Altai Mountains in southern Siberia on the verges of Mongolia. Some Scythians remained in the Altai; their tombs, preserved in ice like the Siberian mammoths, have been discovered and have revealed much about the complexities and sophistications of sixth-century life even outside what we now think of as the early civilized world. The Scythians of the Altai, as we know from archaelogical and other non-literary evidence, kept contact with their relatives of the Royal Horde, who moved west-ward and occupied the Ukraine and Crimea, eventually penetrating Europe as far as Hungary, where their warriors' graves have been found.

The western Scythians traded with the Greeks who had established their mercantile cities on the northern shores of the Black Sea. They welcomed the products of Greek metal-workers and accepted their stylistic influences, as their own artifacts show. But they rejected any kind of cultural assimilation that might have subordinated their nomad concepts of the warrior life to the ways of Hellenic city dwellers. One Scythian chieftain who accepted the Greek way of life during the sixth century was assassinated by his people. The most celebrated Scythian hellenophile, Anacharsis, who lived a while in Athens, would become for Greeks the prototype of what later centuries would see as the noble savage whose primitive virtues contrasted with the degenerate vices of civilized man; nevertheless, he too seems to have paid the price for his acceptance by the Hellenes, for his brother is said to have killed him as a traitor to Scythian ways when he returned from Athens to the Ukrainian steppes.

The eastern Scythians were probably more mobile than the Royal Scyths, who had acquired a source of regular subsistence in the wheatlands of the Ukraine that diminished the need for wandering. But east of the Ukraine the steppes were the beginning of a series of natural grasslands stretching from the Volga to the desert regions of Central Asia and the verges of China, and this provided a corridor of potential communication.

Though they had no direct contact with the Greeks, the eastern Scythians evidently traded with Iran, doubtless through Bactria, for Achaemenian artifacts have been found in their tombs, including the earliest known Persian carpet, a superbly preserved product of the sixth century. In the other direction they were in contact with the nomads of Mongolia, and thus they had at least indirect contact with the Chinese, whose art at this period shows the clear influence of the art of the steppes. My former colleague the Chinese scholar Ping-ti Ho suggests in *The Cradle of the East*:

... the earliest phase of long-range west-east cultural contact, necessarily through many intermediary ethnic groups of the Eurasian steppe, can be synchronized in the main with the invasion and dissemination of horse chariotry; ... the conquest of the immense dry belt of Central Asia eastward to the Kansu corridor had to wait until the nomads of Eurasia had begun to master the art of horse riding, which can be traced back only to the ninth century BC.

A network of contacts between these horse-riding people from the borders of China to the Ukraine and the Caucasus would mean an extension by the sixth century of the ancient trade routes that already linked a great part of Eurasia. One was the north-south route by which amber—that precious resin from which Thales is said to have deduced the phenomenon of magnetism—found its way from the Baltic to the Mediterranean; at the northern end of this route lived the mysterious people known to the Greeks as the Hyperboreans, whose legendary association with Apollo suggests that they were shamanists, possibly of Finnish or Lapp race. The tin route from northwestern Europe was well established by the time the Phocaeans founded Massalia at the mouth of the Rhône in 600 BC, and there were ancient routes that centred on the salt mines of Hallstadt in Austria. Farther east, in Asia, a notable centre from which routes radiated east and west was Badakhshan, on the western slopes of the Hindu Kush. The mines of that region produced a lapis lazuli of a particularly deep gold-flecked blue that was widely sought in the ancient world and that long before our period was being distributed through the Middle East and possibly into China. That precious and easily transportable commodities travelled far at an early age was shown by Schliemann's discovery in the ruins of the Second City at Troy of a piece of white nephrite that must have been found in the mountains of western China.

When a regular route over the steppes became practicable

in historic times the way ran from China through the Kansu corridor and Chinese Turkestan and crossed what are now the Uzbek and Turkmen Soviet Republics in the USSR into Iran. At Dunhuang at the western end of the Kansu corridor a trail from Tibet and India to Mongolia crossed the main route, and somewhere in the north of Afghanistan a side road branched off southward and reached India through Bactra (Balkh), Kabul and Gandhara. At Ecbatana the main route finally divided, the northerly branch going to the Black Sea, the Caucasus and the Urals, and the southerly one to Syria, Palestine and Asia Minor.

This was the great desert trail that eventually became the Silk Road. Silk was certainly being brought over this route and reaching Greece in the fourth century BC, for Aristotle wrote of it with some familiarity, and the route was well established by Roman times. How much earlier the traffic began has not yet been clearly established. Ping-ti Ho suggests that "the silk route did not begin to serve its historic function as the thoroughfare of east-west cultural exchange until the domestication and utilization of the Bactrian camel, which Chinese historical texts can trace back only to the late fourth century BC." However, since camels were used by Cyrus when he attacked Sardis in 546 and were almost certainly of the Bactrian breed with which his Iranian cavalrymen would be familiar, it is likely that these animals were being used on trade routes as early as the sixth century, even if they had not reached China. If the dating of the Stuttgart Celtic tomb that contained a Greek bronze vessel and a piece of Chinese silk fabric is correct, then the trade had begun in some form as early as the seventh century BC and must have been growing in the sixth century. Even in historic times regular caravans did not go the whole way, and in early days the trade would have been carried on by relays of middlemen between China and Europe and also China and India, where silk is also thought to have arrived in the sixth century.

There was another important trade as well as silk that centred on central Asia. In the shadow of the Altai Mountains near the border between modern Russia and China lies an immense and fertile valley known already in ancient times by its present name of Ferghana. The fine horses bred there were celebrated throughout Eurasia. The Royal Scyths, to whom the Greek traders of Crimea paid tribute, rode the tall horses of Ferghana. The Chinese believed that steeds so swift could only be of celestial origin, and certainly by the fourth century the rulers of Cathay were sending emissaries to trade for them; earlier they may have received them indirectly, through trade with the nomads.

There is no record of a Greek merchant and a Chinese trader in this early period having travelled so far from the west and the east that they could have met in Ferghana, though the enterprise shown by the Phocaeans in the western Mediterranean and beyond the Strait of Gibraltar and by Necho's Phoenicians in circumnavigating Africa suggests that such great travels would not have been impossible. Traders are traditionally reticent about the markets or the sources of merchandise they discover and about the ways to reach them; English merchants were secretly exploiting the Grand Banks long before Cabot "discovered" Newfoundland. Except for a few exceptional individuals like Colaeus and Sostratus, we know very little about the activities of individual merchants in the sixth century even as near home as the Mediterranean, and traders who got as far as the Greek settlements in the shadow of the Caucasus may well have been tempted to go farther. But if they did we know nothing of it.

Some evidence does exist of links of different kinds. In the early years of the Christian era the trade routes were much used by scholarly men and spiritual searchers and teachers, particularly the Nestorian Christian and Manichean missionaries who went this way taking their message to China, and the Chinese monks who travelled in the reverse direction so that they could bring back from India the sacred books of Buddhism. Even in the sixth century BC there were men who travelled with aspirations to spiritual or occult knowledge, and of some of them we have a little half-fabulous information.

Even then, as it still is, Central Asia was the home of the kind of ecstatic religion generally known as shamanism. Up to recent times shamanism existed in a great arc from Tibet through Siberia and across the Bering Strait into Alaska, Arctic Canada and British Columbia, where the shaman's rituals were almost identical with those of his counterpart in Siberia. In the sixth century BC, before it was pushed back by the proselytizing activities of Christians and Moslems, shamanism reigned in a much broader territory extending over virtually the whole of Russia and reaching down into Thrace, where the early manifestations of the cults of Orpheus and Dionysus show strong shamanic influences. In the modified forms of the mystery cults it entered Greece during the sixth century and created what one can call an "underground" religion in two senses, since it was subversive of the old Olympian cults and since its ceremonials were linked to symbolic journeys into the underworld or, as Jung would have it, the collective unconscious.

What distinguishes shamanism from other forms of ecstatic religion is, as Mircea Eliade once remarked, the fact that "the shaman specializes in a trance during which his soul is believed to leave his body and ascend to the sky or descend to the underworld." Customarily, through meeting a supernatural being or through some other extraordinary experience, the novice shaman falls into a deep trance. In this trance he encounters the spirit who will be his guardian. As part of the experience he is taken into the underworld, and there, at the hands of the spirits of dead shamans, he undergoes the dismemberment of his body, the reassembling of his bones, and the renewal of his organs. He undergoes, as Eliade put it, "ritual death followed by resurrection." He is symbolically, spiritually and, since he believes the trance as real as any other experience, physically reborn. From this original transformation he has gained the power of further transformation at will. He can change himself into animal form and detach his soul from his body on journeys into the underworld or the heavens. The parallels between such beliefs and the death, dismemberment and resurrection motif in the myths of Dionysus and Orpheus will be obvious.

Yet in these myths, which came indirectly to the Athenians,

it was the god who was killed, dismembered and restored. During the seventh and sixth centuries the pure shamanistic idea, in which the same process happened to the shaman, began to spread in Greece, and E. H. Dodds in *The Greeks and the Irrational* has demonstrated, convincingly to my mind, that this spread began only after the Greeks had established their colonies and emporia on the northern shores of the Black Sea and had come into contact with the Scythians — the first step towards the far orient.

What is especially interesting about the shamans who appear as individuals in the history of archaic Greece is that they do not stand aside, as one might expect, from the philosophic currents of the time. Hermotimus, a Greek of Clazomenae, displayed the characteristics of a true shaman, though there is no indication where he learnt them. We are told that his soul travelled far, observing events in distant places, while his body remained inanimate at home. Greek writers did not universally dismiss Hermotimus as a charlatan, and Aristotle believed that the philosopher Anaxagoras, who came from the same small Ionian city, owed to this trance-wandering shaman his most characteristic idea, that of the *nous* or supreme intelligence, which keeps recurring through the archaic period in various forms, and of which Anaxagoras said, "Other things all contain a part of everything, but Mind is infinite and self-ruling, and is mixed with no thing, but is alone by itself."

Then there is Abaris, the so-called Hyperborean: Abaris is variously reported to have arrived bearing a golden arrow or riding on one, as — it is still asserted in Siberia — the souls of shamans do. Like some Indian ascetics, Abaris claimed to have become so accomplished in fasting that he could finally do without food; he is said to have brought an end to plagues and to have predicted earthquakes; Pythagoras, it is said, knew and discoursed with him. There seems no reason to doubt, from what we know of Pythagoras, that shamanism as well as the doctrines of Indian ascetics was among the influences he accepted, and here again, as in the case of Hermotimus, we can see the shaman playing the same left-hand role in the development of a rational view of the universe as the alchemists and the astrologers played in the early Renaissance. The exploration of states of consciousness to which such ecstatics devoted themselves was not incompatible with the exploration of the nature of the physical universe in which Thales and his successors were involved. The shamans were regarded as being under the protection of Delphic Apollo, one of whose basic rules (devised, we have seen, by Thales) was "Know yourself."

In this matter of the possible links in the sixth century between the Hellenic world and the Far East, it is another Greek who became a shamanic novice and commands our attention. Aristeas from the city of Proconnesus on the Sea of Marmora travelled through the domains of the Scythians in the direction of Siberia. In his poem *Arimaspes* he told of a journey lasting six years during which he went to the country of the Issedonians, who appear to have lived somewhere in the Urals. The length of his absence suggests that his wanderings were long, and his poem was taken seriously by his contemporaries; the Spartan lyricist Alcman treated it as a literal narrative. Although it was widely known in sixth-century Greece, it has not survived, and we can only conjecture on its contents and the experiences that gave rise to it. But the hints and fragments we do have suggest that through the Issedonians Aristeas may have established contact with the Siberians and their shamans, and if he did encounter the Siberians he may well have been the first Greek to hear of the Chinese. In fact Stuart Piggott in *The Druids* gives an interesting twist to Aristeas' claim to have acquired knowledge of those classical will-o'-the-wisps, the Hyperboreans: he suggests they were in fact the Chinese, transformed by rumour:

His informants would have been Central Asian nomads: to semi-savages living hard and dangerously the ordered society of China might well appear as a model of peace, justice and luxury; and to men whose staple food was meat the agricultural Chinese, whose staple food was cereals, could well appear as vegetarians.

Wherever he had been, Aristeas was clearly fascinated by his experience, and when he had written *Arimaspes* he set off once more into the eastern fastnesses and was never heard of again. Yet his reputation and his legend remained so potent and spread so far among the Greeks that according to Herodotus the people of Metapontum in the middle of the fifth century, well over a century after his second expedition and final disappearance, claimed to have seen him several thousand miles away from his reputed travel ground. The important question is not whether Aristeas was actually seen as a *revenant* in Magna Graecia, but why his story so long and so deeply affected the archaic Greek imagination. Was it perhaps because *Arimaspes* provided the most convincing focus for a floating mass of ill-defined information—oral narratives, rumours, trading information surreptitiously transmitted, veiled shamanic initiations—which at this time stirred the imagination of men? The only concrete proofs of even indirect links between China and the European world during or before the sixth century are a very few material objects like Schliemann's lump of jade at Troy and the piece of silk in a Stuttgart tomb. But the highly developed trade that was certainly in existence by the fourth century suggests that in the sixth a probing along the far highways of the steppes and the mountain deserts of Central Asia must already have begun, and that the double interests of trade and shamanic religion may have meant that Greece and China were already the two ends of a long and thickening network of contacts between east and west. This does not imply that the original thinkers who appeared in these centres, however similar their teachings, influenced or were even aware of each other. It does suggest they belonged to worlds whose similarities were more than accidental.

Chapter 12

Debates on the Ganges: The Indian Teachers

Siddharta Gotama, whom we call the Buddha, was born about 563 BC in the foothills of the Himalayas where the border of Bihar touches that of Nepal. Legend made his father a king, but he had no realm; he was one of the Kshatriya chieftains of the warrior republic of the Sakyas. Many such small commonwealths had appeared in the Ganges valley and in the lower Himalayas as the Aryan warriors surged in during the second millenium BC and displaced or subordinated the original Dravidian population. Since none of these little states survived much beyond the end of the sixth century, we do not know a great deal about them, but there appear to have been at least fourteen such republics or leagues of republics at the time of the Buddha's birth. They appear to have been rather like the more rustic states of archaic Greece, oligarchies within which, as in the warrior councils of the Aryan tribes, equality of voice prevailed. The Buddha praised the Licchavis, members of a republic neighbouring on that of the Sakyas, because they held full and frequent popular assemblies after which the people acted in concert, but whether these assemblies included everyone in the community is uncertain. A caste system, simpler than that later developed in mediaeval India, already existed, and it is doubtful if the Sudra, or labourer, caste would be allowed any participation in the affairs even of the republics, though it is possible that the merchants, members of the then powerful Vaisya caste, took their place with the Kshatriyas and the Brahmins in the general assemblies.

The Buddha was so impressed by the virtues of the ancient republics that he used their organization as a model for the order of monks he eventually formed, the *sangha*, which bore the same name as the republican assemblies. But the actual republic of the Sakyas into which he was born was already extinct by the time of his death, swallowed up by the expanding kingdom of Kosala; in his childhood the process of absorbing the republics into the great kingdoms of the Ganges valley, Magadha, Kosala and Benares, had begun, and before these peripheral hill states were destroyed the rich valley lands had fallen under the rule of powerful monarchs.

Northern India in the sixth century was involved in continuing change, and in some respects it must have appeared very much a frontier society. Vast areas of forest remained, providing refuges for religious hermits and robbers alike, and though major routes across the north of the country had been established, they were largely impassable in the monsoon season. The forests provided the material for the perishable buildings erected at this period; stone temples and palaces belonged to the future, and the only actual monuments surviving from this early period are the massive ruins of fortifications like those of Rajagriha.

Before the end of the sixth century the northwest region fell into the hands of the Persians, whose boundary lay somewhere east of Taxila; in the great northern plain the rival kingdoms waxed and waned, and complete unity would not be achieved until Chandragupta established his imperial realm there in the third century BC.

At the same time as the great kingdoms arose, large cities began to grow up, like Shravasti, capital of Kosala, Rajagriha, capital of Magadha, and Benares itself, already a centre of learning that rivalled Taxila. The ideal of a small Aristotelian city was never developed in India, and communities spread without any evident restraint. A great division of labour began, as can be seen from the lists, given in the Buddhist Jataka tales, of the various occupations, their workers organized in guilds and living in separate corners of the cities — carpenters, metalworkers, masons, ivory-workers, leather-workers, braziers, basketmakers, dyers, potters, jewellers, oil millers, painters, garland makers, and so on. The result of this shift in social organization was that the old tribal bonds were broken and the largest basic unit became the joint family; following on this social atomization came — as in Greece at the same period — a growing sense of the importance of the individual, and, in consequence, a more humanistic orientation in philosophic thinking.

Ruthless as they were in their wars of expansion, the Indian kingdoms of this time were not unmitigated despotisms. Kings had their social responsibilities, which verged on religious duties, and they showed an active interest in the teachings of moral philosophers. And if kings had responsibilities, subjects had rights and liberties. The guilds in which working people, even down to labourers, were organized had definite privileges, could frame their own internal laws, and had their representatives in the court of the king. As the stories of the Buddha's wanderings show, it was possible to move freely from kingdom to kingdom, and the highways were well used, particularly by men who had abandoned their occupations to become ascetic mendicants, moving around constantly except during the rainy season, when they gathered in city or forest retreats, and formulating as they went the ideas that made this such a time of philosophic ferment. That they were free to think and speak as they wished seems evident from the Jain and Buddhist reports of debates not only between opposing ascetic philosophers but also between ascetics and Brahmins. India never developed an orthodoxy of the kind that emerged in western religions; Hinduism established its sway over the subcontinent by being tolerant and absorptive, and in the sixth century — a transitional period between the old Vedic religion and the Hinduism of the Christian era — the situation was even more fluid than it later became, for the caste barriers had not yet solidified; there seem as yet to have been no rules of untouchability, and, as A. L. Basham remarks in *The Wonder that was India*, "It is by no means certain that temple worship and iconolatry had developed in India in the sixth century BC.'' Though I use the word "heretic" to define those thinkers whose beliefs broke most sharply with devotional Vedism or Hinduism, the religion of the priests, it must be emphasized that heresy in India was never so damnable and disruptive a phenomenon as it was among Christians. The main difference between Brahmins and non-Brahmin teachers was not in beliefs, which often overlapped, but in privileges and religious duties. The Brahmins alone had the right to perform sacrifices and so to mediate between man and the gods; if, like so many of the heretic thinkers, one was either agnostic or atheist, sacrifice was unimportant, if not repulsive.

The sacrificial privilege lay at the heart of Brahmin pretensions to power, and in these pretensions they were largely successful, for with the formation of the large kingdoms a shift in the relative importance of the two higher castes took place. Brahmins began to replace Kshatriyas as the leading court officials, not entirely because of priestly intrigues. As the king ceased to be *primus inter pares* in the traditional Indo-European warrior community and became instead an absolute ruler, he dared not encourage the presence of powerful rivals of his own class or caste in court, and so he would pick in preference Brahmin officials.

Historians have tended to see in the proliferation of heretical philosophy at this period a manifestation of political as well as doctrinal revolt against the growing power of the Brahmin hierarchy, pointing out that the leaders of the new sects belonged largely to the Kshatriya caste that was being displaced from its ascendant position in the rising monarchies. And certainly there seems no doubt that, when he began his preaching about 525 BC, the Buddha looked back nostalgically to the more secure little world of warrior republics and tried to reproduce that security by giving a republican and egalitarian structure to the *sangha*.

The Buddha's most important contemporary and rival among the new teachers of the time was also a Kshatriya. Like Gotama, Mahavira came from a small knightly republic in a state of transition, somewhere in the lee of the Himalayas.

His real name was Vardhamana. His title of Mahavira, meaning "great hero," was given him by the adherents of the Jain religion, to which, if he did not actually found it, he gave an established doctrine. The transfer of the concept of heroism from the physical to the spiritual battlefield suggests how far these teachers and their followers saw the movements they created as part of a struggle which sought to liberate Indian religion from the domination of the priests, to detach it from the growing multitude of gods in the Brahmin pantheon and from the evil of caste, and to give it a rational, moral and humanistic tone.

In these endeavours the Buddha and Mahavira were not alone. The sixth century in India was a time of daring philosophical proposals, usually advanced by non-Brahminical leaders with ascetic followings. Among the multitude of rivals with whom they debated, the Buddha and Mahavira are perhaps distinguished mostly by the fact that they developed philosophic approaches which were modified by their followers until they became religious systems owing their survival as much to accumulated superstitions as to their original cores of rational thought. Other teachers of the period rivalled them in originality of thought. Many extended the Buddha's agnosticism into materialist atheism. Others, in their attempt to explain the universe rationally, laid the foundations of a scientific approach on which later generations in India failed to build. Certainly such philosophers rank beside their Greek contemporaries, the early natural philosophers of Ionia, and seem to have been inspired by the same desire to observe phenomena in the light of reason rather than of myth.

But it is possible to exaggerate the extent to which, in the Indian context, this constituted or even implied rebellion. The obvious direction for a militant Kshatriya discontent to take would have been armed revolt, but there is no evidence of any uprising. Indian kings tended to be killed by their heirs, not by their generals. Wars were dynastic and territorial in nature, and while the warrior republics defended themselves as best they could against the encroachments of the expanding kingdoms, there is no sign of warrior resentment within the kingdoms themselves acute enough to precipitate revolt. The kings seem to have found nothing unacceptably seditious in the teachings of the Buddha and the other non-Brahminical teachers. Both King Bimbisara of Magadha and his parricide son Ajatasatru appear as patrons in the Buddhist traditions, fully aware of the popular credit to be gained from supporting these teachers, who had gained a considerable following, by their spectacular asceticism as much as by their teachings, among the ordinary people, particularly those of the lower castes.

It is even debatable how much hostility, outside the formal antagonisms of debate, the Brahmins actually showed to the ascetic teachers, whose doctrines in the sixth century represented new philosophical directions rather than new religions. Religious intolerance entered India with the Moslems just as it entered the ancient Americas with the Christians, and it is doubtful if there was any serious religious persecution among the Hindus before that time.

By the sixth century, the original Vedic religion, a cult of herdsmen and warriors propitiating the frightening powers of nature, had already undergone considerable transformations as it became the religion of settled agrarian societies centred on the growing cities, a religion catholic in its breadth and complex in its layers of interpretation.

The Vedas, which the Brahmins transmitted orally, remained the central core of their mythology, but their absorption of the beliefs of earlier peoples, Dravidians or aboriginal tribespeople, increased their pantheon and modified their doctrines, so that orthodoxy, in so far as it existed in Hinduism, did not mean a static complex of beliefs. Numerous gods, with their many manifestations, allowed for multitudinous devotional and ceremonial variations; there could never be an established liturgy like that of the Church of England, or an established body of holy texts sanctioned by revelation like the Christian and Jewish Bibles.

There was not even an institutional hierarchy. Each temple was an autonomous community centred around its deity, and while some of the priests seem to have had wider prestige than others, this was more because of the repute of their shrines than because they had any authority outside them. Even the two great moieties into which the Hindu faith is divided, the Vaishnavites (devotees of Vishnu) and the Saivites (devotees of Siva), have no institution or existence apart from the temples where the two gods are worshipped in their various manifestations.

What has united Hinduism is the caste of the Brahmins, a corporation of priests by right of inheritance. But there has never been a time in Indian history when holy men were all Brahmins. As far back as we can trace, it was customary for men of all castes, often in late middle age, to abandon their worldly concerns and, free of possessions or ties, to seek *moksha* or liberation from the travails of existence. Thus, beside the regular priests with their birthright vocations, there existed a naked or ochre-clad free corps of *sannyasins* or holy men undefined by caste and chosen not by descent but by personal dedication and individual illumination. The unorthodox teachings, called *sramanas* as distinct from the *brahmanas*, emerged from this group, so that the Greek pattern, in which philosophers were also active participants in the worldly life of their time, hardly existed in ancient India. The priests celebrating in their shrines, the hermits meditating in their forests, the wandering beggar preachers with their personal teachings — they have always been present in Hinduism, and in the sixth century the new philosophic and religious concepts that characterized the period, there as in Greece, emerged from the dynamic relationship between these groups. It is a relationship that has continued through the centuries, for Hinduism itself has expanded largely by absorbing the doctrines of its more irregular teachers, from the Buddha and Mahavira down to Gandhi and Vivekananda; the fact that the Buddha was eventually accepted by the followers of Vishnu as one of the avatars of their own great god is a manifestation of this process at work. At the same time, the Buddha, Mahavira and their rivals did to an extent develop trends of thought that had emerged among the more speculative thinkers within the Brahmin community.

This Brahminical speculative trend was represented most

notably by the Upanishads, a series of great religious poems
of which the earliest may have been written towards the end
of the eighth century, but the last of which was certainly composed no earlier than the sixth. Among other things, the
Upanishads drew attention away from the many gods of the
Hindu pantheon and created a substratum of monotheism
below the overt polytheism. Increasingly at this period the gods
were being seen as beings more durable and powerful than
men, but neither universal nor omnipotent. They could be
propitiated and persuaded to favour men, by means of
sacrifice; it was also increasingly believed that they could even
be controlled by occult powers acquired through ascetic disciplines. The Upanishads sought to transcend these ambivalent links between human beings and the traditional deities
by considering the nature of man's relationship with the
universe in general, and, by implication, the nature of his
spiritual destiny.

The thinking of the authors of the Upanishads is essentially
speculative rather than empirical like that of the Milesian
thinkers; Aristotle would probably have classed them among
the *theologi* rather than the *physiologi*, yet their attitude is
not truly theistic. These essentially pantheist texts show little
concern for the operations of the phenomenal world, yet, like
much Indian religious literature, they are pragmatic in the
sense that they are not concerned with acquiring knowledge
about existence so much as with leading the soul toward salvation through realization: everything is relative to that quest.
They proceed by their own special dialectic, reasoning closely
from mystical insights.

Central to the speculations of the Upanishads is the relationship between Brahman and Atman. Brahman can be variously interpreted as the impersonal spirit of the cosmos, of
the All, or, as one writer has described it, as "the ground below
all forms and phenomena" from which the universe, including the gods, emerged. The emergent universe is not separate
from Brahman; it is impregnated with it. And here lies the
secret to the relationship between Atman, the human soul or
self (whose existence the writers of the Upanishads, unlike the
Buddha, never doubted) and Brahman. Brahman in fact

inhabits the human soul, and *is* the individual soul as well as the eternal and infinite All-soul. *Tat tvam asis*, meaning literally "you are that" but by implication that Atman is Brahman, is one of the key phrases of the Upanishadic philosophy. When a human being realizes this truth he is free from the dread wheel of life and death.

The Upanishads contained one of the most remarkable expositions of the mystical quest. The quest represents a different kind of advance from mythology to that of the Ionian philosophers, yet at the same time it shows Indians like Greeks recognizing the tales of the gods and even the gods themselves as of minor importance in comparison with man's direct apprehension of the nature of the universe. Proceeding from premises entirely different from those of the Greeks, the priestly mystics who wrote these great religious poems sought to offer an explanation of the human condition and of man's relationship to the creative forces of the universe on which reason could build. And reason did build upon that explanation, even if often it finally rejected it.

For one cannot generalize about the Indian thinkers of this period any more than one can about their Greek or Chinese contemporaries; they represented an astonishing variety of approaches. Some, particularly the Jains and the Ajivikas, were greatly concerned about the material nature of the universe, whereas the Buddha regarded this as a fruitless route of speculation, since the All was ultimately unknowable to man. In the case of the Jains, their close interest in the phenomenal world was due to their view of karma which, like the Buddhists but in a different way, they accepted as the fatal mechanism that held man on the wheel of repeated existence.

The idea of karma — the law by which in life after life we reap the rewards of our actions and according to which a kind of retributive justice is therefore established — is of course much older than either Buddhism or Jainism, older even than the Upanishads in which the doctrine was first clearly elaborated; it may even derive from the beliefs of the early Dravidians who created the Indus civilization rather than from the less sophisticated cults of the Aryan invaders, for there are no signs of it in the Rig Veda. While teaching that a being will be reborn into the world of suffering again and again until he has acquired the wisdom that will enable him to shed his burden of flaws and slide into the peace of Nirvana, the doctrines of karma preached in the sixth century did not in all cases present the prospect of a closed fate.

Buddhism, for example, introduced the elements of volition and rationality by allowing that a man could change his destiny by recognizing the likely consequences of his acts. Buddhism also differed from the Upanishadic and Jain traditions by rejecting the soul or the self in favour of a view of personality as consisting of a series of mental and physical states with no permanence, so that what passes through karma is not an eternal self seeking release from physical life but a succession of imperfect individualities that lapses when Nirvana is attained.

Because it is indispensable to the search for release from suffering, awareness — an ability to look objectively at one's self and one's world — was for the Buddha and his followers the greatest of virtues. Conversely, in a system of beliefs lacking a concept of sin, ignorance or stupidity became a cardinal fault because it clouded a man's perceptions of the likely consequences of his actions and so kept him on the cycle of rebirths from which enlightenment was the point of liberation. Thus, in a different way, an Indian sixth-century thinker like the Buddha moved towards the same objective as his Ionian contemporaries, to live always in the clear light of reason.

Like the great Chinese teachers who were his contemporaries, the Buddha talked of a Way or a Path, but his was neither the Confucian way of impeccable conduct nor the Taoist way of obedience to the natural powers. It was the way of renunciation, with release from life and sorrow as its end, the way of release into the void called Nirvana. The Buddha called it the Middle Way, and it contained echoes of the moderation stressed by the Greek followers of Apollo. The Buddha

preached it as the Eightfold Path in his famous sermon in the
Deer Park near Benares when he started out to spread his message among the people:

> The monk who takes up the wandering life must avoid
> two extremes. He must refuse the pleasures of the senses,
> which represent the worldly way, but he must also beware
> of the contrary devotion to self-mortification, which is
> both painful and fruitless. Avoiding these two extremes
> he can proceed on the middle way which gives vision and
> knowledge, offers calm and enlightenment, and leads to
> Nirvana.

Attachment leads to desire, and desire to suffering, and so
the goal of the Buddhist is the end of attachment. Not that
Buddhism teaches a dreary doctrine of rejecting joy in life.
Once one has ceased to desire the good things of life, once
one is no longer attached to them and sees them for the illusions they are, then one can enjoy them in all innocence. It
is, ultimately, the degree of attachment that determines the
degree of sorrow. Once the Buddha preached another great
sermon in which he called on his followers to renounce even
family love, even friendship itself, and walk alone like the
rhinoceros.

And, indeed, essential to the pristine doctrine of Buddhism
as developed by the original teacher in the sixth century was
the paradox of its individualism, its teaching of self-sufficiency
even when it urged men to abandon the consciousness of being
inalienable selves. Unlike many later Buddhists who stress the
need for a guru to help one on the road to enlightenment, the
Buddha himself spoke with stark clarity about the personal
search; he emphasized its loneliness as he lay dying, when his
disciple Ananda asked him what instruction he was leaving
for his disciples:

> Why should I leave instructions, Ananda? You must be
> your own light in the darkness. You must be your own
> refuge. Rely on nothing outside yourself. Hold to the
> truth and it will be your light and your refuge. And look
> to nothing and nobody but your own self.

The final paradox of early Buddhism was that the individual
found his way towards enlightenment and salvation through

the community. The search may be personal, but it is still the search for liberation from the demands of the individual considered as the self and is therefore by definition selfless. As Trevor Ling has rightly pointed out in his excellent study *The Buddha*, we mistake the entire nature of true Buddhism when we imagine it, as many westerners do, as "a private cult of escape from the real world": "The teaching of the Buddha was not concerned with the private destiny of the individual, but with something much wider, the whole realm of sentient being, the whole of consciousness."

The Buddha's involvement in the social and political world of his time was constant. He knew the rulers of the great kingdoms personally and advised them, but he also knew the citizens of the warrior republics, and, we have seen, he modelled the structure of the *sangha* on these small states. Always he stressed, among the duties of a Buddhist and especially of a Buddhist ruler, the alleviation of distress among the people, the encouragement of peaceful relations between men, the cultivation of compassion for all living beings and of respect for the world of nature; all of them were conducive to the moral life that led to enlightenment. This social direction achieved its most notable expression in the attempt of Ashoka, more than two hundred years after the Buddha's death, to establish a Buddhist kingdom.

It is true that Buddhism eventually turned into a religion rather than the moral and social philosophy it had originally been, and that then the perspective of the Buddhist did tend to narrow to a search for individual salvation. But that came about only after the pristine doctrine had been notably corrupted. If there was anything that clearly distinguished the teaching of the Buddha from that of his contemporaries, it was less its rejection of the individual soul, which other teachers of the time shared in their own ways, than the essentially social direction of its philosophy, its relating of personal enlightenment to changes within the community — an attitude unique in the India of the Buddha's time, though it had counterparts in both China and Greece, in the ideas and efforts of Confucius and of Solon and his fellow lawgivers of the archaic age to establish just societies. Indeed, the Greek *polis* as a deliberate construct was perhaps the nearest political institution to the Buddhist *sangha*, itself a model for the Ashokan kingdom.

Mahavira and his followers, who called themselves Jains, also taught in the sixth century a doctrine based on gaining release from karma and the cycle of rebirth through the practice of virtue, and particularly through *ahimsa*, the non-harming of other beings, a concept that millenia later provided the foundations for Gandhi's teaching of non-violent civil disobedience. The Jains have always claimed that their tradition is ancient, and Mahavira himself, in the legendary history they developed, counted as the twenty-fourth and last in the present era of the Tirthankaras or Ford-makers, the great teachers who appeared during each cycle of universal history. Mahavira seems originally to have belonged to a sect called the Nirgranthas ("those free from bonds") founded in the eighth century BC by Parsva, who eventually counted as the twenty-third of the Tirthankaras and may well have been an actual historical figure. Certainly Jainism does not have the new-made appearance of Buddhist philosophy, and, while its rationalization by Mahavira took place in the sixth century, there is an overlay of myth which does not seem entirely the accretion of later generations, and also a feeling of special relationship with the animate world — which for Jains included not only animals and plants but also the four elements themselves — that appears to have stemmed from pre-Aryan cults of earth-spirits and genii. In archaic, as in twentieth-century, India, shrines were maintained to these spirits by the rural people, and around them the early Jain teachers and other holy men established themselves to find a ready source of alms and an audience for their teachings.

These teachings, as Mahavira developed them, were anti-theist rather than atheist; they did not deny the existence of gods, but regarded them as beings like any other who had a limited role in the natural order. The gods had no hand in the creation of the world, nor could they destroy it; it functioned according to a universal system which regulated the elaborate processes of its cycles and also the fates of individual souls. In souls, or *jivas*, the Jains, unlike the Buddhists, firmly believed. The universe contained an infinite number of souls, which inhabited not only human beings and animals and trees but also rocks and running waters, extending into the microscopic realms, for, by reasoning alone, the Jains came to the correct conclusion that if there were forms of life so small as to be barely visible, there must be others that were invisible. Water and air, they believed, were inhabited by such animalculae, and so to this day Jain monks will strain their drinking water and wear gauze veils over their mouths and nostrils to prevent such creatures being ingested and killed. In this way, without instruments, they anticipated the microbiologists of later centuries.

The Jains taught a quasi-materialist doctrine which held that the pristine brightness of the soul was marred by accretions of matter in the form of invisible dust, and that this material impediment was karma, which other systems like the Buddhist interpreted immaterially and psychologically. The deposit of dust varied from soul to soul, so that some were more dimmed than others. It resulted from activity; the more harmful the activity, the heavier the deposit. This dust clogging the soul could be removed only by refraining from harmful acts — hence the emphasis on *ahimsa* — and by performing rigid penances, so that, unlike the Buddha, who had condemned extreme asceticism as the mirror image of extreme sensual indulgence, the Jains laid great stress on austerities. The true saint destined for liberation was the holy man who starved to death, as Mahavira is said to have done, or otherwise immolated himself. Liberation for the Jain consisted in the final clarification of the soul, at which point it would rise above the highest heavens and remain, inactive and all-knowing, in perpetual bliss through all eternity. Those who did not achieve that bliss were condemned for endless eons to the transmigratory process. Thus the Jain soul, indestructible despite its bondage, stands complete, in contradiction to the loose and impermanent bundle of impulses and characteristics which is the Buddhist non-soul.

The Jain teachings, far more closely concerned with

individual salvation than early Buddhist doctrines, had no specific social content, but the doctrine of *ahimsa*, the refusal to harm others, resulted in Jain laymen playing a positive role in Indian society; they were enjoined to be honest in business dealings and frugal in their living, using their surplus to sustain their holy men and their temples, but also to help unfortunate beings, human and animal alike.

Like Buddhism, Jainism was eventually corrupted by theism, and Mahavira and the earlier, legendary Tirthankaras came to be worshipped as if they were gods. But the model of the virtuous Jain life persisted, and so did the austere intensities of the religious life among the monks, who were traditionally divided between the Svetambaras, or White-Clad, who wore simple and spotless robes to proclaim their dedication to purity, and the Digambaras, or Sky-Clad, who went naked because, like Mahavira himself according to the legends, they held nudity to be a symbolically necessary declaration of their independence of earthly ties.

Just as the resemblances between early Buddhist attitudes and contemporary Delphic exhortations to moderation and self-knowledge are evident, so are those between the austerities and simplicities of living practised by the Jains and those which Pythagoras enjoined on his followers at roughly the same time. As the generations went by, other groups of Greek philosophers like the Stoics followed analogous paths.

None of the other ascetic schools that were in the process of formation at the same time as Jainism and Buddhism had the same staying power, and none of them developed into a religion that existed separately from Hinduism. But at least two of these traditions — those of the Ajivikas and the Carvakas — persisted well into the Christian era and made their contribution to the syncretic and absorptive religion that Hinduism eventually became.

The teachers who led these movements stood up as rivals to the Buddha and Mahavira and contributed to the discussions that took place during the period. As personalities they are ill-defined, but their ideas retain a certain solidity even in the accounts of obviously unsympathetic Buddhist chroniclers.

Some of their ideas appear also in the Jain scriptures, notably those of Makkhali Gosala, who was apparently Mahavira's travelling companion for about five years, until they disagreed fundamentally. And indeed it is hard to imagine a doctrine more remote from Jain and Buddhist ideas regarding the freedom with which the individual can change his karma by a combination of will and action (or inaction in the case of the Jains) than the strict determinism to which Gosala and his Ajivika followers eventually came.

Like most Indian teachers of the sixth century, Gosala and his associates, Purana Kassapa and Pakudha Macayana, believed in transmigration and eventual enlightenment and liberation. But they rejected the idea that man had any freedom to influence his destiny. Anticipating nineteenth-century scientific determinists, they believed that the whole universe in all its elaborate details was ruled by an impersonal cosmic principle, which they called *niyati* or destiny. Though Gosala enjoined on his followers an extreme asceticism, he stressed that they were ascetics only because fate had made them so, and that each man would achieve liberation not through effort but because of the eventual automatic working of fate. It was not a teaching without hope, but one had to wait for the hope to materialize in its own good time.

Since the Ajivikas held that "human effort is ineffectual," their ethics were necessarily antinomian. Since whatever we do will not change the course of destiny, the notions of compassion and good living so prominent in Buddhism and Jainism were really irrelevant to the Ajivikas. Gosala was notorious for the scorn with which he regarded other men's religious activities, and he is said to have endured beatings from angry crowds for mocking openly at bridal processions and other popular ceremonial acts. Because of their theoretical amoralism, the Ajivikas were often accused by their opponents of licentious behaviour, but they seem to have been too convinced of their fate of ascetic living to lapse often into sin.

Some at least of the Ajivikas went beyond the Buddha's agnosticism regarding the nature of the world and, like the Milesian physiologues, sought explanations of the functioning and substance of the universe. Pakudha Macayana believed in seven elements, which he described as earth, air, fire, water, joy, sorrow and life. These elements were indestructible; like some of the Ionians, Pakudha believed that the actual substance of the universe remained always the same, neither increasing nor decreasing. "What *is*," he argued, "cannot be destroyed; out of nothing comes nothing." This, of course, strikingly anticipates the dictum of the Greek philosopher Democritus in the next century, "Out of nothing arises nothing; nothing that is can be destroyed." And Pakudha, in further anticipation of Democritus and his teacher Leucippus, was also an atomist, certainly one of the first, though atomic theories were fairly widespread in India at this time, having been developed by some of the Brahmin thinkers as well as the ascetic philosophers.

These ideas were derived not from observation and experiment but from logical reasoning. It was observed that material entities occurred in diminishing proportions to the verge of invisibility, and presumably there must be other smaller entities invisible to the naked eye, which was all the Indians of this period had as an instrument of observation. But for matter to exist at all, it was reasoned, there must be a primal grain or substance of which everything according to its nature was constituted. This was the atom, differing in characteristics according to the various elements. Atoms could only be seen when they formed aggregates, similar to molecules, called *bhutas*; the density with which the atoms came together determined the physical character of an object, and the diamond had a high density while the bamboo stem had a loose one.

Among the other teachers who were Buddha's contemporaries the most interesting seems to have been Ajita Kesakambalin, or Ajita of the Hair Blanket. Ajita, the forerunner of the Carvakas of later centuries, differed strikingly from the writers of the Upanishads and from teachers like Mahavira, the Buddha and even the Ajivikas, not only by

denying the gods rather than ignoring them, but also by rejecting the belief in transmigration which the other teachers, all
in their various ways, sustained. He taught that there was no
karma because there was no survival after death. An atomist
like Pakudha, he went beyond him in declaring that matter
is all that exists. Man, like everything else, is a transient
aggregate of all the four elements, earth, air, fire and water.
When he dies these elements are released and the consciousness vanishes. Ajita was even more extreme in his denial of
an eternal soul than the Buddha, for he believed that nothing
survives bodily death. Everything happens according to the
working out of material processes, and since there is no survival, there cannot be any karmic reward for virtuous acts,
which thus become pointless, as vicious acts also do. Despite
such negative views, Ajita gathered around him a group of
disciples, who draped themselves in goat's hair robes to distinguish them from their naked Ajivika and Jain rivals, and
from the Buddhist monks, who wore orange robes or even,
in those early days, garments patched together from the discarded clothes of laymen. What the disciples of Ajita did we
are not told, but A. L. Basham was probably correct in his
assumption that, like the Epicureans, they chose to avoid
unhappiness by living a peaceful and simple life together.

It is certainly the Ajivikas and men like Ajita of the Hair
Blanket who seem to have the closest affinities with the Greek
physiologues, for they like the Ionians were concerned with
discovering and describing how the universe was constituted
and how it operated. In the case of Democritus in the fifth
century one seems to be moving towards something more than
affinity, for his views are uncannily close to those of the Indian
atomists. Perhaps we should not reject as forthrightly as most
scholars have done the ancient assertions that Democritus, who
was certainly a great traveller, got beyond Persia into India.
In his day India was under Persian rule, and a resolute traveller
could have got to Taxila even if he had taken a long time to
do so. Certainly from this time the links between Greece and
India become more feasible than they would have been in the
earlier part of the sixth century, before Darius moved his

armies over the Hindu Kush into Gandhara. But the parallel
urges in sixth-century Greece and India to escape the domination of myth and confront the universe with the eyes of
human reason seem even more striking if we assume there was
no connection.

Chapter 13

The Ways of Men and Nature: The Chinese Sages

In Chinese history the sixth century was an era as politically turbulent as the same period in the Mediterranean world, the Middle East or the Ganges valley. Social patterns were changing; structures of power were shifting. But where in India the cause of turbulence lay in the fact that new kingdoms were establishing themselves and increasing at the expense of the older warrior republics, and monarchy was replacing tribalism by an authoritarian society largely oriented towards urban living, in China it was a long-established and once powerful empire that was disintegrating. The great kingdom of Chou had replaced the more primitive Shang empire at the end of the twelfth century; the shift of power had been part of a vast social transition from a tribal to a feudal order, accompanied by a technological transition from a Bronze to an Iron Age — transitions similar to those that took place a little later in India and the Hellenic world.

The Shang view of the universe was largely dominated by animist attitudes, which have never entirely disappeared in China. Spirits were feared and placated, and the ancestors, whose worship had already begun, tended to be distrusted at the same time as they were honoured, since they too belonged to that mysterious world, beyond human ken, which was ruled by Ti, the tribal god of the Shang, who as the lord of hosts, the arbitrary giver of rewards and punishments, at times seems remarkably like the Yahweh of the early Jews. In Chou society there was a gradual but important shift in attitudes, an evolution rather than a revolution. The ancestors continued to be honoured, because the joint family structure was a part of the feudal social fabric, but they were no longer feared or regarded as having power to solve the problems of the living. The rule of the whimsical tribal deity Ti was replaced by the Mandate of Heaven (Ti'en), which was essentially an impersonal universal law beyond man's control by supplication or magic. Nevertheless, an understanding of the Mandate of Heaven, manifested by virtuous deeds, made it possible for man to control his destiny to a great extent by intelligent choices, particularly as technological changes, such as the growing use of iron and the development of irrigation and drainage, gave humanity a greater power over its physical circumstances; the Chinese were one of the first peoples to attempt the extensive shaping of their environment. Out of these trends, towards the rejection of an anthropomorphic concept of deity in favour of an impersonal one, and towards a confidence in man's capabilities in dealing with the natural world, there arose a humanist attitude that tended to shape Chinese philosophy, dominate Chinese art, and largely replace theistic and devotional kinds of religion by a peculiarly Chinese combination of pantheism and pragmatism whose extremes came eventually to be represented by Taoism and Confucianism.

By the sixth century, during the period known as the epoch of Spring and Autumn, the fabric of the Chou kingdom had begun to break apart as the feudal family structure showed signs of disintegration and the realm itself became dominated by rival principalities whose rulers defied the authority of the emperor and fought each other continuously like the war lords of early twentieth-century China. Matters were to become even worse in the fifth century, the epoch of the Warring States, but even in the sixth century the people suffered from tyranny and want as result of these perpetual conflicts. In *The Book of Odes*, the anonymous anthology that is the first known work of Chinese literature, dating from the epoch of Spring

and Autumn and dubiously attributed to Confucius, the
suffering of the people is the subject of some of the darker
poems:

The people are mown down with misfortune.
They need peace and heaven only sends
Famine and plagues, and everywhere
There is death and disorder.
The voice of the people is dark,
And their grief is uncomforted.
The heavens are pitiless!
The strife is unceasing.
Everywhere it grows
And the people beg for peace.

In such turbulent times, when society is seeking new bear-
ings, important cultural developments often begin, and in
China at this period the first stirrings of philosophy emerged
in the movement, lasting from the sixth to the third centuries, that is traditionally called, with the Chinese passion for
even numbers, the Hundred Schools. The two most important of these schools emerged in the sixth century; they were
those associated with two great teacher figures, K'ung Ch'iu,
known to westerners as Confucius, and Lao-tzu, whose name
means the Old One or the Old Teacher. Confucius was
definitely a historical personage, born about the middle of the
sixth century, a few years after the Buddha, and also dying
a few years after him. Like Thales, Pythagoras and the
Buddha, Confucius was an oral teacher, and his doctrines,
as we know them, seem to have been transmitted mouth to
ear by his disciples for several generations after his death.

Lao-tzu is a much more shadowy figure. Some scholars have
argued that he did not exist at all, that his name was a pseu-
donym used by a group of later Taoists who compiled the *Tao-
te Ching*, or Book of the Way and its Power, which is
attributed to him. But the traditions pointing to his existence
are strong. They tell us that his real name was Li Tan and
that he was an archivist in the kingdom of Chou — the Chinese
were conscious of the importance of keeping records long
before the Greeks. Moreover, the traditions of Lao-tzu are

interwoven with those of Confucius, with whom he is said to have discoursed, reproaching him for his reliance on government. Since Confucius undoubtedly did exist, this strengthens the tradition of Lao-tzu, just as the traditions of the Buddha and Mahavira strengthen each other.

Equally important is the internal evidence of the *Tao-te Ching*. There is a consistency of voice and outlook to this book which suggests that it was produced by a single intelligence and not by a committee, and a simplicity to its expression of Taoist ideas, as compared with the later writings attributed to Chuang-tzu in the fourth century, which suggests that the book was in fact written about the time traditionally allocated to it, the sixth century BC. So we can assume there was a teacher at this time who has since become known as Lao-tzu — the Old One — and we can accept this as a convenient name for an elusive personality. Who exactly he may have been is doubtless as unprofitable a subject of debate as the real identity of the poet Homer. The traditions which tell us that such men existed are reasonable enough to be respected as in a general way true. The identification of Lao-tzu with Li Tan seems plausible, since an archivist would have been inclined to write his thoughts down in a book, while a professional tutor like Confucius would be more likely to rely on the effect his spoken words had on his followers.

In no strict sense was either Confucius or Lao-tzu a religious leader; they were moral philosophers as the Buddha and Mahavira were in their lifetimes, though in the pragmatic Chinese way their cults did become quasi-religions and so allowed for the retention of ancient animistic and ancestral cults. Both teachers evaded metaphysical speculation, taking the gods for granted as representing the inexplicable aspects of the universe, but not attempting to define them any more explicitly than the Buddha did. Myths, as such, did not interest them, though they recognized their metaphorical uses. Both were concerned with teaching a *tao* or Way, by which was meant a pattern of true living, just as the Buddha taught his Eightfold Path. But there was a great deal of difference between what Confucius meant by a way and what Lao-tzu did, and that difference reflects the variegation of thought which characterized the awakening of the age of reason in ancient Chinese civilization.

For Confucius it was the moral Way, the Way of virtue and integrity, to be followed by individuals and communities if society were to become peaceful and healthy; a way not very different from that of Solon or the Buddha in its social aspects. For Lao-tzu the Way was something far less social and tangible. It was really the Ground of the universe, the unnameable and indescribable Non-Being from which Being constantly emerges. It is not far from the Brahman of the Upanishads or, for that matter, from the impersonal all-moving God of Xenophanes. A Chinese friend, an artist closely attuned to the non-human animistic world, described it to me simply as "the Nature." Each living creature and each thing, even if apparently inanimate, derives its own power of specificity from the *tao*, and so the good life is the life that is lived according to one's true nature. Nothing could be further removed from the Jain view of the struggle that each soul must wage to cleanse itself of the natural world, though on another level, in giving souls to all animate and inanimate things, the Jains resembled the Taoists.

In broader terms there are haunting resonances between the teachings of these old Chinese philosophers and the ideas of the Greek sages in the sixth century. What Confucius repeatedly taught about the balanced life could easily be interpreted as an elaboration of the first of the two famous maxims carved in the temple of Apollo at Delphi, "Nothing to excess." Like the archaic Greeks, like the Buddha, he held to the Middle Way. The second great Delphic maxim, "Know yourself," the more ultimately subversive of the two, can be seen as a parallel to the Taoist teaching that a man need only find and follow his own nature to live the good life.

In later centuries Confucianism and Taoism became influential philosophies with some of the power if not the institutional structure of churches — Confucianism as the basic system of Chinese political ethics, and Taoism as a pragmatic, popular system of belief that incorporated into its essential pantheism the animistic and ancestral cults and even the magical practices that had survived from earlier eras. This development was not accidental; in many ways, the teachings of Lao-tzu and his successors, notably Chuang-tzu, refined and rationalized the essence of ancient nature worship.

To judge Confucius as a historical figure, we have to see him apart from his admirers and his critics, for the official Confucianism of later centuries was clearly in many ways a distortion of what he actually taught. His Taoist rivals, representing the only other teacher of the Hundred Schools whose doctrines continued to be influential, always presented him in ways that favoured their own founder, so that Lao-tzu is shown beating Confucius in all arguments until the latter bows down before the Old One and compares him to a dragon riding high in the winds and cloud. That Confucius, whose philosophy led him to respect age and wisdom, appeared deferential to the older man is likely, but that he felt diminished by this, or that his followers thought him so, is unlikely.

When we observe Confucius apart from the flattering and the deprecatory traditions, we see a man who made no claims to high ancestry, to holiness, or to any other privileged distinction. Living in a feudal world, he seemed to stand apart as the forerunner of a more open society where men would be judged by their personal qualities and individual accomplishments.

He may have come from the minor gentry, but he was orphaned in boyhood and grew up poor; at first he had to be content with menial employments like supervising the state granaries. He may have educated himself, for there is no tradition of his having studied under any master, but by diligent application he eventually gained the repute of being the most learned man of his time. This did not help him greatly in gaining the kind of employment that would enable him to put into action the idea of a just and humane society he was developing in his young manhood, between 530 and 520 BC. He offered gratuitous advice to the princes of Lu, his native state, but they were not interested in teachings critical of their feudal system and its economic consequences, and he never gained the high administrative post that might enable him to put into practice his teachings about the ideal way of government and the ideal relationship between rulers and their peoples.

While he wandered over China waiting for the opportunities that never came, Confucius established a role for himself as perhaps the first private teacher of morals and political skills in Chinese history; he accepted students of all classes, and, in easy, seminar-like gatherings, sought to broaden their knowledge of history, literature and socially beneficial rites, and also to teach them how to behave in a variety of human relationships and problematical situations.

Confucius began from the simple premises, "Virtue is to love men. And wisdom is to understand them." In its humanism and in the pragmatic agnosticism that made Confucius avoid all attempt to explain or indeed to speculate on the supernatural (while stating that the virtuous man must stand in awe of the incomprehensible will of Heaven), his general viewpoint so anticipated that of the European Enlightenment more than two millenia later that it might have found a reasonable summation in Pope's couplet:

Know then thyself, presume not God to scan;
The proper study of mankind is man.

The study of man, for Confucius, was inseparable from the study of society, and individual virtue was inseparable from social virtue:

The truly virtuous man, desiring to establish himself, seeks to establish others; desiring success for himself, he seeks to help others succeed. To find in the wishes of one's heart the principle of one's conduct towards others is the method of true virtue.

That is not far from the ancient Jewish injunction of *Leviticus*, "Thou shalt love thy neighbour as thyself," which may well have attained its present form at the hand of some rabbi in Babylon about the time Confucius was teaching.

But the man who would practise these social virtues must himself be transformed into a moral being, and this realization led Confucius to aim at developing the being he called "the superior man": "Of three things the superior man stands in awe. He stands in awe of the commands of Heaven. He stand in awe of great men. He stands in awe of the words of wise men."

For Confucius the moral life must find expression in meticulously correct behaviour, based on the proper relationships between ruler and ruled, between parents and children, between husbands and wives. If the right rules were established and inculcated, men would eventually live morally without thinking about it, as Confucious claimed had happened to him:

At the age of fifteen I made up my mind to learn. By thirty my ideas were established. By forty I had shed all my doubts. By fifty I knew the will of heaven, and by sixty I was prepared to accept it, so that now I am seventy I can do what I wish without offending righteousness.

This kind of moral existence, in the individual and in society, would be achieved only by the development of a high degree of awareness, resembling the mindfulness enjoined by the Buddha, that would result in a rational and critical view of existence: "To hear much, select what is good and follow it; to see much and take careful note of it; these are the steps by which one ascends to understanding."

Good government, essentially, was the application on a broader scale of the same ethics as men must observe in daily intercourse. Confucius was appalled by the misrule he saw around him in those turbulent days as the Chou empire tottered towards collapse. The wars seemed endless, while the rulers taxed the people without mercy and conscripted them constantly for forced labour. In the world Confucius saw around him, the sole aim of government seemed to be that of giving pleasure and power to the ruler. For him the only true end of government was the happiness of the ruled.

Confucius conceived a state in which all classes would co-operate. He never went so far as to suggest the abolition of aristocratic rule, or to propose any form of democracy like that which the Buddha adumbrated in the *sangha* or which Solon and Cleisthenes developed in the Athenian constitution, but he believed a hereditary ruler should become what we now think of as a limited and constitutional monarch, confiding administrative responsibility to ministers chosen not for their class but for their ability and virtue. He seems to have envisaged replacing the absolute rule of a single king or emperor with a kind of Platonic bureaucracy dependent for its success on the goodness of its members. As immediate measures to start the process of fostering the happiness of the people, he called for the reduction of taxes, the abandonment of cruel punishments, and the search for peace rather than the pursuit of unnecessary wars. These must have seemed radical, even subversive, proposals at a time when the right of the feudal lord to rule as he wished was regarded as inviolate, and it is hardly surprising that Confucius never found himself appointed to a position in which he could put them into practice.

What strikes one immediately about the approach of Confucius is its rational optimism. It is the doctrine of a period when technological advances were giving men confidence that they would control their environment, and when a tendency towards self-examination was leading them to believe that through self-improvement they could find means to improve human society, to reshape it not for the times of scarcity, when only the privileged could enjoy material well-being, but for the times of abundance, when every man could be assured material sufficiency and freedom from oppression. There is no mystification about Master K'ung's teachings; the supernatural powers are never called on for assistance; man himself must make the best of his life on earth. Respect for the commands of Heaven is to be understood as a realistic recognition of what later European philosophers would call Necessity — the natural forces, the events like ageing and death that place their inescapable limitations, which the wise man respects, on human ambition and achievement.

Virtue, in this vision, will bring an automatic reward, by making society harmonious and man therefore more happy. It is a thoroughly humanistic approach; other beings assume peripheral roles. The Way of Master K'ung is man's way, and he — not the intangible forces of Nature as in Taoism — must seek actively to control it.

This means that Confucian aims were virtually centred on this life, on seeking the good society, as it was put by Wordsworth (whose thought in many ways resembled that of Confucius):

. . . in this very world, which is the world
Of all of us, — the place where in the end
We find our happiness, or not at all!

There was little stress on an after-life. The idea of karma and of striving for release from the wheel of existence only entered China centuries later when Buddhism was imported, and it was probably the aspect of Buddhism that struck the shallowest roots, for the Chinese have never been afflicted by the *taedium vitae* which is so striking an aspect of the Indian psyche, and for them happiness on this earth has usually seemed sufficient. Ideas of divine reward and punishment like those developed in the Judeo-Christian-Islamic tradition did not enter the thoughts of Confucius. When his favourite disciple died, he cried out in his grief, "Heaven has destroyed me!" not "Heaven has punished me!" Misfortune and good luck he clearly believed came through the inscrutable operations of the law of the universe (the will of Heaven), and though in this life a failure to follow counsels of moderation would bring its natural consequences, there was no sense of an invisible account being built up that might determine the courses of future lives, as Indian thinkers believed, or might destine us either to Heaven or to Hell, as, round about this time, the Jews under the influence of the Persians were beginning to believe. Nor was there any eschatological element, envisaging a Kingdom of God or a secular utopia in some distant future, in either of the two great native Chinese philosophies that began to develop in the sixth century.

The delight in the visible world and the desire for a good life here and now, which gave Chinese art and poetry their poignant immediacy, were already governing the Chinese attitude to the world. In this, if they had known each other, the archaic Greek philosophers and their Chinese contemporaries might have found themselves in virtual agreement. Both saw as their destination a good life lived for its own sake with awareness.

In this sense we can see more in common between Taoism and Confucianism, or rather between the teachings of Lao-tzu and those of Confucius, than the tradition of their opposition at first suggests. Though Confucius puts his stress on man in relation to society, and Lao-tzu on man in relation to nature, both are essentially humanist and both proclaim the reality of the physical world and of the individual ego; in this sense their teachings are notably different from those of Buddhism. Neither adopted the Indian pessimism which regarded suffering as inevitable and the only escape from it a release from the chain of life. Each in his own way saw the possibility of happiness here and now, in Master K'ung's case through a right relation with our neighbours, and in Lao-tzu's case through a right relation with nature. It was the Ways that differed.

The teachings of Confucius, like those of the Buddha, represented a new and original approach to the world. Nobody before his time had thought or dared to develop a philosophy on which one might base a social and political order designed to further not the gain of the ruler but the good of the people. In this sense he was even more innovatory and radical than Lao-tzu. He was the first true political philosopher in China, as Solon was in Greece.

Though we have no mythological records, Taoism seems, like Jainism, to have preceded its first known master as a tradition emerging out of a fairly recent past of animism, magic and ancestor worship, and perhaps in the more distant past out of the shamanism that underlay ancient Chinese as well as ancient Siberian structures of belief. Essentially it was a nature cult; from it Lao-tzu and his successors like Chuang-tzu distilled a philosophy that over the centuries has carried the name of Taoism.

In its own way it involved an interpretation of history, but a specifically anti-progressivist one. For Lao-tzu civilization was a degradation of the natural order, and the more complex political and social arrangements became, the greater the distress rather than the well-being of the people. The aim of true philosophy must be to return the world as far as possible to its pristine innocence.

This was why Lao-tzu was represented as so strongly opposed to Confucius. Confucius believed that by reforming government, by making it less corrupt and more solicitous for the welfare of men, men could increase their happiness. Lao-tzu believed the opposite — that government was a self-perpetuating disorder, and that political action never mitigated the effect of government but rather created the need for more government, a truth history has in fact done nothing to refute.

Lao-tzu and his followers opposed the arguments of Confucius by contending that man is a social and peaceful being whose potentialities are realized by living according to nature, which — in another use of the word — his own true nature manifests and yearns for. Civilization and government impose limits on the development of our true natures, which will more clearly assert themselves the less we are governed.

Central to Taoist thought was the paradoxical expression, *wei wu wei*. The nearest to a literal translation is "Do without doing" or "Act without action," and its most positive meaning, I think, is that one must flow with the Way and move according to the power that is given by obeying one's nature. If one attempts to shape the world, disaster will follow, since the world has its own shape and changes according to its own nature. The wise man understands the world by "sitting in forgetfulness," by emptying his mind in meditation and being ready to receive what cannot be grasped, which is the Way:

You can know the World
without leaving your house.
You do not need windows
to see the Way.
The farther you journey
the less you learn.
Therefore the wise man learns without going,
perceives without seeing,
and does without acting.

Taoism as Lao-tzu preached it is the least systematic of philosophies. It could quite plausibly be described as an anti-philosophy embodying an anti-ethics as well as an anti-politics. The lists of virtuous attributes, the programmes of meritorious behaviour that figure so prominently in other Asian philosophies of the period, find no place in Taoism precisely because as soon as we categorize a virtue it ceases to be such. Playing on the Confucian ideal of the "superior man," Lao-tzu invented his own idea of superiority, posing the Taoist as the truly superior man and the Confucianist as the truly inferior: "The man of superior virtue is not virtuous, and that is why he has virtue. The man of inferior virtue never strays from virtue and that is why he has no virtue."

And if virtue cannot be prescribed, neither can the Way that mysteriously embodies it be defined, for it exists in the spaces between definition:

You build a house with walls
but you live in the space
between the walls, which is empty.
You use a bowl because of
the part that is empty
but the emptiness
depends on the bowl.
We live by what is
and the void within it.
There is no map to be had
of the Way, there are
no words to describe it.
It exists, and is not.

But if the Taoist is unwilling to describe his world, he has no sense of its being an illusion. The sage who "strolls in the origin of all things" is not apprehending a non-existent universe; he is making contact with a natural world that is given and immutable and instinct with meaning and that provides the body for Taoism's essential pantheism:

The sky has been there for ever
and the earth is ancient.
They survive because they exist
not for themselves. The wise man

effaces himself
and so he is foremost.

But even the wise man who effaces himself has not become a non-being; on the contrary, he has become the being through whom the *tao* flows, so that of everything he does it can be said that "it happened of its own accord." In some ways the recommendations of the Taoist sages, like those of the Buddha, are practical and material. Lao-tzu was no less prone than Confucius to offer advice to rulers — indeed the *Tao-te Ching* is meant as such — but the advice was of self-effacement. The ruler in Lao-tzu's anti-politics becomes an anti-ruler. He must be as nearly invisible as possible, and above all must refrain from inculcating virtue and what usually passes for wisdom; he will be better occupied in the material task of filling bellies than the intellectual task of filling minds, in building up the bones of his people rather than building up their ambitions. As for war, he will avoid it — "whoever has conquered in battle should be received with rites of mourning." War, we can assume, was for Lao-tzu the ultimate offense against nature, the ultimate perversion of the Way.

It is impossible to say, at this distance in time, which came first, that extraordinary sense of the immanence of meaning in the natural world which one gains from the poetry and art of all the great Chinese periods, or the Taoist philosophy, which gave this kind of awareness a rationale peculiarly Chinese in that it presented a reasonable approach that claimed no omniscience, relied on no myth, and offered a pragmatic vision of living one's life by flowing with the Way, at the same time as it laid out no path for salvation and indeed no reason for seeking it. More than any of the great philosophers who emerged in the sixth century and saw the world anew, Lao-tzu projected the sense of knowledge as an opening out of man's nature to all experience.

PART V

ARCHAIC
BORDERLANDS

Chapter 14

Peoples in Waiting

I

History belongs to the literate; peoples who did not keep records, or kept them in scripts yet undeciphered, remain almost as elusively in the shadows of the past as those who, like the Australian aborigines in living memory, remained the mental inhabitants of the great dream time of myth.

This does not mean such peoples are without historic significance. One of the striking aspects of the sixth century BC is that in the background to the more dramatic activities of the period, in which the Greeks and the Persians, the Indians and the Chinese, were principally involved, other peoples emerged who underwent profound developments that would manifest their full significance only in later centuries; we have already seen the Jews as one such group. Some peoples who developed distinctive civilizations at this time lived even farther away from the centre of the archaic world than the Chinese; among them were the early precursors of the great pre-Columbian civilizations of the ancient Americas. But other groups, particularly in Europe, began to develop their special civilizations at the same time as they came into contact with more sophisticated peoples, and notably with the Greeks. In some instances such conjunctions between civilized sophistication and barbarian vitality produced collective forces so strong that they would eventually change the course of history and help determine the shape of our world twenty-five centuries afterwards. The full influence of the sixth century on the world we inhabit today can be appreciated only by taking such emergent cultures into account, even if the lack of literary traditions makes it harder for us to enter into the minds and motives of their people.

The Romans, whose appearance late in this period would have dramatic consequences for almost the whole of Europe as well as for western Asia and northern Africa, provide the most striking instance. The real history of Rome, like that of the Jews, began modestly at the end of the sixth century, when the Roman republic came falteringly into being.

Early in the century the Romans were merely the leading tribe among a group of Latin-speaking peoples in central Italy. Culturally, they had come under the influence of the Greek colonies of Cumae and Neapolis, from the former of which they acquired not only an alphabet but also an oracle, the Cumaean Sibyl. But politically, until almost the end of the sixth century, they were under the domination of the Etruscans, a people whose origins have puzzled historians, and whose language, despite the familiar-looking alphabet also adopted from the Greeks, has still been incompletely deciphered.

Though some historians still argue that the Etruscan culture was a development of the native prehistoric Villanovan culture of northern Italy, most are now inclined to accept the tradition recorded by Herodotus, that at least the Etruscan upper class were emigrants from Lydia. Herodotus was writing of an early period, perhaps in the eighth century BC, when Lydia was afflicted by a long famine, and King Atys finally divided his people into two groups, chosen by lot, one of whom stayed at home, and the other of whom set sail from Smyrna, where they had built ships, and, after touching on many lands, finally settled in central Italy, where they called themselves Tyrrhenians after their leader, the king's son, Tyrrhenus.

The people whom Herodotus called the Tyrrhenians are the people we call the Etruscans, and the route they followed is suggested by the fact that on the Aegean island of Lemnos there still lived in the sixth century a people called the Tyr-senoi who left inscriptions in a language that seems to be related to Etruscan. The strong oriental elements in Etruscan culture and the rapidity with which it emerged in Italy make any slow evolution from the markedly different Villanovan culture most unlikely; as in Herodotus' day, the Lydian hypothesis still seems the best solution to the problem of this mysterious people's origins.

The Etruscans were a vigorous, intelligent people, with a society of strong city states in which women enjoyed a greater freedom and influence than anywhere else in the ancient world. They did not use the alphabet they had acquired from the Greeks of Magna Graecia to leave a written heritage of his-tory or poetry or philosophy, but in their vivid tomb paint-ings and expressive terracotta sculptures they left the image of a way of life in whose amiable hedonism later interpreters like D. H. Lawrence found a vibrant vitality. They were highly innovative engineers and urban planners who first developed the arch and attended with great practical sense to such basic urban problems as the disposal of sewage; they were also accomplished metallurgists who exploited the abundance of ores in the parts of Italy they inhabited and on offshore islands like Elba.

Relations between the Etruscans and the Greeks of Italy were at best uneasy. Etruscan pirates attacked Greek traders, and they allied themselves with the Carthaginians to drive the Phocaeans out of Corsica. In southern Italy Etruscan armies advanced into the Campania and established Capua as a rival to the Greek settlements. It was only the military skill of the Cumaean tyrant Aristodemus, who twice defeated the Etrus-cans in the later sixth century, that saved Cumae, Neapolis, Poseidonia (Paestum) and the other Greek cities of the region from submergence.

Yet at the same time the Etruscans imported large quanti-ties of pottery from Corinth and metalwork from Laconia, and their own art was so much influenced by the Greek that the murals in their famous tombs are interesting not only for what they tell us about Etruscan life and beliefs but also for what they may reveal about Greek painting techniques of the period; some surviving Greek murals in the tombs of Paestum suggest that the derivations may have been very close, and that what Lawrence, looking at the tombs of Etruria, took for the Etruscan spirit may actually have been the archaic Greek spirit transported and modified. In some Etruscan ports there were whole Greek quarters where the traders built their own temples dedicated to Hellenic deities. Greek craftsmen, especially potters, settled in the Etrurian cities and introduced from Corinth the art of clay statuary which the Etruscans so dramatically developed. Spina on the Po delta, founded about 520 BC and developed as a kind of early Venice, with canals for streets, provided an interesting variation on the usual pattern, for here the majority were Greek traders who left in their cemeteries a superb collection of fine Athenian vases, and who seem to have lived amicably side by side with the strong Etruscan element in the population. It was even asserted by Pliny the Elder that the Etruscan Tarquin family, which ruled in Rome during the sixth century, were Greeks by race, descended from a wealthy Corinthian merchant named Demaratus who settled in Tarquinia and imported three clay-modellers who introduced the techniques of clay statuary into the city.

It was through these alien rulers that Greek and Etruscan influences combined to civilize the Romans, for under the Tarquins Rome itself developed from a cluster of rustic villages into a city. One at least of this line, Servius Tullius, was remembered kindly by the Romans as a good and humane king, and all seem to have contributed notably to the physical transformation of the city and its emergence as the dominant Latin community.

But the last of the dynasty, Tarquinius Superbus, Tarquin the Proud, was an arrogant and tyrannical ruler, less concerned with the welfare of the Roman people than with the vast building programmes directed by the Etruscan technicians from whom the Romans learnt their vaunted skills as engineers. Tarquin spent much of his time and Rome's wealth and the labour of the people on planning and constructing the vast temple to the Capitoline Jupiter, with its great terracotta statue of the god executed by Vulca, the Etruscan sculptor. As the historian Livy remarked,

Tarquin acted on the belief that if the proletariat were allowed to be idle, they would be a drag on the state, and when his major works did not absorb all the unemployed, he sent the rest off to found settlements that both increased Roman territory and created new outposts against invasion from both land and sea.

Some of the works of Tarquin and his predecessors undoubtedly benefited the Romans long after the dynasty came to an end. One was the Cloaca Maxima, the great complex of underground pipes and culverts that carried off the city's sewage and storm water and at least in part still functions to this day; it was the most imaginative work of public hygiene in its time, and an engineering feat more than equal to the contemporary tunnel of Eupalinus on Samos. Others of Tarquin's works were aimed at ensuring the safety of the state. Yet they did not endear this proud alien king to a people who had grown tired of Etruscan rule and who, as a result of the unity the Tarquins had imposed on them, were beginning to become conscious of their own strength. The Roman aristocrats began to plot against him. The event that became the excuse to turn their discontent into rebellion has a special place in English literature:

From the besieged Ardea all in haste
Borne by the trustless wings of false desire,
Lust-breathéd Tarquin leaves the Roman host,
And to Collatium bears the lightless fire,
Which, in pale embers hid, lurks to aspire
And girdle with embracing flames the waist
Of Collatine's fair love, Lucrece the chaste.

The poem is of course Shakespeare's prolix apprentice work, *The Rape of Lucrece*, whose plot he derived mainly from Livy. The Tarquin of the poem is Sextus, son of Tarquinius Superbus. He raped Lucretia, wife of the Roman patrician Collatinus. She committed suicide from shame, and her death was the spark for an uprising led by Lucius Junius Brutus, who swore before the assembled Romans, as he drew the dagger from Lucretia's heart, to take revenge. The Romans followed him, and what had begun as a family vendetta ended as a revolution. Tarquinius Superbus fled to Cumae, where Aristodemus gave him refuge. Despite Tarquin's efforts to regain his throne, and the attempts by other Tuscan lords like Lars Porsena of Clusium to take the city for themselves, the Roman republic survived to begin its spectacular career in history.

But for many years after the Republic was established, it was still one of many small Italian states struggling for survival against each other and against such formidable enemies as the Etruscans, the Carthaginians and the Greek colonies of southern Italy and Sicily. In the sixth century the Romans did no more than emerge, like the Jews, as a distinct and historic people establishing their independence and asserting the beginnings of a national consciousness. It was their future that would make their emergence so historically important.

II

Even the Greeks, who by the end of the sixth century were demonstrating in their writings a sharp interest, both philosophical and commercial, in the known world, and an inclination to speculate about *terrae incognitae* and to travel to them, had as little to say about the Romans as they did about the Jews. On the other hand, they were much aware of the great conglomeration of tribes known as the Celts, who were already spread over a large area of France, southern Germany and Bohemia.

Hecataeus, who called them the *Keltoi*, remarked that they lived near the Ligurians, the inhabitants of what we now call the French and Italian Rivieras, and his successor Herodotus equally correctly remarked that the Danube rose in the land of the Celts. They probably owed their knowledge to the Phocaean settlers who founded the city of Massalia east of the Rhône delta in 600 BC. The Massaliots found the trade with local tribes so rewarding that within a few years they had established lesser trading posts that eventually became cities at Antibes, Nice and Monaco, as well as at Emporia on the Spanish coast, and had moved inland to establish settlements at Arles and at Glanon (the Roman Glanum) near St. Rémy. Even when the Carthaginians expelled them from Tartessus, southern Spain and the Balearic Islands, and the Etruscans made their position on Corsica untenable, the descendants of the Phocaeans retained control of their settlements on the southern French coast and in northern Spain, and the continuing wealth and importance of Massalia was shown by the rich gifts it dedicated at Delphi during the sixth century.

The Phocaeans came into contact with the Ligurians along the coastline, probably as far west as Massalia itself, and with the Iberians in Spain, but the main trade was carried on up the Rhône with the Celts, an Iron Age people whose contemporary Hallstadt culture was named from a salt-mining centre in Austria, where an immense cemetery, rich in relics, was discovered at the junction of trading routes that carried the precious mineral in all directions.

To the sixth-century Greeks, the Celts were barbarians, semi-nomadic people who did not live in cities, who were devoted to warfare, adventure and feasting, yet who were willing to obtain what they wanted by trade if that were the only way; in other words, a people much like the Greeks' own pre-Homeric ancestors, who had put an end to the Mycenaean civilization. The trading routes of Europe must in fact have been protected by truces or taboos of some kind, for there is no record of the Greek merchants having experienced any difficulties carrying on their commerce, which seems to have extended far into the interior of France.

One of the great sixth-century centres of this trade, to which tin and amber were brought from various parts of northern Europe, and pottery, metalwork and amphorae of wine from the Greek cities of the Côte d'Azur, was at Vix, now a tiny village on the headwaters of the Seine just over the Côte d'Or from Burgundy. In historical times Mount Lassois, overlooking the village, was traditionally regarded as the site of an ancient castle, and in 1929, when sceptical archaeologists at last began to excavate its summit, they found the remains of a whole trading town, in which they dug up more than a million pieces of pottery, most of it Greek of imitated from Greek originals, as well as hundreds of weapons, indicating the presence of a warrior aristocracy, and splendid jewels of worked amber from the Baltic and polished coral from southern seas.

In 1953 the most splendid grave of all was excavated at Vix. It was that of a young woman of high rank, with a diadem of pure gold on her head; around her were ranged black-figure wine cups from Athens, copper beakers from Etruria, amphorae that must have contained wine from Massalia or Greece itself, the wheels of one of the ceremonial carts often found in tombs of the Hallstadt period, and a great bronze crater five feet high, decorated with a frieze of Greek warriors on foot and in chariots, and probably made for the French trade at Taras (Taranto) in southern Italy.

The rulers who could afford such luxuries obviously levied tolls on a very profitable commerce, with tin coming up the Seine from Brittany and Cornwall, and being transported over the Côte d'Or by packtrains or in carts, and thence shipped down the Saône and the Rhône to the Greek cities of the coast, from which trade goods were transported on the return journey. How far the trade was directly in the hands of the Greek merchants is not certain. The example of Hallstadt, which flourished as an active commercial centre at this period without Greek involvement, suggests that the Celtic chieftains were themselves active in trade, perhaps exploiting the labour of other peoples whom they had conquered in their sweep over Europe.

On the the other hand, like their Phocaean ancestors, the Massaliots of this period were hardy and enterprising travellers. One of them, Euthymenes, sailed through the Strait of Gibraltar down the west coast of Africa until he came to rivers infested with crocodiles. It is unlikely that a community with such daring traditions of travel and trade would fail to send its representatives up the Rhône into the country of the great Celtic chiefs, and one can envisage the crater of Vix being taken there under the careful supervision of a Massaliot merchant who rightly believed he had a unique object in his hands, and was seeking a king or a queen rich enough to buy it. Certainly one Greek architect must have found his way at this period deep into the Celtic heartland, for in the fortress of Hueneburg on the upper Danube, which contained Etruscan and Greek artifacts, some of the walls and bastions were built of air-dried brick on stone foundations in a style familiar in archaic Greek military architecture but to be found nowhere else in the Celtic world of the time.

How far society in the Celtic heartland was influenced by the presence of the Greeks on the Mediterranean coast it is hard to establish. It certainly varied from class to class. The kings and chieftains imported Greek pottery and metalwork, and drank wine from Chios and later from Massalia, while their subjects continued to drink beer. As John Boardman remarks in *The Greeks Overseas*, "The first wine to be drunk in Burgundy was Greek wine from Marseilles." Indeed, anything foreign that might enhance their prestige as rulers or satisfy their taste for novelty they accepted, so that, as Boardman also points out, "Inland, along the tin routes and in the richer Celtic 'Hallstadt' cities, the volume of Greek finds grows less, but more spectacular." At sites in Wurtemburg, Bavaria and Switzerland intricate and costly bronze vessels, from Laconia or Magna Graecia, have been discovered, indicating that in these wealthy Celtic principalities fine Greek metalwork was as valued as it was at the same period in the mobile camps, far to the east in the Ukraine, of the Royal Scyths, with whom the Celts seem to have maintained some kind of contact in the borderland of the Carpathians, based on a mingling of trade and warfare.

But, like the Royal Scyths, the Celts in the central and northwestern European heartlands tended to treat the imports that came through Massalia from all parts of the Hellenic world as the rewards of power, its exotic ornaments, rather than allowing their way of life to be affected in any profound way by Hellenic influences. They remained primarily pastoral marauders, and only after they had spread in the sixth and fifth centuries across the Pyrenees into Spain and across the

Channel into Britain and Ireland, and the limits of nomadic expansion had been reached on the western seacoasts, did they settle down unwillingly to an agrarian life.

It was in the south of France, roughly in the areas we now identify as Provence and the Languedoc, that Greek influence in the sixth century and later was most marked. The Romans who came later acknowledge this, for in the third century AD their historian Justinus said that

> from the Greeks the Gauls learned a more civilized way of life and abandoned their barbarous ways. They set to tilling their fields and walling their towns. They even got used to living by law rather than force of arms, to cultivating the vine and the olive. Their progress, in manners and wealth, was so brilliant that it seemed as though Gaul had become part of Greece, rather than that Greece had colonized Gaul.

One may discount the hyperbole with which this passage ends and still acknowledge the immense economic transformation which the introduction of the vine and the olive must have brought about throughout the southern regions of France, and the exemplary influence that well-organized city governments like those of Massalia and its dependencies must have wielded. The establishment of the Greek colonies in the sixth century in fact created a cultural continuity that persisted through the Roman period and into the Middle Ages, when even the rigours of the crusade against the Albigensian heretics did not entirely eliminate the element of Hellenic paganism in Provençal life, any more than centuries of Catholic domination eliminated it in Magna Graecia.

The strength of the Greek presence in southern France and in northeastern Spain was shown by the vigour with which, even when obscure changes shifted the balance of power in central Europe and the inland trade up the Rhône came to a halt, the cities on the Côte d'Azur were sufficiently well-established, with bases in local agriculture, to continue with a restricted commerce and also to resist the threats posed by Carthaginian and Etruscan raiders. It was only the Hellenization of local Ligurian and Celtic communities that gave the

Greek cities the strength they needed to survive and continue their civilizing influence over this whole region south of the Côte d'Or and the Massif Central.

How far these Hellenic cultural influences on the southern Celts, the Ligurians and the coastal Iberians were paralleled by philosophic influences it is hard to determine. That there was an overlapping of religious practices between the Greeks and local peoples is shown by the example of the shrine at Glanon near St. Rémy, which began as a sacred grove of the Ligurians, centred on a holy spring. Later the Celts went there to worship their own water gods, and eventually, when the Greeks arrived, they treated it as a nymphaeum, so that all three peoples worshipped their own deities in the same place in full harmony. Glanon seems also to have been a kind of spa, whose waters were credited with healing powers, and it became a meeting place where merchants of several races could gather and carry on their commerce under the benign supervision of their various gods. But the phenomenon may perhaps be more easily explained by the religious tolerance of the ancient Greeks rather than by any interest of other peoples in Greek religion.

There may have been Celts or Ligurians who, like Anacharsis the Scythian, became interested in Greek philosophy, but there is no record of them. Indeed, the only link of a philosophic kind — and that a very tenuous one — is between the religion of the Druids and the philosophic speculations of Pythagoras. This link was first proposed by Hellenistic writers of the second century BC, who attributed to Zalmoxis, the Thracian slave whom Pythagoras manumitted, the transmission to the Celts of various doctrines, notably that of reincarnation. By the time, in the early Christian era, the theory had reached such Fathers of the Church as St. Clement and St. Cyril in Alexandria, the situation had been reversed, and the Druids were credited with the invention of such doctrines, which Pythagoras is said to have borrowed from them.

It is possible that some Pythagoreans, dispersed from Croton by the hostility that forced Pythagoras to retire to Metapontum, may have found their way as far as the Greek towns of the French coast. The real problem lies in isolating what part of Druid doctrine may in fact have been derived from Pythagoras. The Druids indeed believed in reincarnation, but as the passing of the indestructible soul from one human body into another. The theory Pythagoras advocated and shared with the Indian philosophers assumed that the souls of men might enter into animals or even, it seems, into beans, but there is no evidence that the Druids shared such beliefs. The idea of the indestructibility of the universe which Strabo credited to the Celts is one they appear to have shared with many contemporary Greek philosophers, but our lack of knowledge of how the Celtic belief was formulated makes it impossible to decide whether they actually borrowed it from the Greeks or whether it was one of those ideas that sprang up in many places with such a strange and apparently spontaneous similarity during the sixth century.

Indeed, if the Celts were influenced at all by Greek thought during this period, it is more likely, as Stuart Piggott suggests in *The Druids*, to have been through astronomy and mathematics than through metaphysics. There is evidence that between the sixth century and the invasion of Gaul by the Romans the Celts developed an inclination, resembling that of the Ionian philosophers of the archaic period, to enquire into the nature of the universe. Caesar remarked that they had "much knowledge of the stars and their motion, of the size of the world and the earth, of natural philosophy," and Hippolytus asserted that "they can foretell events by the Pythagorean reckoning and calculation." Pythagorean or not, the Druids, like their megalithic predecessors who built Stonehenge, had clearly acquired considerable calendrical knowledge. Their cycles seem to have been based on the same principles as those the Greeks borrowed from the Babylonians — a 19-year solar corresponding to a 235-month lunar cycle. It is here, among a people much concerned with celestial phenomena, that Greek ideas transmitted through Massalia may have had their strongest appeal. But perhaps the most important fact of all to emerge from a discussion of this subject is that the Druids, whom we must regard as the philosophers of the Celts, were moving, like thinkers in Greece and Persia, in India and China, towards a concept of the universe that would not depend on myth, but would be acceptable to human reason because it was based on observation aiming at the accurate description of phenomena.

III

Half a world away from the Mediterranean, and a whole ocean from China, the emergent cultures of the Americas were pursuing their own apparently independent courses. From time to time, theories have appeared about maritime links between ancient China and the pre-Columbian civilizations of Mexico and Peru, and some puzzling pieces of evidence do suggest that there may have been intermittent contacts between the cultural regions of the western and eastern Pacific. How else, for example, can one explain the presence among the Aztecs of types of jade that in their natural state have been found only in Burma? Investigators moving on the verge of accepted ethnographical research, like Thor Heyerdahl, have turned up fascinating scraps of evidence suggesting trans-Pacific cultural links. But there is little in this miscellany of facts that seems to relate to a period as early as the sixth century BC.

Nevertheless, this was a time when, in various parts of the Americas, people racially related to the inhabitants of China, Mongolia and Siberia had developed the earliest American civilizations, some of which, by the sixth century, seem even to have been entering on cycles of decay. The sacred complex of Chavin in Peru, which seems to have been begun in the middle of the second millenium BC, may well have been abandoned already by this time, though its influence survived to permeate later Peruvian cultures. In Mexico the Olmec culture had been flourishing for several centuries south of Vera Cruz, and had developed elaborate trading networks to bring the stone needed for the strange Cyclopean heads, sometimes ten feet high, of creatures resembling helmeted American footballers, which were its most striking artifacts, and the jade and obsidian needed for its smaller works of art; it had reached its peak in the islanded sanctuary of La Venta, and newer cultures were gathering strength in the Mayan highlands of Tabasco and in the valley of Oaxaca, where the construction of the great ceremonial complex of Monte Alban in the overshadowing hills appears to have begun in the sixth century.

The lack of written records prevents us from making plausible conjectures about intellectual developments in the Americas at this time. The highly sophisticated prehistoric cultures of Peru never developed a system of records more elaborate than the mnemonic devices of knotted strings which sufficed to administer the affairs of a considerable empire. In Mexico by the middle of the first millenium BC the Mayans and the Zapotecs, like the Babylonians, developed elaborate calendars and even devised a hieroglyphic script to record their complex and remarkably accurate observations of the heavens. The sixth century, indeed, may have been a crucial one in the development of Central American astronomical science. But we are still left, because the scripts that were developed seem to have been almost as narrowly utilitarian as those of Minoan Crete and Mycenae, with no way of access to the minds of these materially advanced early Americans. We can see what they created in terms of impressive artifacts. We can admire their architecture, their mural painting, their stone and ceramic sculpture, the baroque ingenuity of their imagery. We can even get a fair idea of what they saw in the heavens and admire the accuracy of their mathematical calculations. But we have little idea of their history until a relatively late period, and virtually no knowledge of the personalities who controlled their lives before the Spaniards came. The myths that have been sketchily recorded, largely by hostile Catholic missionaries, give us some idea of their gods and their views of the creation of the universe, and we can relate this information, perhaps not always accurately, to what their art represents.

It seems likely that, like the early Aryans in India and the pre-literate Greeks, these pre-Columbian peoples had an extensive body of oral tradition and poetry and an unwritten lore relating to medicine and the practical arts, though little of this has come down to us. We know nothing more about the lives of common people than the fragmentary objects recovered by archaeologists can tell us, though we can reasonably conjecture that the astronomical observations and calculations of the priests, like the rituals enacted at the great pyramids and ceremonial platforms that early became standard features of Mesoamerican architecture, were closely linked with the cycles of vegetable fertility on which these cultures, which had few domestic animals, mainly depended.

We know a little about the cosmogenies of later peoples like the Aztecs, but again it is largely projected through Christian mental lenses, and we know virtually nothing of the intellectual lives of these peoples with high material civilizations. We have no hint whether, parallel to those who sustained the priestly theogonies, there were speculative thinkers like the Ionians and the Indian ascetics, framing and orally transmitting phenomenal explanations of the universe and moral systems based on reason. Given what happened elsewhere at the same time, this does not seem impossible. But all one can say in the absence of a literary record is that the sixth century in the Americas, as elsewhere, was a time of social vitality that may have been friendly to a pattern of intellectual search and speculation out of which the more highly developed later cultures, like those of the Mayas and the Incas, may have derived their impetus.

PART VI

CONCLUSION

Chapter 15

Vibrations in a Single Thought: The Age in Far Perspective

I

Herodotus, the first historian whose work has come down to us virtually entire, wrote his account of the stirring events of the sixth century and shortly afterwards "lest the great and wonderful deeds performed by Greeks and barbarians should be lost to fame." And reading his *History* one gets the sense of a man looking back on a remarkable and triumphant age already past.

The consciousness that the sixth century was a great and exceptional era has inspired many successors of Herodotus. They have seen it as an age of awakening, an age of intellectual renewal, and some cultural historians, like Lewis Mumford in *The Conquest of Life*, propose it as a model for our age:

> . . . here and there in history one notes a sudden concentration of energies, a more favourable constellation of social opportunities, an almost worldwide upsurge of prophetic anticipation, disclosing new possibilities for the race; so it was with the worldwide changes in the sixth century BC symbolized by Buddha, Solon, Zoroaster, Confucius and their immediate successors, changes that gave common values and purposes to people too far separated physically for even Alexander the Great to unite

them. Out of still deeper pressures, anxieties, insecurities, a corresponding renewal on an even wider scale now seems about to open for mankind.

The debt that anyone writing on the sixth century owes to Herodotus must be immense. The first true historical genius, he tells us far more than any single author of his time about the political and social background to events in that era, not only in the Hellenic world but thoughout the Middle East and the Mediterranean basin and even in such remote areas as the Scythian steppes, to which he travelled at considerable discomfort in his search for knowledge.

Yet perspectives, whether of space or time, change as they lengthen, and the viewpoint from which a modern author writes is necessarily different from that of Herodotus. His aim was to extract from recent events the lessons that might help his fellow Hellenes direct their affairs more wisely in the future. Like all antique Greek writers, he was unashamedly didactic; like all the early Greek sages, he was practical and pragmatic at the same time. He tended to see the importance of men reflected in their deeds, and in this he retained the spirit of an earlier age, that of the rhapsodic bards who celebrated in their epics the half-mythical heroes of a remoter past. Yet he was also a man of his own urgent time, and the most remarkable aspect of the opening statement to his *History* is that, in setting out to credit both Greeks and barbarians with "great and wonderful deeds," he displays the universalism of thought that was emerging everywhere in his age — that was reflected by Aeschylus in *The Persian Women*, where he gave compassionate expression to the idea of a common humanity embracing one's enemies, and, in a different way, by Xenophanes and Zoroaster and the Buddha and the post-exilic Jews, who shaped philosophic attitudes that projected a universal God or a universal way of liberation, and hence a universal morality, extending not merely to all mankind but even, in the case of Buddhists and Jains, to all living beings.

Writing today one sees the sixth century not only from a far greater distance in time than Herodotus — twenty-five centuries compared with two generations — but also through a screen of experience that has changed our ideas of the relative importance of events and even of personalities. One must admire the remarkable critical awareness of social realities and of rapidly changing political forms that Herodotus manifested. Only a society acutely attuned to the day-to-day exigencies of the Hellenic city state could have produced this kind of insight. Yet Herodotus, who mentioned only Thales of all the pre-Socratics, clearly had little if any idea how important the speculations of the natural philosophers who lived in the century before him would become in fostering the growth of a scientific cast of mind. He was indeed impressed by the achievements of the applied sciences in his time, the practical inventiveness that inspired the great public works of the age, and particularly those of Samos. But later generations of Greeks, perhaps because of their much wider use of slave labour, turned away from the rapid process of technical development which characterized the archaic period, and in the long run the speculative philosophers of Ionia offered more, even in determining the goals and practices of scientific research, than the technocratic innovators like Eupalinus and Theodorus, whose tradition lapsed so quickly.

What the natural philosophers offered were not actual scientific discoveries, except for some minor geometrical and geological insights, or even theories that would ultimately be acceptable, for nobody now takes seriously the notions of Thales or Anaximander or Anaximenes concerning the essential substance of the universe or the structure of the cosmos. They called on men to be guided by the evidence of the five senses instead of by the voices of myth, and they refused to accept anything merely on authority. They stood on their own reason and their own experience, and here was their revolutionary significance. Talking of Xenophanes and Heraclitus, Walter Kaufman remarks in *Tragedy and Philosophy*:

> It is not enough to note that their writings mark the beginnings of man's emancipation from mythical thinking . . . . they took a further step of the utmost significance: they broke with exegetical thinking; they were anti-authoritarian.

As Kaufman also points out, it was the rejection of myth and of any authority other than one's own experience and one's own reasoning that also distinguished the Indian contemporaries of the pre-Socratics and notably the Buddha. Indeed, in terms of significant scientific anticipations, the Indians may have preceded the Greeks, since it was they who developed the one great insight of the sixth century that has played a dominant role in modern science, the atomic theory.

But the Buddha was not, in the same sense as Thales or Anaximander, a philosopher concerned with the nature of the universe. What concerned him was the suffering of that fragile bundle of psychic states he saw as a human being, and the problem of ending that suffering. He directed his attention to the spiritual ganglion where moral and psychological concerns meet, and the ultimate substance of the world — or of the gods for that matter — concerned him very little. Perhaps we may find an affinity among the Greeks in Heraclitus, whose statement that "the world is an ever-living fire" was strangely paralleled in the Buddha's own Fire Sermon, and whose concerns were essentially psychological, rather than physical as in the case of Thales.

Yet we must be on our guard against interpreting the pre-Socratic preoccupation with the physical world as essentially materialistic: it was in conncection with the Milesian physiologues, after all, that Aristotle made his remark, "And some say that soul is intermingled with the universe, for which reason, perhaps, Thales also thought that all things were full of gods." Heraclitus, in his turn, matched Thales' pantheist vision of a world permeated by the divine with the idea of a spirit whose freedom was infinite: "You will not find the limits of the soul, though you follow every path, so deep and broad it is."

Here we are not merely writing about philosophy. We are making contact with a new kind of religion, a religion based not on responses to the commands of irrational tribal deities or on obedience to the dictates of a hieratic state like Egypt or Babylon, but on the attempt to explain the universe in rational rather than mythical terms, and to create a humanistic morality, related to the needs of man rather than to the imagined requirements of the gods.

This is the other area where Herodotus and the other historians of the ancient world had no conception of the vast effects that would stem from the transformation of the philosophic urges that appeared in their period into what we now call the "higher religions." Buddhism, Jainism and Zoroastrianism, as we have seen, all sprang from the preachings of moralistic teachers in the sixth century who set themselves up as critics of the established cults. Nobody at that time could possibly have imagined that Buddhism, a philosophic brotherhood in the small cities along the Ganges, would become a world religion, or that, through its encounter with the teachings of Zoroaster, Judaism would not only be transformed into a universalizing religion, but would also give birth to two other great eschatological creeds, Christianity and Islam, as well as to the secular religion of Marxism.

It is thus with a knowledge of developments in philosophy and religion and ultimately in science which Herodotus could not have foreseen that we now look back on the sixth century, and as we do so we find ourselves seeking to preserve and celebrate not so much the "great and wonderful deeds performed by Greeks and barbarians" as their great and wonderful thoughts, which irrevocably transformed our perceptions of experience and the world.

One need not deny that the deeds men performed in that post-epic age had profound effects on the world which grew up after the archaic age faded away. The Achaemenian Empire was a "new model" of a secular empire uniting many peoples in an atmosphere of religious and cultural tolerance; its exemplary influence would not be played out until the British Empire finally dissolved after World War II. The great conflict between the Greeks and the Persians created a rift between the East and the West that even now is unhealed. The invention of money by the Lydians transformed not only economic but also social relations. Spartan totalitarianism and Athenian democracy provided opposing political paradigms whose influence has remained strong over the ages.

Yet Solonian democracy in Athens, like Confucian bureaucracy in China, had its origins in thought before action, and even political systems, like the Achaemenian and the Spartan, that came into being without the intervention of any known philosophers would be most effectively projected into the future through the writings of thinkers who idealized them, as Xenophon did the Achaemenian system in *Cyropaedia* and as Plato and Plutarch did the Spartan system in *The Republic* and the "Life of Lycurgus" respectively. One may wonder whether Alexander would have been inspired to take over and revivify the moribund Achaemenian Empire if he had not read Xenophon, both the *Anabasis* and the *Cyropaedia*, and whether Sparta would have stirred the imaginations of European revolutionaries and English public school masters if it had not been for the eighteenth-century translations of Plutarch.

In every age, at least since the invention of literacy, there have been individuals, notably thinkers and poets, who to their successors seem in some outstanding way to express and even symbolize their age. What characterizes the sixth century is not only the considerable number of such individuals, but also the fact that they gave expression to their age's innovatory impulses and did so in astonishingly similar ways. All of them, whether consciously or not, seemed to gaze towards the future while their predecessors had gazed towards the past. Historians dealing with the ancient world have noticed this fact and have left a provocative question hanging in the air. As Jacquetta Hawkes puts it, without venturing an answer, in *The Atlas of Early Man*,

> It is worth noting the extraordinary number of great thinkers living in this sixth century BC . . . . Nearly all of them were alive at the same time and were in their various ways striving to relate man to the universe not by the old means of myth and rite, but by new modes of intuition, morality and reason. How to account for it? The homes of the sages were strung out over many thousands of miles and most knew little of one another.

Some, indeed, knew nothing of the rest.

II

Three interrelated questions offer themselves at this point. Why did so many seminal thinkers appear in so many widely separated places, from the Mediterranean to the shores of the China Seas, during the same few decades? Why, given the profound differences between their cultures and their traditions, were their basic insights so remarkably similar? And why, given that these insights implied a rejection of authority and an assertion of the importance of enquiry and free reasoning, did such a revolutionary change of attitude take place anywhere, let alone everywhere, at this time?

These are questions that may ultimately be unanswerable, given the distance from which we view that long-past century and the erosion of concrete evidence. They may even be unanswerable in another way, since we are concerned with a series of physical and mental events whose effects are evident and unquestionable, but whose causes, like those of so many creative moments in history, remain obscure and perhaps impenetrable.

But there are hypotheses regarding the causes of events in the ancient world that deserve consideration for what they may contribute towards a possible explanation, and the obvious place to begin, since we are concerned with cultures spread over so vast an area, is the diffusionist theory, which was based on the idea that civilization had originated in a single centre, usually the Middle Eastern area of the two great rivers, Nile and Euphrates, and had thence spread outward. Some of the more extreme diffusionists found in the megalithic monuments of western Europe and in the great ceremonial platforms of the ancient American cultures the descendants of the great pyramids of Egypt. After more exact dating methods had proved that Stonehenge and many of the other megalithic monuments in fact predated the pyramids, these more extreme and unsupported variants of diffusionism fell into discredit. But this did not invalidate the fact that at certain times in history techniques and styles have spread rapidly and over large distances. The diffusion of the ironsmith's skills over the con-

tinent of Africa in a few centuries from the original centre
of Meroe is an example. And, nearer the centre of the Mediterranean world, there is no doubt that while Egypt set out to
close itself off from all alien influences, the younger and more
open civilization of the Hellenes not only received much in
the way of cultural influences but also passed them on freely
to other peoples like the Etruscans, the Scythians and the Celts.

Yet there are difficulties about applying a merely diffusionist
interpretation to everything that happened in the sixth century. First of all, there is the case of China. Considering the
great world civilizations, Arnold Toynbee has classed the Sinic
as one that arose by spontaneous "mutation" from a pre-
civilizational situation without impulse or content coming from
outside, and recent Chinese historians like Ping-ti Ho have
supported him with convincing evidence and arguments. There
are, as we have seen, no indications in either Chinese or
western records of direct links between the two areas or even
awareness of each other as early as the sixth century. Even
Herodotus in the fifth century knew of India but not of China,
and Herodotus was an assiduously enquiring man, travelling
far and listening carefully. The only record of Greek travel
even as far east as Siberia is that of Aristeas, who just may
have heard of a people who might have been the Chinese; no
Chinese equivalent of him has yet been discovered. At most
we can assume that there existed what some historians have
called the Scythian Trail, but it was almost certainly no more
than a trail by which the nomads carried on a tenuous commerce across the central Asian mountains and deserts, passing on goods from one nomad group to another, which would
explain the early Chinese silk found in Stuttgart and the
Achaemenian carpet found in the Altai; no artifact from the
west dating as early as the sixth century has yet surfaced in
China. It is true that in later centuries, during the early Christian era, when regular caravans followed the Silk Road, Buddhist monks and Nestorian missionaries turned the Asian trails
into powerful channels for the diffusion of ideas and styles
in life and art, but we can reasonably assume that no such
cultural traffic found its way over the Scythian steppes and

the deserts beyond them during the sixth century or for long afterwards.

The case of India is not unlike that of China, since the kind of contact between western and Indian centres of civilization that might have led to cultural diffusion did not exist during most of the sixth century. Scylax and his exploration party crossed the Hindu Kush in 517 BC, and got back in 514. Only then did Darius send his troops over the mountains and annex most of the Punjab. But all this happened very near the end of the sixth century, and it is unclear how far, by the Buddha's death in 483 BC, influences from Persia and the west had affected the farther India of the great Gangetic plain, for there is no record of any contact, hostile or pacific, between the Persians and the kingdoms of Kosala and Magadha. And while among Indian philosophers of the time, as among Chinese to the east and Greeks to the west, we find the same turning away from myths to seek an explanation of the nature of experience in rational concepts, there is no evidence of any intellectual influence having passed from the west eastward during the early period of Persian intrusion. By the time the Persians came, in any case, the ascetic thinkers had already formed their basic attitudes, and any derivations on their part were from earlier Indian sources. In the case of the one major scientific insight they shared with the Greeks, the development of an atomic theory, it is clear that the Indians were first in the field.

Thus there is little to be said in support of a diffusionist explanation of the emergence of the new sixth-century philosophic attitudes in China or India. The same would apply to the isolated Bactrian uplands at the time when Zoroaster developed his revolutionary adaptation of the ancient Aryan religion. It is true, indeed, that the Greeks were the willing beneficiaries of many forms of cultural influence. Yet their example seems to show the limitations, as a cultural determinant, of diffusion. However much it received from other societies, Hellenic civilization retained its specific character virtually unchanged, and Greeks retained a strong sense of the unity and uniqueness of their culture.

Greek sculptors and architects learnt a great deal technically from the Egyptians, but they rapidly adapted what they learnt to new formal conceptions, so that in a relatively short time the distinctive archaic style appeared in sculpture, possessed of a life and fluidity quite different from the stiff manner of contemporary Egyptian statuary; the major Greek temples which began to appear at this period were different in spirit and form from the great temples of Thebes and Memphis, fitted to another landscape and in clear lines and carefully calculated proportions projecting the rationalizing tendencies emerging in the Greek world.

Similarly, the Greeks borrowed an alphabet from the Phoenicians, but applied it to a language already rich in oral epic, and quickly produced a broad literature, mentally vital and formally sophisticated, quite beyond the capabilities of the narrow commercial culture of the Phoenicians. The Greek imagination worked in a similar transformative way when it originated drama out of the derived cult of Dionysus, an achievement beyond the capabilities of the Thracian tribal world where the god originated.

In politics during the sixth century the Hellenes followed their own genius without much perceptible influence from outside and developed patterns quite distinct from those characteristic of other civilized areas. While the Middle East evolved from one kind of imperial rule to another, and in China an early empire went through the throes of disintegration, and in India small republics were swallowed up by large monarchies, the Greek world continued in its own pattern of compact city states, each choosing its own administrative form within a general progression that in most instances led from oligarchy through tyranny towards democracy. Democracy was in fact an invention of the Greek sixth century unparalleled in the other civilizations of the time. The Greeks, in other words, originated their political institutions and their political ideas; in the archaic age they borrowed in this field from nobody.

In the world of ideas we can detect possible borrowings from Egypt and Babylon among the early Greek philosophers, which suggest minds open to inspiring hints, to techniques of observation and recording, but there is ultimately little in common between the myth-bound world views of Egyptians and Babylonians and the search of the Ionian physiologues for a rational model of the universe that accords with observation and experience.

What seems certain in the sixth century is that whatever diffusion took place, whatever derivations were accepted and, in the case of the Greeks, eagerly welcomed, the dynamic civilizations of the period retained their distinctiveness. Each developed its own political and social patterns independent of the others; each developed its own philosophic attitude, borrowing the detail of content rather than the essential form, and in cases where influence seems to have touched on a fundamental issue, we usually find it was a matter of strengthening a trend already present within the influenced culture, as the contact with Zoroastrian Persians confirmed and strengthened the monotheism already developed within the Jewish religion and gave it a new eschatological direction.

Yet the sustained autonomy and distinctiveness of all the major cultures of the sixth century make it all the more astonishing that, over spaces so far and time so brief that diffusion is impossible, they all developed, within two or three decades in the second half of the sixth century, similar clusters of revolutionary attitudes, involving the replacement of myth by reason and of authority by speculation and enquiry, the emergence of individual and responsible personality as a factor in human societies, and the demotion of the capricious will of the gods in favour of a morality based on human needs.

III

All at once awareness is moving everywhere in a newly opened world; it is moving individually, from mind to mind, like Auden's "scattered points of light," and not through hieratic structures. It is moving fast. As Julian Jaynes remarks in *The Origin of Consciousness in the Breakdown of the Bicameral Mind*, "Chinese literature leaps into subjectivity in the teaching of Confucius with little before it," and the same applies to the other civilizations of the time. As Jaynes further remarks, "It is the century where, for the first time, we can feel mentally at home among persons who think in somewhat the way we do."

The origins and transformations of civilizations are processes in their own ways as mysterious as the origin of life and its evolution. Some historians, like Oswald Spengler and Franz Borkenau, have compared civilizations to natural organisms and envisaged their rise and decline as similar to the process by which a man or an animal passes through childhood, youth and maturity on his way to old age and inevitable death. But this is a determinist view based on a false analogy, for, as Toynbee remarks in his criticism of Spengler in *A Study of History*,

> . . . societies are not in fact living organisms in any sense.
> In subjective terms they are the intelligible fields of study;
> and in objective terms they are the common ground
> between the respective fields of activity of a number of
> individual human beings, whose individual energies are
> the vital forces that operate to work out the history of
> a society, including its life-span.

Yet if Toynbee rightly rejects the repetitious and predetermined destinies that Spengler proposes for all civilizations, he does believe that a society, through the interplay of individual energies, develops a kind of collective existence and evolves as a collectivity. It does not merely evolve in the steady progression of cause and effect; it can also undergo rapid and unforeseeable changes, analogous to mutations in the natural world. As Toynbee remarks, "A civilization can emerge through the spontaneous mutation of some pre-civilizational society."

In the sixth century, of course, we are involved in something much more complex — a transcivilizational mutation affecting within one brief period the whole of the literate world. How can it be explained?

Certainly not in the simple environmental terms which the early Greek historians tended to favour, as Herodotus did when he tried to account for the special character of the Egyptian civilization:

The climate in which the Egyptians live is quite different from ours, and, as well as that, their river is something unique. This explains why they have developed for themselves manners and customs that, in general, are entirely opposite to those of the rest of humankind.

Such an explanation may in somewhat general terms be applied to a single rather static civilization, but it clearly loses its relevance in a situation where similar changes took place in a variety of places whose geographical, climatic and economic conditions were as different as their histories. There was no common environment in the sixth century, just as there was no common history, but in spite of these differences of tradition and ancestry and physical setting, a radical transformation of the same kind took place in civilizations out of touch with each other in the vast sweep of the earth that extended from the Mediterranean to the Indian Ocean and the China Seas.

But when we have ruled out the influence of immediate environment, there remain other approaches that might be called paraenvironmental, since they are based on an unwillingness to believe that, given the slow progress man made during the long eras of the Stone Age, he could have developed, in the brief six or seven millenia since the first emergence of civilization beside the Euphrates, the extraordinary series of rapid developments that have led us to the perilous complexities of the modern world.

In general terms, the paraenvironmental approaches can be divided into the interventionist and the catastrophic. The interventionists, unconvinced by the intellectual potentialities which early *Homo sapiens* displayed in the caves of Lascaux and Altamira, seek to refurbish the old myths from which men everywhere shook themselves free in the sixth century. Those myths attributed to the gods, or to titanic beings like Prometheus, the basic discoveries that in the end marked off the human from the animal. The interventionists return to the myths which the rationalists of the sixth century had rejected and attempt to revitalize them by claiming that the gods were not in fact deities but were mortal beings who travelled from outer galaxies, impregnated Cro-Magnon maidens, and endowed them, as Prometheus did in legend, with the arts of civilization. There have been several popular books along these lines, but their evidence, except for the myths discarded by sixth-century men, is mainly fanciful interpretations of ancient inscriptions; one such interventionist, for example, assumed that every pointed cylindrical object in a Babylonian stele was meant to represent the rocket craft on which the benefactors from other worlds reached the earth. Nowhere is such fantasy haunted by the problem: if human beings needed other beings to civilize them, how were the civilizers in their turn civilized? But there must, at one point, have been an origin without mediators.

For the moment at least, the catastrophists appear to stand on firmer ground, for we live in a threatened age, horizoned by atomic apocalypse, and it is not surprising that conjunctions of the planets and the activities of comets should have moved out of the charts of astrologers and into the minds not merely of popularizing interpreters of the past but also of bona fide scientists. Alongside somewhat sensational writers like Emmanuel Velikhovsky, who speculate with a degree of scientific plausibility on the way prehistoric and even marginally historic events may have been affected by the ruinous approaches of bodies from outer space, contemporary astronomers have become largely catastrophic in their interpretations of the origins and fates of worlds, while palaeontologists studying the world's distant prehistory have attributed the extinction of the dinosaurs to the destructive visits of heavenly bodies.

More recent disasters have been credited with catastrophic effects on human civilizations, and with some apparent degree of justification. In a vast eruption round about 1500 BC the island of Thera (now Santorin) virtually exploded, and it is believed that the great showers of debris, carried over large areas and ruining cultivation, and the tidal waves that destroyed fleets and communities, were the cause of the sudden decline of the Minoan empire, and that the widespread distress caused by the eruption may have set off the great migrations of the Sea Peoples around the eastern end of the Mediterranean.

But, as the effects of the Thera eruption seem to show, catastrophes do not invigorate cultures; they destroy or retard them. And even if disasters might sometimes have positive and creative results, the sixth century was a remarkably uncatastrophic era as far as natural disasters go. There were few great earthquakes or eruptions, and by this period men were beginning to learn how to deal with such misadventures as flood and drought, as the Chinese of the time did by embarking on large-scale drainage and irrigation. Despite man-made disturbances, like the overthrow of Assyria, the imperial conquests of Persia, and the chronic disunities of Hellas and China, men on the whole seem to have lived better than they had in past eras; the Athenians, for example, had changed from barley-eaters into wheat-eaters and the cultivation of the vine spread far and wide. Civilization was directed more than it had ever been towards meeting the needs of men rather than the capricious will of the gods.

And here we may have to move from the search for objective causes to the consideration of subjective factors. We may, like contemporary physicists, have to abandon ordinary views of cause and effect. Historians, in fact, often find themselves faced with situations in which an explanation in materialist terms is insufficient. A great deal can be discovered about an age from economic or technological data, but rarely enough to capture and define its true spirit. As Toynbee remarked, the introduction of the human personality into a historical situation brings an unpredictable element into the pattern. Toynbee in fact presents himself in *A Study of History* as a historian who followed the determinist path and found it inadequate:

The effect of a cause is inevitable, invariable and predictable. But the initiative that is taken by one or the other of the live parties to an encounter is not a cause; it is a challenge. Its consequence is not an effect; it is a response.

Here we are offered an alternative way of regarding

sequences of events involving human beings, and one that is related to the emergence of conscious individuality in human affairs, which was the most striking aspect of the sixth century in all those parts of the world about which we retain literate knowledge. Perhaps the most important reason for the slow progress that humanity made in developing the techniques of living during the long eons of the Stone Age was that, just as herding animals obey instinct, a way of collective thinking, more slavishly than the individualist predators, so early man lived according to highly circumscribed patterns of tribal custom, of ritual and taboo, that reduced his life to a pattern of mechanical repetition in which change was inevitably slow. Once conscious individuality, or personality, has emerged, two other related factors begin to react strongly on each other — the awakened reason and the personal will detached from the tribal consciousness.

Writers like Toynbee release us from the habit of seeing history in rigid determinist patterns of cause and effect. But in doing so they do not entirely detach us from scientific thought, for many evolutionists have realised that types of mutation have to be considered when the gradual process of ordinary adaptive evolution does not offer a satisfactory explanation, and when originative — or creative — factors outside the normal pattern of causality play some part. Even developments in the emergent science of genetics have brought us no nearer a resolution of such problems, for attempts to explain genetically every aspect of human personality have patently failed, as did attempts to explain the rise and fall of civilizations on purely genetic lines. Always there is a missing factor — the creative impulse to which even genetic patterns and their mysterious mutations owe their origins.

The revolution that occurred in the sixth century over the whole civilized world happened among peoples whose genetic patterns had been differentiated over many millenia. No form of inheritance can explain why Greeks, Jews, Indians, Persians and Chinese all broke loose within the same generation from mythical into rational ways of thought. There was a vast worldwide *change of mind*.

IV

When we generally talk of a change of mind, we mean that for some intellectual or emotional reason a person abandons one opinion or intention for another. But in the situation of the world's philosophers in the sixth century we are not talking merely of a change of opinion, like whether to vote Liberal or Tory or not at all in the next election. We are talking of new ways of perceiving the universe and its moving forces that are so different from those generally accepted a mere generation beforehand that we have to assume a worldwide transmutation of mental processes, a change of mind in the sense of an alteration among large numbers of people in the way the mind works.

An interesting and controversial book which relates to the great change of mind that took place in the sixth century and the immediately preceding decades is *The Origin of Consciousness in the Breakdown of the Bicameral Mind* by Julian Jaynes. The first virtue of *The Origin of Consciousness* is that it recognizes the problem: the heroes who figured in the *Iliad* and even the poets who devised the epic did not merely see the world in a different way from later men; they thought in a different way. The second virtue is that it attempts an explanation that is necessarily largely conjectural but does make use of the available knowledge about the period.

For Jaynes, the deities who appeared and spoke to the Homeric Greeks and to the inhabitants of the early kingdoms of the Middle East had no objective existence. They were auditory and sometimes visual hallucinations resulting from a different functioning of the brain. His argument is that the relationship between the two lobes of the brain was then different. Today the active speech areas of the brain are in the dominant left lobe, the lobe that inspires the intelligence and disposes us to rational and objective thinking, formulates our thoughts and motivates what we have to say. The right lobe is regarded as the silent area of the brain from which emotions and intuitions arise.

But, according to Jaynes, the right lobe was not always

silent. The speech functions were once active in both chambers of the brain, but in the right, not adapted to the practical uses of the left lobe, they tended to be externalized, so that what man heard were the hallucinatory voices. The gods, then, were the products of a primal schizoid functioning of the brain, and when the speech function fell out of use in the right lobe, the gods departed and only the rational, unseeable, inaudible God of the monotheists remained. In attempting to explain the changes that took place in the functioning rather than the form of the brain, Jaynes suggests that "the brain is more capable of being organized by the environment than we have hitherto supposed, and therefore could have undergone such a change from bicameral to conscious man mostly on the basis of learning and culture." In other words, he is posing a fundamental change in the *use* of the brain rather than a structural change in the brain itself.

Jaynes's arguments have to be considered because they make a serious attempt to deal with the historical problem this book concerns. There are indeed initial difficulties about his definition of consciousness and his argument that a thinking being is not necessarily a conscious being. Most of the definitions of consciousness centre around the idea of inward awareness, and it is hard to conceive of thought without such awareness. What he is really talking about is self-consciousness, the growing sense during the two or three generations preceding the sixth century of the human personality as an autonomous entity detached from the mythical continuum that subjected man to the power of prophetic and minatory hallucinations and from the tribal continuum that subjected him to the rigid laws and customs and taboos supported by the sense of living with the ancestors as continuing presences, ghosts or gods.

The phenomenon he describes dominates our view of the sixth century, whether one thinks of it in Jaynesian terms as the origination of consciousness or in my terms as the individuation of an already existing consciousness. The way men perceived the universe and in consequence thought about it shifted profoundly just before and during the sixth century, and in consequence the character of all the world civilizations was changed.

Jaynes sees the influences that determined the change beginning in the breakdown of the cultures that fostered the bicameral mind, the hieratic cultures in which men seemed to be in perpetual inner contact with the gods. The cause of this breakdown, as he sees it, was largely catastrophic — a series of crises that shook apart the old myth-ridden realms of the dawn of civilization. He invokes the eruption of Thera, linking it to large-scale subsidences of land bordering the Aegean Sea (hence, in his view, the myth of Atlantis).

Apart from the eclipse of the Minoan civilization, the consequence of these events was probably the great migration of peoples already mentioned, which the old Egyptian kingdom resisted but which transformed Assyria into the first great military empire. Military necessities, according to Jaynes, induced men to look at their world objectively, and so a historic awareness emerged for the first time in the annals of the Assyrian kings. Sustained by the introduction of a viable and convenient form of writing through the Phoenician invention of the alphabet, and by the rise of trading practices which stressed the differences as well as the similarities between men, the awareness of history led to personal thinking. As a result of these factors, Jaynes suggests, men were no longer god-motivated members of the tribe. They were individuals thinking their own thoughts as well as responding to outside influences. They were ready for the great philosophic revolution of the sixth century.

The Origin of Consciousness in the Breakdown of the Bicameral Mind presents an interesting exercise in environmental determinism in which Jaynes explicitly rejects an explanation in terms of genetic determinism. But he still brings us back to the situation we have already recognized as untenable, that of external and material factors entirely shaping the fate of humanity, and he rejects or at least evades an explanation that would recognize the human mind as a factor in its own liberation. According to his theory, the mind changes because it is subjected to external forces, but there is never a suggestion of that factor of challenge-and-response between human beings that, as Toynbee remarked, has always operated alongside material causality in shaping human societies.

There are other ways in which Jaynes's theory fails to provide an adequate explanation of what happened in the sixth century. The environmental changes he evokes occurred only in the eastern Mediterranean and the Middle East. But we are considering a revolution in perception that took place also in Iran, India and China, none of which can have been affected by the results of the Thera eruption. It was a revolution that took place with amazing rapidity and with little warning at least six and probably eight centuries after the Thera disaster. The developments we can regard as truly premonitory, like the strange emergence of a modern personality in the *Odyssey*, or the sudden assertion of individuality in seventh-century Greek poets like Archilochus, actually occurred a comparatively short time before the sixth century dawned, but the revolutionary breakthrough in philosophy took place entirely in the sixth century and the first two decades of the fifth. It did so with a remarkable simultaneity, within a generation or so, in places far apart and virtually unknown to each other. And if no gods descended, and if the Jaynesian hypothesis seems at best dubious in relation to this period, how are we to explain this extraordinary and ubiquitous change of mind?

V

The clue may lie in the most striking features of the situation, the factors of simultaneity and similarity. Here is something too sudden for diffusion to explain, and too widespread to be attributable to coincidence. Chance cannot possibly govern a situation where so many men, so widely separated by distance and mutual unawareness, developed within so short a time the same rejection of myth in favour of reason and of the gods in favour of humanity, or the same purification of the divine by its final dissociation from the human image. And since we have no adequate explanation in terms of material causality for this phenomenon, we can only proceed by a mixture of logic and conjecture, our sole certainty being that the connections are meaningful.

And here our best guide may well be the great unorthodox psychoanalyst Carl Jung, writing on the problem of synchronicity, by which he meant the existence of series of events that do not seem to be causally linked yet whose connection with each other is evident and meaningful. In his work as a psychiatrist Jung had repeatedly encountered clusters of linked events. Often the link between the events appeared to be psychic in character, as in the case of two scientists, like Darwin and Wallace, making a discovery unbeknown to each other at the same time, or a person experiencing a certain knowledge of another person's death at the very time the death happens in a remote place. What unites such events, Jung has remarked, is not a causative link, yet it is a "meaningful" one, and this meaningfulness outside causality characterizes the phenomenon Jung calls synchronicity.

In *The Secret of the Golden Flower* Jung offers a definition of synchronicity that seems to have a close bearing on the problem before us:

It seems indeed as though time, far from being an abstraction, is a concrete continuum which contains qualities or basic conditions that manifest themselves simultaneously in different places through parallelisms that cannot be explained causally, as, for example, in cases of the simultaneous occurrence of identical thoughts, symbols, or psychic states.

The "simultaneous occurrence of identical thoughts" is of course precisely the situation with which we are now dealing, even though in magnitude the sixth century BC offers a much more dramatic example of synchronicity than most of those Jung discusses, because of the vast distances over which it took place and the different cultures it involved. In posing the existence of an alternative principle to causality, a principle which elsewhere he described as "acausal orderedness," Jung was of course reviving an ancient tradition, the tradition that finds the meanings of the universe in "correspondences" as well as causes.

The tradition goes back to primitive man and his magic;

it flourished in the Middle Ages; it was reflected in the thinking of Renaissance philosophers like Leibnitz; exemplified
most strikingly in the *I Ching*, it dominated Chinese thinking
until modern times; it provided a philosophic justification for
the poetry of Symbolism from Baudelaire down to W. B.
Yeats. Most important, it is a tradition whose basic assumptions reappear whenever philosophers or even scientists find
themselves faced with discontinuities in the chain of cause and
effect that call for the recognition of some other kind of relationship existing between phenomena that are clearly linked.
As Jung himself says, "Synchronicity is a modern differentiation of the obsolete concept of correspondences, sympathy
and harmony. It is based not on philosophical assumptions
but on empirical experience and experimentation." The connections embraced in synchronicity are objective if acausal;
very often, for example, they centre around the combination
of a physical and a psychic event, as in the case of premoni-
tions, but they can also consist of the correspondences between
events enacted in the world and not merely within men's
minds, such as the phenomenon we are here considering, of
sages posing similar questions at the same time in widely separated places.

One of the characteristics of the connections embraced in
synchronicity is that, in accordance with their acausality, they
cannot be anticipated. They happen at random, and, as Toynbee the historian observed as clearly as Jung the psycholo-
gist, when acausal factors like the human personality are
involved, we cannot rely on what seem to be similar sets of
circumstances producing similar results. In this realm everything is gratuitous or appears to be so. As Jung remarks, "synchronicity is not a phenomenon whose regularity it is at all
easy to demonstrate. One is as much impressed by the dishar-
mony of things as one is surprised by their occasional
harmony."

It is obvious that we are dealing with a class of events quite
different in the manner of their initiation from those that fall
within a causal pattern. And so we have to assume the existence of a principle distinct from causality but operating
parallel to it. In *Synchronicity* Jung leads us to the definition

which many people find hard to accept because it poses anew the principle of creativity that liberal thinkers have long thought discredited:

Synchronicity is no more baffling or mysterious than the discontinuities of physics. It is only the ingrained belief in the sovereign power of causality that creates intellectual difficulties and makes it appear unthinkable that causeless events exist or could ever occur. But if they do, then we must regard them as *creative acts*, as the continuous creation of a pattern that exists from all eternity, repeats itself sporadically, and is not derivable from any known antecedents.

The concept of creativity, as Jung presents it, has little relationship with the process of creation described in Genesis, since it does not imply that creation is the affair of a personal God. It poses a universe in which from time to time, without motivation, spontaneous change takes place outside the pattern of causality. But if we are to imagine a creator of any kind, or even a creative principle, as I suspect Jung intends, we return by a different route to the concept of causality; not a mechanically determined causality, but a spontaneous causality inspired by will. What kind of a will then becomes the problem.

This will Jung would doubtless find in what he called "the collective unconscious," meaning not only the medium that may transmit so-called psychic messages like a resonant membrane, but also the great memory bank of archetypal images that populate our dreams and provide us with the potent symbols which dominate our art and, though we are usually unaware of it, affect much of our daily thinking and our ongoing fantasy life.

Clearly it is hard to conceive such a situation as that which occurred in the sixth century except by the transmission of insights through some kind of intuitional continuum that took no count of distances. But Jung's collective unconscious seems too passive a continuum to engender the creative impulses which such a situation implies. Even if one conceived such an unconscious as linking all human beings in a pattern of shared images and a membrane of common awareness that offers intermittent and erratic communication in despite of space, Jung's concept lacks the factor of activity necessary for a concept of creativity.

At this point it may be helpful to return to the sages of the sixth century and see what hints and suggestions they have to offer. They were men who by a sudden act of rebellion put aside the mythological concept that served more ancient civilizations. By this rejection they were faced with two alternatives: either like the Buddha to declare that what is beyond experience cannot be known and is therefore not worth speculating about; or to attempt a new, unmythical explanation of the universe both by self-examination (hence their constant exhortations to "know" oneself, or "search out" oneself as Heraclitus boasted to have done) and by seeking a rational explanation of the universe based on the observation of things as they are. As Heraclitus put it, "Wisdom has a single aim, to learn by the use of true judgment how all things are steered through all." They had no illusions about the difficulty of the task. Heraclitus also said, "the real constitution of things is accustomed to hide itself," and warned that reason is not always sufficient to discover what is hidden. Intelligence works best aided by intuition, and sometimes one must be prepared to receive the flash of spontaneous insight: "If one does not expect the unexpected one will not find it out since it is not to be searched for and is difficult to grasp."

The extraordinary feature of the thinking of all these sixth-century sages is that although they have broken away from a variety of religious traditions, they are strikingly alike, not only in their negations of the mythical assumptions of the past but also in the positive visions of the universe that came into their minds. The concept of a single substance to the universe, changing constantly but neither increased nor reduced, occurs surprisingly often, even if at times one of the characteristics of that unity is its inner conflict between opposing elements. The anthropomorphic gods are universally expelled, among other reasons because their caprices diminish the image of divinity, but only among a few of the Indian contemporaries of the Buddha does one encounter a strictly materialist attitude to the universe.

Among the really important thinkers of the time there is always an awareness of the material as moved by the immaterial, whether in the sense of the "gods" that for Thales inhabited all things, or the "souls" that Mahavira and his followers believed to reside in everything, animate and inanimate. Yet, divided though spirit might become between various entities, there was the sense of a governing unity, God as distinct from the gods; of an impersonal divinity, all-embracing, all-permeating yet all-permeated, containing within himself all likenesses and all opposites. As Heraclitus had it,

> God is day and night, winter and summer, war and peace,
> satisfaction and hunger; he undergoes changes of form
> in the way that fire, when it is mixed with spices, takes
> on in turn the scent of each of them.

God, in this sense, is not far distant from the *tao* of Lao-tzu and his followers, which is far more than a "way" in any ordinary sense. The *tao* exists yet, when we seek to define it, eludes us. It is all-permeating yet imperceptible. By letting ourselves be carried on its current we act without acting and all is well, yet when we seek to lay hold of it our hands are empty:

> We live by what is
> and the void within it.
> There is no map to be had
> of the Way, there are
> no words to describe it.
> It exists, and is not.

And that is very close to the concept of Heraclitus which Aristotle, that most literal-minded man, quoted with some puzzlement:

> Things taken together are whole and not whole, some-
> thing which is being brought together and taken apart,
> which is in tune and out of tune; out of all things there
> comes a unity, and out of a unity all things.

And when we seek for an image of that unity we come back to the great vision of Xenophanes, whom Heraclitus disliked yet in so many ways resembled:

[God] is one, undifferentiated, undivided,
sees all, hears all, and without labour
sets all things in vibration
with a thought.

Here, surely, is a perfect deist statement before deism
existed, a description of God by a deeply religious man cast-
ing aside supernatural revelations and proceeding by reason
and by the knowledge of the natural world. But it also offers
us, from the sixth century itself, a concept of thought moving creatively through the universe.

It is when we seek to explain how this can happen that, as
the Buddha realized from his own speculations, we find ourselves confronted with the unknowable. Human observation
can explore whatever is material in the world with notable
intricacy, extending our knowledge constantly into the realms
of the infinitesimal and the infinite. The goal of total understanding is not reached; such goals never are. But we know
far more about the stars and the atoms than we do about psychic and even psychological phenomena; the process of magical transmutation by which the material cells of the brain
collect and store data and then transform them into all the
manifestations of intelligence has still to be explained by something more precise than conjecture; the instant of imaginative impulse that leads to a human creative act remains
impenetrably mysterious.

But if the human brain can both transmute and create
without our being able to explain its action, how much more
inexplicable, as well as proportionately more potent, must be
the action of a universal intelligence, which is really what
Xenophanes postulates when in his own way he talks of God.

Once we speak of a universal intelligence, we are thinking
again of a continuum, but a dynamic one as distinct from the
passive continuum of Jung's collective unconscious. And once
we have envisaged that dynamic continuum, that all-moving
tao; once we have sensed that, as Thales variously argued,
"the mind of the world is god" and "all things are full of
gods," then the distinction between creation and intelligence
becomes as irrelevant as the distinction between the personal

and the universal mind. One is implied and contained within the other, in an everlasting exchange of roles. And if, as modern men conditioned by scientific clichés, we are baffled by the working of the universe, that is doubtless because, except at fleeting moments of insight such as mystics claim from their experiences, the part, which is the human intelligence, can never comprehend the whole, which is the universal intelligence. It can only be conceived metaphorically; one cannot describe it literally.

Such an evocation by clustering metaphors perhaps brings one closest to an understanding of the sixth century BC and the extraordinary revolution in thought that then took place. There was an authentic transmutation, in the Yeatsian sense of "all changed, changed utterly: a terrible beauty is born." Philosophy was initiated, science was foreshadowed, history was begun and religion was irrevocably transformed. It was, moreover, a transmutation that happened at the same time in all the civilizations that then had the means of recording their histories. The *tao* became positive mental action; "all things" were set "in vibration with a thought"; the universe changed gears from causality into creation, and in the marvellous century, the sixth century BC, the human world we know came into sudden being.

A READING LIST

Aharoni, Yohanan, and Michael Avi-Yonah. *The Macmillan Bible Atlas.* Revised edition. New York: Macmillan, 1977.

Akurgal, Efrem. *Ancient Civilizations and Ruins in Turkey.* Istanbul: Mobil Oil Turk A.S., 1969.

Allchin, Bridget and Raymond. *The Rise of Civilization in India and Pakistan.* Cambridge: Cambridge University Press, 1982.

Andrewes, Anthony. *The Greek Tyrants.* London: Hutchinson,1956.

The Greeks. London: Hutchinson, 1967.

Andronicos, Manolis. *Olympia.* Athens: Exdotike Athenon S.A., 1980.

Aristotle. *The Athenian Constitution.* Translated by P.J. Rhodes. Harmondsworth: Penguin Books, 1984.

Aristotle. *The Politics.* Translated by T.A. Sinclair. Harmondsworth: Penguin Books, 1962.

Bachofen, J.J. *Myth, Religion and Mother Right.* Translated by Ralph Manheim. Princeton: Princeton University Press, 1967.

Bacon, Edward, ed. *The Great Archaeologists and their Discoveries as originally reported in the Illustrated London News.* London: Secker & Warburg, 1976.

Barnes, Jonathan. *The Presocratic Philosophers.* 2 vols. London: Routledge & Kegan Paul, 1979.

Barrow, R.H. *The Romans.* Harmondsworth: Penguin Books, 1949.

Basham, A.L. *A Cultural History of India.* Oxford: Clarendon Press, 1975.

History and Doctrines of the Ajivikas. London: Luzac, 1951.

The Wonder that was India. New York: Macmillan, 1954.

Bean, George. *Aegean Turkey.* London: Ernest Benn, 1966.

Bengston, Hermann. *The Greeks and the Persians from the Sixth to the Fourth Centuries.* London: Weidenfcld & Nicolson, 1968.

Beye, Charles Rowan. *Ancient Greek Literature and Society.* Garden City, N.Y.: Doubleday, 1975.

Blakeney, Raymond P. *The Way of Life: A New translation of the Tao Tê Ching.* New York: New American Library, 1955.

Boardman, John. *Athenian Red Figure Vases: The Archaic Period*. London: Thames & Hudson, 1975.

   Greek Sculpture: The Archaic Period. London: Thames & Hudson, 1978.

   The Greeks Overseas: Their Early Colonies and Trade. New and enlarged edition. London: Thames & Hudson, 1980.

   and N.G.L. Hammond, eds. *The Cambridge Ancient History*. 2nd edition. Vol. III, Part 3. *The Expansion of the Greek World, Eighth to Sixth Centuries B.C.* Cambridge: Cambridge University Press, 1982.

   Jasper Griffin and Oswyn Murray, eds. *The Oxford History of the Classical World*. Oxford: Oxford University Press, 1986.

Boyce, Mary. *Zoroastrians: Their Religious Beliefs and Practices*. London: Routledge & Kegan Paul, 1979.

Branigan, Keith, and Michael Vickers. *Hellas: The Civilizations of Ancient Greece*. New York: McGraw Hill, 1980.

Breasted, James Henry. *A History of Egypt*. New York: Scribner, 1905.

Burney, Charles. *From Village to Empire: An Introduction to Near Eastern Archaeology*. Oxford: Phaidon, 1977.

Bury, J.B. *A History of Greece to the Death of Alexander*. 3rd edition, revised by Russell Meiggs. London: Macmillan, 1951.

   S.A. Cook and F.E. Adcock. *The Cambridge Ancient History*. Vol. IV. *The Persian Empire and the West*. Cambridge: Cambridge University Press, 1972.

Butterfield, Herbert. *The Origins of History*. New York: Basic Books, 1981.

Campbell, D.A. *Greek Lyric*. Vol. I. Translated by D.A. Campbell. Loeb Classical Library. Cambridge, Mass.: Harvard University Press, 1982.

Campbell, Joseph. *The Masks of God: Occidental Mythology*. New York: Viking, 1964.

   The Masks of God: Oriental Mythology. New York: Viking, 1962.

   The Masks of God: Primitive Mythology. New York: Viking, 1959.

Chang, Kwang-Chih. *The Archaeology of Ancient China*. 3rd edition. New Haven: Yale University Press, 1977.

Charles-Picard, Gilbert, ed. *Larousse Encyclopedia of Archaeology*. Translated by Anne Ward. London: Hamlyn, 1972.

Coles, J.M., and A.F. Harding. *The Bronze Age in Europe*. London: Methuen, 1975.

Conze, Edward. *Buddhism: Its Essence and Development*. Oxford: Bruno Cassirer, 1951.

Cook, J.M. *The Greeks in Ionia and the East*. London: Thames & Hudson, 1962.

Cotterell, Arthur, ed. *The Encyclopedia of Ancient Civilizations*. New York: Mayflower Books, 1980.

Craik, Elizabeth. *The Dorian Aegean*. London: Routledge & Kegan Paul, 1980.

Crawford, Michael, and David Whitehead. *Archaic and Classical Greece: A Selection of Ancient Sources in Translation*. Cambridge: Cambridge University Press, 1983.

Cunliffe, Barry. *Rome and Her Empire*. New York: McGraw Hill, 1978.

Dal Maso, Leonardo B., and Roberto Vigli, eds. *Southern Etruria*. Florence: Bonechi, 1975.

Davies, J.K. *Democracy and Classical Greece*. London: Fontana, 1978.

Davis, Nigel. *Human Sacrifice in History and Today*. New York: Morrow, 1981.

Davis, Norman. *Greek Coins and Cities*. London: Spink & Son, 1967.

de Bary, Wm. Theodore, ed. *Sources of Indian Tradition*. 2 vols. New York: Columbia University Press, 1964.

de Coulanges, Fustel. *The Ancient City*. Garden City, N.Y.: Doubleday, 1956.

Dickinson, G. Lowes. *The Greek View of Life*. Ann Arbor: University of Michigan Press, 1958.

Dodds, E.R. *The Greeks and the Irrational*. Berkeley: University of California Press, 1951.

Durrell, Lawrence. *The Greek Islands*. New York: Viking, 1978.

Edmonds, J.M. *Greek Elegy and Iambus*. Vol. 1. Translated by J.M. Edmonds. Loeb Classical Library. Cambridge, Mass.: Harvard University Press, 1931.

Fairservis, Waller A. *The Roots of Ancient India*. 2nd edition. Chicago: University of Chicago Press, 1975.

Farrington, Benjamin. *Greek Science*. Harmondsworth: Penguin Books, 1953.

Feder, Lillian. *Crowell's Handbook of Classical Literature*. New York: Lippincott & Crowell, 1964.

Finegan, Jack. *Archaeological History of the Ancient Middle East*. Boulder, Col.: Westview Press, 1979.

Finley, M.I. *Ancient Slavery and Modern Ideology*. New York: Viking, 1980.

    ed. *Atlas of Classical Mythology*. New York: McGraw Hill, 1977.

    Early Greece: The Bronze and Archaic Ages. London: Chatto & Windus, 1977.

    Economy and Society in Ancient Greece. New York: Viking, 1982.

    ed. *The Legacy of Greece*. Oxford: Clarendon Press, 1981.

Fitzgerald, Patrick. *Ancient China*. New York: Phaidon, 1978.

Fornara, Charles W. *Translated Documents of Greece and Rome*. Vol. I, *Archaic Times to the End of the Peloponessian War*. Baltimore: Johns Hopkins University Press, 1977.

Frankel, David. *The Ancient Kingdom of Urartu*. London: British Museum Publications, 1979.

Fränkel, Hermann. *Early Greek Poetry and Philosophy*. Translated by Moses Hadas and James Willis. Oxford: Blackwell, 1975.

Frederic, Louis. *The Art of India: Temple and Sculptures*. New York: Harry Abrams, n.d.

Frye, Richard N. *The Heritage of Persia*. London: Weidenfeld & Nicolson, 1963.

Ful, Alexander, and Ivan Morazov. *Thrace and the Thracians*. New York: St. Martin's Press, 1977.

Garratty, John A., and Peter Gray, eds. *The Columbia History of the World*. New York: Harper & Row, 1972.

Ghirshman, R. *Iran*. Harmondsworth: Penguin Books, 1974.

Goetz, Hermann. *India: Five Thousand Years of Indian Art*. New York: McGraw Hill, 1959.

Goodrich, L. Carrington. *A Short History of the Chinese People*. New York: Harper & Row, 1963.

Gordon, R.L., ed. *Myth, Religion and Society*. Cambridge: Cambridge University Press, 1981.

Gorman, Peter. *Pythagoras: A Life*. London: Routledge & Kegan Paul, 1979.

Grant, Michael. *The Etruscans*. New York: Scribner, 1980.
  The History of Ancient Israel. New York: Scribner, 1984.
  History of Rome. New York: Scribner, 1978.
  Myths of the Greeks and Romans. New York: New American Library, 1962.

Graves, Robert. *The Greek Myths*. 2 vols. Harmondsworth: Penguin Books, 1953.

Grimal, Pierre. *The Dictionary of Classical Mythology*. Oxford: Blackwell, 1986.

Guido, Margaret. *Sicily: An Archaeological Guide*. London: Faber & Faber, 1967.

Guirand, Felix, ed. *New Larousse Encyclopedia of Mythology*. Translated by Richard Aldington and Delano Ames. London: Hamlyn, 1968.

Guthrie, W.K.C. *The Greeks and their Gods*. Boston: Beacon Press, 1950.
  A History of Greek Philosophy. 1. The Earlier Presocratics and the Pythagoreans. Cambridge: Cambridge University Press, 1962.
  A History of Greek Philosophy. 2. The Presocratic Tradition from Parmenides to Democritus. Cambridge: Cambridge University Press, 1965.

Hafner, German. *Art of Rome, Etruria and Magna Graecia*. New York: Harry N. Abrams, 1969.

Hamilton, Edith. *The Greek Way to Civilization*. New York: New American Library, 1948.

Mythology. New York: New American Library, 1953.

and Huntingdon Cairns. *The Collected Dialogues of Plato including the Letters*. Princeton: Princeton University Press, 1961.

Hammond, N.G.L. *A History of Greece to 322 BC*. 2nd edition. Oxford: Clarendon Press, 1967.

Harden, Donald. *The Phoenicians*. London: Thames & Hudson, 1962.

Harrison, Jane Ellen. *Themis: A Study of the Social Origins of Greek Religion*. New York: Meridian, 1962.

Hauser, Arnold. *The Social History of Art*. Vol. 1. New York: Vintage Books, 1957.

Havelock, Eric A. *The Literate Revolution in Greece and its Cultural Consequences*. Princeton: Princeton University Press, 1982.

Hawkes, Jacquetta. *Atlas of Ancient Anthropology*. New York: McGraw Hill, 1974.

The Atlas of Early Man. New York: St. Martin's Press, 1976.

The First Great Civilizations. London: Hutchinson, 1973.

ed. *The World of the Past*. 2 vols. New York: Alfred A. Knopf, 1963.

Hay, John. *Ancient China*. London: Bodley Head, 1973.

Heath, Thomas. *A History of Greek Mathematics*. Vol. 1. *From Thales to Euclid*. Oxford: Clarendon Press, 1921.

Henderson, John S. *The World of the Ancient Maya*. Ithaca, N.Y.: Cornell University Press, 1981.

Herm, Gerhard. *The Celts*. New York: St. Martin's Press, 1976.

The Phoenicians. New York: Morrow, 1975.

Herodotus. *The Histories*. Translated by Aubrey de Selincourt. Harmondsworth: Penguin Books, 1954.

Ho, Ping-ti. *The Cradle of the East*. Hong Kong: Chinese University of Hong Kong, 1975.

Hopkins, Adam. *Crete: Its Past, Present and People*. London: Faber & Faber, 1977.

Hopper, R.J. *The Early Greeks*. New York: Harper & Row, 1976.

Hughes, E.R., ed. *Chinese Philosophy in Ancient Times*. London: J.M. Dent, 1942.

Hume, Robert Ernest. *The Thirteen Principal Upanishads, Translated from the Sanskrit*. 2nd edition. Oxford: Oxford University Press, 1931.

Humphreys, Christmas. *Buddhism*. Revised edition. Harmondsworth: Penguin Books, 1955.

Hussey, Edward. *The Pre-Socratics*. London: Duckworth, 1972.

Huxley, G.L. *The Early Ionians*. Shannon: Irish University Press, 1972.

Ikeda, Daisaku. *Buddhism: The First Millenium*. Translated by Burton Watson. Tokyo: Kodansha International Ltd., 1977.

Irving, Clive. *Crossroads of Civilization: 3000 Years of Persian History*. London: Weidenfeld & Nicolson, 1979.

Jacobsen, Thorkild. *The Treasures of Darkness: A History of Mesopotamian Religion*. New Haven: Yale University Press, 1976.

Janson, H.W. *History of Art*. New York: Harry N. Abrams, 1969.

Jaynes, Julian. *The Origin of Consciousness in the Breakdown of the Bicameral Mind*. Toronto: University of Toronto Press, 1978.

Jeffery, L.H. *Archaic Greece: The City States, c.700-500 BC*. London: Ernest Benn, 1976.

Johansson, Rune E.A. *The Dynamic Psychology of Early Buddhism*. London: Curzon Press, 1979.

Johnson, Paul. *The Civilization of Ancient Egypt*. London: Weidenfeld & Nicolson, 1978.

Jung, C.G. *Synchronicity: An Acausal Connecting Principle*. Translated by R.F.C. Hull. Princeton: Princeton University Press, 1973.

Kaufman, Walter. *Tragedy and Philosophy*. Princeton: Princeton University Press, 1968.

Keller, Werner. *The Bible as History*. New York: Morrow, 1964.

Kinder, Herman, and Werner Hilge Mann. *Atlas of World History*. Vol. 1. Harmondsworth: Penguin Books, 1974.

Kirk, G.S. *The Nature of Greek Myths*. Harmondsworth: Penguin Books, 1974.

    and J.E. Raven. *The Presocratic Philosophers*. Cambridge: Cambridge University Press, 1957.

Kitto, H.D.F. *The Greeks*. Harmondsworth: Penguin Books, 1951.

Knobloch, Edgar. *Beyond the Oxus*. London: Ernest Benn, 1972.

Landels, J.C. *Engineering in the Ancient World*. London: Chatto & Windus, 1980.

Langer, William H., ed. *An Encyclopedia of World History*. Revised edition. Boston: Houghton Mifflin, 1972.

Laufer, Berthold. *Sino-Iranica*. Chicago: Field Museum of Natural History, 1919.

Lee, Sherman E. *A History of Far Eastern Art*. New York: Harry Abrams, n.d.

Levi, Peter. *Atlas of the Greek World*. New York: Facts on File, 1980.

Licht, Hans. *Sexual Life in Ancient Greece*. London: Routledge & Kegan Paul, 1932.

Ling, Trevor. *The Buddha: Buddhist Civilization in India and Ceylon*. Harmondsworth: Penguin Books, 1976.

Livy. *The Early History of Rome*. Translated by Aubrey de Selincourt. Harmondsworth: Penguin Books, 1960.

Lloyd, G.E.R. *Early Greek Science: Thales to Aristotle*. London: Chatto & Windus, 1970.

Lloyd, Seton. *The Art of the Ancient Near East*. New York: Prager, 1963.

MacKendrick, Paul. *The Greek Stones Speak*. New York: Norton, 1962.

McNeill, William. *Plagues and Peoples*. Garden City. N.Y.: Doubleday, 1976.

Marshall, George M. *Buddha: The Quest for Serenity*. Boston: Beacon Press, 1978.

Mascaró, Juan. *The Upanishads: Translations from the Sanskrit*. Harmondsworth: Penguin Books, 1965.

Matheson, Sylvia. *Persia: an Archaeological Guide*. London: Faber & Faber, 1972.

Miller, Madeleine S., and J. Lane. *Harper's Encyclopedia of Bible Life*. New York: Harper & Row, 1978.

Moore, Charles A. *The Indian Mind: Essentials of Indian Philosophy and Culture*. Honolulu: University of Hawaii, 1967.

Mumford, Lewis. *The City in History*. New York: Harcourt Brace, 1961.
The Condition of Man. London: Secker & Warburg, 1944.
The Conduct of Life. London: Secker & Warburg, 1952.

Murray, Oswyn. *Early Greece*. London: Fontana, 1986.

Neumann, Erich. *The Great Mother: An Analysis of the Artifact*. Translated by Ralph Manheim. 2nd edition. Princeton: Princeton University Press, 1963.

Oates, Joan. *Babylon*. London: Thames & Hudson, 1979.

Pallotino, M. *The Etruscans*. Harmondsworth: Penguin Books, 1955.

Papathanassopoulos, G. *The Acropolis: Monuments and Museum*. Athens: Krene Editions, 1977.

Pausanias. *Guide to Greece*. 2 vols. Translated by Peter Levi. Harmondsworth: Penguin Books, 1971.

Piggott, Stuart. *The Druids*. London: Thames & Hudson, 1968.

Pliny. *The Letters of the Younger Pliny*. Translated by Betty Radice. Harmondsworth: Penguin Books, 1963.

Plutarch. *The Rise and Fall of Athens: Nine Greek Lives*. Translated by Ian Scott-Kilvert. Harmondsworth: Penguin Books, 1960.

Postgate, Nicholas. *The First Empires*. New York: Phaidon, 1977.

Pritchard, James B. *Recovering Sarepta, A Phoenician City*. Princeton: Princeton University Press, 1978.

Rice, Tamara Talbot. *Ancient Arts of Central Asia*. New York: Prager, 1965.
The Scythians. London: Thames & Hudson, 1957.

Richardson, Emeline Hill. *The Etruscans: Their Art and Civilization*. Chicago: University of Chicago Press, 1964.

Riepe, Dale. *The Naturalistic Tradition in Indian Thought*. Seattle: University of Washington Press, 1961.

Roberts, J.M. *The Hutchinson History of the World*. London: Hutchinson, 1976.

Roberts, Martin. *The Ancient World*. Basingstoke: Macmillan Education, 1917.

Robinson, Richard R., and Willard J. Johnson. *The Buddhist Religion: A Historical Introduction*. Encino, Cal.: Dickenson Publishing, 1977.

Roux, Georges. *Ancient Iraq*. London: Allen & Unwin, 1964.

Ruffle, John. *The Egyptians: An Introduction to Egyptian Archaeology*. Ithaca, N.Y.: Cornell University Press, 1977.

Sandars, N.H. *The Sea Peoples: Warriors of the Ancient Mediterranean*. London: Thames & Hudson, 1978.

Sauneron, Serge. *The Priests of Ancient Egypt*. New York: Grove Press, 1966.

Scully, Vincent. *The Earth, the Temple and the Gods: Greek Sacred Architecture*. Revised edition. New Haven: Yale University Press, 1979.

Sealey, Raphael. *A History of the Greek City States, 700-338 BC*. Berkeley: University of California Press, 1976.

Sharma, J.P. *Republics in Ancient India, c.1500 BC - 500 BC*. Leiden: E.J. Brill, 1968.

Smith, Huston. *The Religions of Man*. New York: Harper & Row, 1958.

Snodgrass, Anthony. *Archaic Greece: The Age of Experiment*. London: J.M. Dent, 1980.

Soothill, William Edward. *The Analects of Confucius*. Oxford: Oxford University Press, 1937.

Spengler, Oswald. *The Decline of the West*. 2 vols. New York: Alfred A. Knopf, 1926-28.

Starr, Chester G. *The Economic and Social Growth of Early Greece, 800-500 BC*. New York: Oxford University Press, 1977.

Steindorff, George, and Keith R. Seele. *When Egypt Ruled the East*. 2nd edition. Chicago: University of Chicago Press, 1957.

Swaddling, Judith. *The Ancient Olympic Games*. London: British Museum Publications, 1980.

Thapar, Romila. *A History of India*. Vol. 1. Harmondsworth: Penguin Books, 1966.

Thomas, Edward J. *The Life of Buddha as Legend and History*. 3rd edition. London: Routledge & Kegan Paul, 1949.

Thomas, Hugh. *History of the World*. New York: Harper & Row, 1979.

Thomas, Ivor. *Greek Mathematical Works*. Vol. 1. *Thales to Euclid*. Translated by Ivor Thomas. Loeb Classical Texts. Cambridge, Mass.: Harvard University Press, 1980.

Thomson, George. *Studies in Ancient Greek Society: The First Philosophers*. London: Lawrence & Wishart, 1955.

Thucydides. *The Peloponnesian War*. Translated by Rex Warner. Harmondsworth: Penguin Books, 1954.

Toynbee, Arnold. *The Greeks and their Heritage*. Oxford: Oxford University Press, 1981.

A Study of History. A New Edition revised and abridged by the author and Jane Caplan. Oxford: Oxford University Press, 1972.

Trypanis, Constantine T., ed. *The Penguin Book of Greek Verse*. Harmondsworth: Penguin Books, 1971.

Warmington, E.H. *Carthage*. Harmondsworth: Penguin Books, 1964.

and M. Cary. *The Ancient Explorers*. Revised edition. Harmondsworth: Penguin Books, 1963.

Welch, Holmes, and Anne Seidel, eds. *Facets of Taoism*. New Haven: Yale University Press, 1979.

Wender, Dorothea. *Hesiod and Theognis*. Translations by Dorothea Wender. Harmondsworth: Penguin Books, 1973.

Wheeler, Mortimer. *Early India and Pakistan*. London: Thames & Hudson, 1959.

Flames over Persepolis. London: Weidenfeld & Nicolson, 1968.

Wilson, John A. *The Culture of Ancient Egypt*. Chicago: University of Chicago Press, 1959.

Wolpert, Stanley. *A New History of India*. New York: Oxford University Press, 1977.

Woodcock, George. *The Greeks in India*. London: Faber & Faber, 1966.

Zavitukhina, M.P., and others. *Frozen Tombs: The Culture and Art of the Ancient Tribes of Siberia*. London: British Museum Publications, 1978.

Zimmer, Heinrich. *Myths and Symbols in Indian Art and Civilization*. New York: Harper, 1962.

Philosophies of India. New York: Meridian Books, 1956.

Index

255